Publish'd Dec 31 1788 by T. Malton N.º 6 Conduit Street.

SHERIDAN
OF DRURY LANE

RICHARD BRINSLEY SHERIDAN ESQ.

From the painting by Reynolds, engraved by Hall
Courtesy of Kennedy & Co.

SHERIDAN
OF DRURY LANE

A biography by
ALICE GLASGOW

WITH ILLUSTRATIONS FROM OLD PRINTS
AND PORTRAITS

FREDERICK A. STOKES CO.
New York · 1940

To F. H. G.

Contents

Prologue: BEFORE THE CURTAIN 3

CHAPTER

I. THE SETTING 11

II. SIRENS AND PERFECT SYLLABLES . . 31

III. PUPPET PROMENADE 41

IV. INFANT PASSION TO DISCLOSE . . . 55

V. ELOPEMENT À TROIS 71

VI. WHILE REASON'S BLIND 87

VII. THE WONDERFUL YEAR 99

VIII. SCHOOL FOR SCANDAL 125

IX. MEMBER FROM STAFFORD 139

X. THE PRINCE'S MAN 153

XI. THE TRIAL OF WARREN HASTINGS . 165

XII. THE KING IS MAD 179

XIII. TIME OF TORTURE 189

XIV. A VAIN EXPECTATION 203

XV. TREASURER OF THE NAVY 225

XVI. NEITHER PLACE NOR PURSE . . . 241

Contents

CHAPTER

XVII. THE LAST SPEECH 259

XVIII. CURTAIN 273

EPILOGUE 293

BIOGRAPHICAL SUMMARY 299

BIBLIOGRAPHY 301

INDEX 302

List of Illustrations

RICHARD BRINSLEY SHERIDAN, *from the engraving by Hall, after the painting by Reynolds* . . . . *frontispiece*

FACING PAGE

ELIZABETH LINLEY SHERIDAN, *from the drawing by Ozias Humphry* 34

ELIZABETH LINLEY SHERIDAN AS ST. CECILIA, *from the painting by Reynolds* 50

CHARLES JAMES FOX 130

HESTER JANE OGLE, SHERIDAN'S SECOND WIFE 146

GEORGE FREDERICK, PRINCE OF WALES, *from the painting by Lawrence* 226

MRS. FITZHERBERT, *from the painting by Russell* 242

DRURY LANE THEATER, 1809, *from an old engraving* 282

THE CRESCENT AT BATH, 1786, *from the engraving by Malton. Courtesy of Kennedy & Company* . . . . . . *front end-paper*

THE CIRCUS AT BATH, 1784, *from the engraving by Malton. Courtesy of Kennedy & Company* . . . . *back end-paper*

SHERIDAN
OF DRURY LANE

Before the Curtain

IT IS nine o'clock on the morning of December 11, 1757, the year in which Clive commenced his conquest of India. The Poet Laureate's man servant, returning to his master's bedroom with the customary early-morning pot of chocolate, finds that Colley Cibber has died in his sleep. With him, although it is not apparent to the servant, has departed an era.

Cibber had been an actor, a poet, a dramatist, and a manager. He had portrayed almost all the great rôles in the English theater and had written several notable plays. Chief among them were *Love's Last Shift, The Careless Husband,* and *The Provok'd Husband* in which he had collaborated with Sir John Vanbrugh. He had trod the boards with Garrick, of whose universally admired talents Cibber himself had a very low opinion, and the stages of Covent Garden and Drury Lane had resounded with his successes.

With Cibber, on that biting December morning, an epoch in the history of the English stage had snuffed itself out. The man who was to take the scepter from the Laureate's cold, relaxed fingers, was over six

[3]

years old now — a bright-haired, precocious Irish boy named Richard Brinsley Sheridan. Between Cibber's death in 1757 and the initial performance of the bright-haired boy's first play, *The Rivals,* in 1775, nearly twenty years were to elapse. Between the two play-wrights, the fulsome Colley Cibber, actor-author and briefly Laureate of England, and the gay, incisive Sheridan, there was a difference in technique, in theme, in viewpoint and in critical approach, of not merely twenty years but two hundred.

Fundamentally the stage and the theater of the eighteenth century — before Sheridan — were identical with those of the Restoration. When on August 21, 1660, Charles II granted letters patent to Sir William D'Avenant and Thomas Killigrew for the incorporation of two companies of players, it was understood that the theater was to resume its existence where it had left off when the Puritans in 1642 had decreed that all actors were "to be punished as Rogues, according to Law." But this was not to be the case. Londoners who could stretch their memories back to the days of the new King's father recollected that under Charles I the theater was a simple place, free from display, indulging in " neither Scenes, nor Decorations on the Stage, but only old Tapestry, and the Stage strew'd with Rushes. . . . Whereas ours now for Cost and Ornament are arriv'd to the heighth of Magnificence." [1] By the beginning of the

---

[1] From a contemporary writer.

century the property man was assuming an important part in the life of the acting company, holding as he did his very realistic mirror up to the face of an art which was even more realistic than Nature itself. One of the property lists at Drury Lane in 1709 included:

1. Three Bottles and a Half of Lightning.
2. One Shower of Snow in the finest French Paper.
3. Two Showers of a browner Sort.
4. A dozen and a Half of Clouds trimmed with black, and well conditioned.
5. A Mustard Bowl, to make Thunder with.
6. The Complexion of a Murderer in a Bandbox, consisting of a large Piece of Burnt Corke and a Coal Black Peruke.

The elegant Nicholas Rowe went backstage, and charmed with what he saw there, wrote verses:

Hung on the selfsame Peg, in union rest
Young Tarquin's Trowsers and Lucretia's Vest . . .

. . .

Near these sets up a Dragon-drawn Calash;
There a Ghost's Doublet, elegantly slashed,
Bleeds from the mangled Breast, and gapes a frightful Gash.
Here stands a Throne, and there the Cynick's Tub,
Here Bullock's Cudgel, there Alcidas' Club;
Beads, Plumes and Spangles in confusion rise,
Whilst Rocks of Cornish Diamonds reach the Skies.
Crests, Corslets, all the Pomp of Battle join
In one Effulgence, one promiscuous Shine.

Besides movable scenery which enchanted the spectator, there was music to sweeten the entr'actes, sometimes the entire play. And most exciting of all, those feminine rôles formerly played by young boys were now performed by actresses. The type of play too had changed. While Roundhead and Cavalier had been pursuing their fortunes in England, writers in France had adopted the classical ideal of the drama and were carefully constructing their plays to conform to it. French criticism was sound, French influence incalculable. When the theaters reopened their doors in 1660 they ushered in the Age of Classicism.

The " cult of correctness " rapidly won supporters. The dramas of the Elizabethans, rarely produced now, were soon entirely out of favor. A new-fashioned play had superseded them. Written in accordance with all the rules of the ancient dramatists, these new plays were characterized by a flawless technique — and were at the same time completely devoid of human passion and understanding.

This was the age of the youthful dramatist — Wycherly was only twenty-three when *The Old Bachelor* was first performed in 1693 — and of the gentleman-amateur like Sir John Vanbrugh, who flirted coyly with the Muse in the time he could spare from architecture and from the never-ending round of the Man of Pleasure. His *The Relapse,* written in 1696, became the model nearly one hundred years later of young Dick Sheridan's *A Trip to Scarborough.* Diversion was the sole aim of the Restoration play, and wit was the only bright reason for its existence.

Still another type of play was slowly coming into

fashion. This was the "drama of sensibility," of bathos and of tears; in later years Oliver Goldsmith christened it the "bastard tragedy." In January, 1696, there was presented at Drury Lane Colley Cibber's first success, *Love's Last Shift* or *The Fool in Fashion*. To the audience at the première was accorded a strange experience. They were made to sympathize with, to weep over, the anguish of the virtuous heroine, instead of being asked to sneer knowingly at her simple innocence. At the end they were permitted to thrill with rapture at her triumph. Cibber had, unwittingly, founded a school. He had started a trend. For the next century the boards would be sodden by the tears of Virtue cast down and trampled upon, and the rafters would ring with noble sentiments relating to Love and Chastity and Filial Devotion.

The size of the theater had been altered. In the latter years of the seventeenth century a number of smaller playhouses mushroomed around London. There was the *Little* in Goodman's Fields, the *Little* in Lincoln's Inn Fields, and the *Little* in the Haymarket. These are the names associated with Peg Woffington and David Garrick, and with the grand old Cibber himself. Here in these intimate houses the love of what was termed "subtle acting" was kept alive. The audience could hear an overtone and perceive an innuendo in an actor's voice; they could comprehend and retain every movement, every significant gesture and expression.

[7]

The Licensing Act of 1737 silenced and sealed forever these small theaters. Ostensibly limiting the number of playhouses and providing that no play should be produced without a license, it was in reality directed against the scurrilous political satires of Fielding and Vanbrugh. It is said that one such play, *The Golden Rump,* was so offensive that when the manager, Giffard, showed it to Walpole he promptly brought in a Bill which would forever remove such indecencies. Despite Lord Chesterfield, who signified his opposition to the Bill in a celebrated address, it became a law, and in February 1738 one William Chetwynd was sworn in as Licenser under the Lord Chamberlain at a salary of four hundred pounds a year. Many of the plays submitted failed to satisfy the Licenser's stern eye, and the fee demanded for a performance was in most cases prohibitive. Theater after theater dismissed its companies and closed its doors. Drama concentrated in Covent Garden and Drury Lane. The few playhouses which survived the Licensing Act grew in size to accommodate the increase in their audiences. Across drafty, echoing stages actors raised their voices and waved their arms. They ranted and raged and sawed the unpitying air. All innuendo vanished, and the aside was virtually lost. Any theater in London could furnish a troupe which nightly defied Hamlet's sober injunction and " tore a passion to tatters."

Queen Anne had avowed no interest in the playhouses. As for the first George — he could not have understood a word had he gone to a theater. In consequence the actors and their managers were forced to turn for the first time for patronage from the king to the public.

In the seventeenth century many aristocratic families, finding themselves impoverished and facing the rigors of debtors' prison, had allied themselves shudderingly with " persons in trade." These members of the lower orders, elevated suddenly into the world of fashion, had adopted its plaything, the theater. Some of its vices and immoralities they adopted also. Still they did succeed in injecting into the drama a certain lofty moral note.

Lackeys filled the theater's upper galleries until their rowdy behavior and the unsavory nature of their practical jokings brought about their ousting. From the boxes, perfumed and patched and periwigged, leaned the ladies of quality and their gallants. They nodded to the actors on the stage, frowned at the vulgarities of the gallery, and flirted with the critics and the beaus in the pit below them. Candles hissed behind tall shields at the stage's edge, and the hot wax sputtered in the tin trough. A violin scraped and quivered reedily. In his airless hutch the prompter turned the stiff pages of the playbook, pursuing with an indefatigable forefinger the crisscrossed meanderings of the text. The heroine sobbed, the hero protested, the villain expostulated and thundered, and the heroine's confidante had an eye cocked alertly toward the gentlemen in the boxes. And the audience listened and clapped politely, and trained its eyeglasses upon the house during the intervals. All around them — although of its existence they were completely unaware — raged a struggle more thrilling than the one which engrossed them from the stage. On the one side were the forces of intellectual callousness as evidenced by the "bawdy play," the licentious comedy. And on the other the forces of incipient humanitarianism, glimpsed in scenes of bathos, in sermonizings and moralizations, and in those passages of "sentiment" which young Mr. Sheridan would presently imitate so cleverly. The struggle was soon to cease, with "sentiment" the unchallenged victor. The tastes of the middle class had triumphed. It was to please this same middle class, as well as gracefully to caricature its affectations, that young Mr. Sheridan would soon write the first of his plays.

CHAPTER ONE

The Setting

THE violins discourse softly a tune which has the rippling grace of water. Flutes take it up, reiterating it again and again with a piercing sweetness. The voice of the horn insists, and the leader's baton, descending, has brought from the tall harp in the corner a shower of bright sound. On the walls, against the ceiling, on low tables everywhere candles blaze; in the still air their flames stand pointed and tall. But their light is a fine golden haze through which the dancers move with soft shufflings to the music.

The heads of the ladies are white as spring clouds, and as they sway and dip the feathers in their headdresses bend gracefully, like palm fronds. For women of the Great World are already, in the year 1772, affecting head-feathers — although this pretentious plumage has not yet reached the extravagant height it was to attain a few years later, when the indignant *Times* sputtered: " The ladies now wear feathers of exactly their own length, so that a woman of fashion is twice as long upon her feet as in her bed." The coats of the gentlemen bloom through the figures of the minuet like sullen tropical flowers, and the ladies who touch their fingers and move without effort beside them are as vivid as gardens. It is warm. Outside the tall windows scarcely a breeze lifts through the trees. Within, in patterns elaborate and intricate, pass and repass the yellow chintz gowns and the stiff Italian damasks, and those stuffs with queer Indian names, for hot nights like this, bafts and dimities, taffaties and teapoys.

With a swift succession of chords the music has stopped. There is a genteel spatter of applause, and from his dais the rotund orchestra leader is bowing, all his buttons agleam. His name is William Herschel, and although he is an accomplished musician — has he not been bandmaster for the Duke of Cumberland's own regiment? — he has recently found something to tempt him even more than his music. For the man who will one day discover the planet Uranus has already, in 1772, looked through his first telescope into infinity.

The hour is just on nine. At six, with the playing of a minuet, the dancing had started; now there is the usual pause for the gentlemen to hand tea to the ladies, and for the musicians to wet their tired throats. To-night being something of an occasion there will be supper as well, and behind screens footmen are busily laying a long table with cold ham and pheasant, biscuits, sweetmeats, jellies and wine. And now the Master of Ceremonies in plum satin and paste buckles offers his arm to the ranking lady present, Her Grace the Duchess of Marlborough, and together they swing across the room. Behind them rustle the others, Her

Grace's inferiors. Countesses and ladyships, wealthy tradesmen's wives and daughters, the mothers and mistresses of bone-setters and shipbuilders and swindling gamesters, all come to Bath to taste the salubrious "Spaw" waters at the Pump Room, to take the cure, to ogle their partners at balls at the Assembly Rooms — and best of all, to be stared at themselves in return.

The position occupied by Bath in eighteenth-century England was unique. There were other spots in the Kingdom which possessed medicinal springs — Tunbridge and Epsom and Hampstead — but all these were definitely lower in *ton,* and Epsom was decidedly raffish. Besides, nowhere save at Bath could one drink the healing waters and bathe one's affected limbs as well.

Legends clustered thickly about Bath, some romantic and fanciful, others ludicrous. The city's origins stretched back into the misty reaches of unrecorded time. It was said that the Celts and the Picts had known of the health-giving properties of the springs and had brought their sick to them to be cured. This knowledge they imparted to their Roman conquerors, who created on the shores of the Avon a replica of those resorts which already existed in Italy. They built roads and viaducts. In the construction of the baths and other public edifices they utilized the grayish-golden native sandstone which still gives to Bath its unusual luster and charm.

Another set of legends places the founding of the city in the time of the British King Bladud, son of King Hudibras and father of the unfortunate Lear. The young Prince is reputed to have been banished from his father's court because he was " afflicted with a Leprosie." Morose and disheartened, he hired himself out as a swineherd to a wealthy thane, and spent his time roaming up and down among the low hills which fringe the Avon. One day he noticed that his charges appeared ill and were covered with filthy scabs. Groaning and sweating they dragged their heavy limbs along to a "muddy morass," in which they wallowed. When at last they were led home Bladud discovered that the sores had disappeared. Wisely the Prince concluded that the waters which had cured his hogs might have a salutary effect upon him. He bathed, and emerged free from all traces of his disease. He returned the hogs to the thane and restored himself once more to his parents. And in the year of grace 1741 certain citizens of Bath, retelling the old tale of Bladud and the swine, added the following footnote: " We, whose names are herewith written, natives of the city of Bath, having perused the above tradition, do think it very truly and faithfully related . . . as witness our hands, this first day of November, 1741."

It is certain that there was a general belief which persisted until late in the eighteenth century that the Baths could cure leprosy, for one of them was called the Lepers' Bath, and an inscription near it recounted the healing of one " William Berry, of Galthorp near

Melton Mowbray, County of Leicester, cured of a dry leprosy by the help of God and the Bath, 1737." And weary invalids, returning from the baths on sultry summer afternoons, were grateful to King Bladud for the only place of shade in a long hot walk. This was an octagonal tower with seats for the bathers, a stone balustrade, and a statue of the King.

But in Sheridan's day the sceptic was troubled by doubts as to the actual therapeutic value possessed by the waters. In *St. Patrick's Day*, Sheridan makes Dr. Rosy bemoan his wife's untimely end in these words: "Why, she could decipher a prescription, and invent the ingredients, almost as well as myself; then she was such a hand at making foreign waters! — for Seltzer, Pyrmont, Islington, or Chalybeate, she never had her equal; and her Bath and Bristol springs exceeded the originals. — Ah, poor Dolly! she fell a martyr to her own discoveries!"[1]

But whatever the story of its origin, Bath had become by the first years of the seventeenth century the citadel of the aristocracy. Magnificently conceived and planned by England's ablest architects, it rested on the Somerset hills as a series of semicircles, terraces and crescents, all executed in the same grayish-golden sandstone. The world of fashion made it a place of play. It became the mirror of the vanities and vices of the age.

Gallants rented houses in the North Parade and the

[1] *St. Patrick's Day*, Act I, Scene 1.

Circus, and hard upon their heels trod gamesters and tipsters and trollopes, the refuse and sweepings of the town. " Wherever people of fashion came," said Oliver Goldsmith, " needy adventurers were generally found in waiting. With such Bath swarmed." Goldsmith was writing the life of one of these needy adventurers — of that Richard Nash whom men called " Beau," who until his death in 1761 reigned in Bath as an uncrowned king whose displeasure was feared even by royalty.

It was largely through the skill and tact and the amazing perspicacity of this same Richard Nash that Bath rose from an obscure English " spaw " to a watering-place whose brilliance and elegance were renowned all over the civilized world. Nash disapproved of the wearing of swords, and suddenly dueling, which had been for so many years the chief occupation of the gentleman, was considered unfashionable. Himself a gambler, he established in Bath several gaming-houses in which he maintained an interest. Besides Ombre and Lanterloo and Hazard the country soon was playing Nash's new game called " Eo." Indeed, gaming was becoming a passion all over England. Everyone played cards, and cards were decorated with every conceivable and fantastic adornment. There were cards to commemorate Marlborough's victories. There were cards for Brag, for Whist, or Whisk, for Rolly Polly, Pharaoh, and Post and Pair. There were Sacheverell cards, cards from Vigo, after the battle in 1702, and innumerable sets of Proverb cards. " What is Eng-

land now?" mused Horace Walpole in 1773,—"A
sink of Indian wealth, filled by Nabobs and emptied
by Macaronis." At one sitting the Duke of Northumberland lost twenty thousand pounds at quadrille.
Everyone would take a wager—on anything. Young
bloods idling at Brooks' placed serious bets as to
whether a man knocked down by a carriage was dead
or alive—but no one moved from his chair to help
him! Gaming was largely responsible for the aristocratic highwaymen who infested society. It was no
unusual thing to encounter on Hampstead Heath or
Blackheath one's dinner partner of the week before,
armed and wrapped in a heavy cloak, and to be bidden
summarily to stand and deliver.

When he was fourteen, Charles James Fox had been
taken abroad by his doting father to Spa, and there,
with a nightly allowance of five guineas for the tables,
initiated into the fascinations of play. At sixteen he
had been elected to Almack's Club — afterwards
Brooks'. There he and his friends would sit from ten
o'clock at night until six the following evening, while
a tired waiter stood beside them to remind each drowsy
player whose deal it was. Thousands of pounds were
tossed on the tables between them. They began "by
pulling off their embroidered clothes," wrote Horace
Walpole, who had frequently observed such a scene,
"and putting on frieze greatcoats, or turned their coats
outwards for luck. They put on pieces of leather, such
as are worn by footmen when they clean knives to save
their lace ruffles ; and to guard their eyes from the light,

[17]

and to prevent tumbling their hair, wore high-crowned straw hats with broad brims and adorned with flowers and ribbons."

Besides ruining young gentlemen so that they were driven to try their fortunes as " gentlemen of the road," the prevalence of gambling had still another effect upon society. Men who could hazard all they possessed or could borrow upon a single throw could not be expected to watch very diligently the expenditure of the public funds. Corruption was consequently an open and accepted fact.

It was an age of great and lusty drinkers. Even ladies drank porter with their lobsters, and gentlemen sat for eight or ten hours at a time over claret or port, or rock-punch and brandy. Drunkenness was an admitted fact which required no concealment. On the contrary, one's prowess with the bottle was as much a source of pride and vanity as one's luck at cards or one's success with the ladies. Thus a " three-bottle man " had acquired a dimension, a stature, which stamped him unmistakably. Pitt the Elder drank port profusely. " He was observed," the *Morning Chronicle* noted in 1772, " in walking to his carriage after a Canterbury Corporation banquet, to oscillate like his own Bills." And Richard Sheridan, himself a hardened drinker, wrote in *The Duenna:*

> A bumper of good liquor
> Will end a contest quicker
> Than Justice, Judge or Vicar.

It was an age of scandal, openly discussed and disseminated, in many cases openly invented. Privacy was the prerogative only of the humble and the obscure. Newspapers depended for their circulation upon a restricted class of readers. They fed the insatiable and prurient curiosity of the middle classes by lurid bits of gossip from the Great World. The gentleman or lady of fashion recognized with a satisfied smile the names of his or her friends in the columns of some lying sheet; or perhaps he saw his own, and realized with horror that neither age nor sex nor position rendered one immune from the filthy fingers of the gossip-writer. So wrote David Garrick in his Prologue to *The School for Scandal:*

Give me the papers, Lisp — how bold and free!
Last night Lord L. (sips) was caught with Lady D.
For aching heads what charming sal volatile!
If Mrs. B. will still continue flirting,
We hope she'll DRAW, or we'll UNDRAW the curtain.

. . .

. . . A certain lord had best beware
Who lives not twenty miles from Grosvenor Square,
For, should he Lady W. find willing,
Wormwood is bitter — Oh, that's me, the villain!
Throw it behind the fire, and never more
Let that vile paper come within my door!

And in *The Critic* Sheridan himself condemned them: "The newspapers! Sir, they are the most villainous, licentious, abominable, infernal — Not that I ever read them! No, I make it a rule *never* to look at a newspaper!"

It was an age when upstarts from the ranks of "trade" lent money at staggering rates of interest. Everyone gambled; the times were insecure and unrest was prevalent; everyone was in debt — and the usurers flourished in the land. It was an age of ostentation and display. Of florid *roulades* in music, of "Gothic" over-ornamentation in architecture and landscaping, of pretentiousness in dress. The toilette of the man or woman of the world took hours of careful thought; when completed it was a work of art. The ambition of every young man from the Prince of Wales to the stock-broker's clerk was to be a beau, a macaroni, although only a scant few achieved that distinction.

It was an age when the voice of poverty was inaudible, and when the man of wealth could and did buy anything — talent, position, political preferment. Edmund Burke was practically supported for years by "gifts" from Pitt, Lord Rockingham, and Joshua Reynolds. Charles James Fox found a way to defray his enormous expenses by the "subscriptions" of his friends. Even Sheridan, burdened with debts as he always was, gladly contributed. Fox was adept at securing government pensions for people whose services to the nation might be considered dubious. He obtained one for Miss Willoughby, his natural daughter, and one for the beautiful "Perdita" Robinson, once the mistress of His Royal Highness the Prince of Wales. The younger Pitt invented the post of Third

Secretary for Dundas, thereby causing Sheridan to remark in a speech in 1795, "We certainly had a most
gentlemanlike administration, and Mr. Secretary
Dundas was three times as much a gentleman as any
of them, for he had three places." This was that same
Dundas to whom Sheridan once replied after a debate
in the House of Commons: "The Right Honourable
Gentleman is indebted to his memory for his jests, and
to his imagination for his facts."

Money could even buy for its possessor a title; the
traffic in titles was become a vast and profitable business. In the first thirteen years after his rise to power
Pitt made more than eighty new peers, and before his
death he had conferred almost one hundred and fifty
coronets.

It was an age of oratory — on the stage as well as
in Parliament. The words were unimportant. It was
the inflection, the gesture, which rated with the discerning. "The whole world knows," Sheridan stated
in a speech on the proposed Irish union, "that never
was there a time when fine speeches more powerfully
affected the public, and never a time when the public
has appeared less profoundly eager to examine any
question."

It was an age when nobody worked, when the possession of a visible means of support was most frequently an insurmountable barrier against admission
into the world of Society. Money must be inherited.
One might own lands in England or even in the Colonies — in America or in the magical West Indies —

but persons "in trade" were kept from rising in the fashionable world by the weight of their own business enterprises. Wrote Selleck Osborn:

> My father's trade! — why, blockhead, art thou mad?
> My father, sir, did never stoop so low;
> He was a Gentleman, I'd have you know!

It was an age when gentility and excessive refinement rubbed elbows with the most astonishing coarsenesses of speech, with vulgarities of behavior, and with a cruel and sadistic delight in physical deformities and suffering. The madhouse at Bedlam and the gallows upon Tyburn Hill were still the two most popular pleasure-spots in all London.

In short, it was an age when, said the urbane Chesterfield, ".Everybody's son married nobody's daughter."

All these men came to Bath, crowding its streets, drinking its waters: the fortune-hunter, the place-seeker, the debtor, the gambler, the tradesman and the rogue. Beau Nash knew that in his rôle of Master of Ceremonies he must be tireless, unflagging, if he was to keep Bath orderly and civilized. The rules which he laid down for good behavior in his little principality he enforced strictly, and to him the visitors owed the rapid improvement in the baths and in the town itself.

A hundred years before Nash's advent conditions in Bath had become literally so malodorous that the Cor-

poration, meeting in September, 1646, enacted several
"Bye-Laws," which were consistently disregarded
until enforced by the Beau himself. These laws provided against the throwing "into the said Baths" of
any "dog, bitch, or other live beast," or of a person's
clothing, and emphatically stated "that no persons
shall disorderly or uncivilly demean themselves in the
said Baths, on pain of forfeiting five shillings." Lodgings were squalid, uncomfortable, and in many in-
stances actually filthy. And since Bath existed for
the ostensible purpose of healing the sick, its association with the medical profession was necessarily an
intimate one. That is to say, there were more quacks
in Bath than even in London.

The doctors in their handsome waistcoats and pow-
dered wigs called for their chairs and descended in
avid swarms upon each new arrival. They bled him
and purged him. Learnedly they rubbed their noses
and said "Hrumph!" while listening to his symptoms.
Then they prescribed for the sufferer restoratives and
remedies straight from the realm of necromancy:
"Live Hog Lice, Burned Coke quenched in Aqua Vitæ,
Red Coral, New-gathered Earthworms, Live Toads,
Black Tips of Crabs' Claws, Man's Skull, Elk's Hoofs,
Goose Dung gathered in the Spring of the Year and
Dry'd in the Sun, and Powder'd Unicorn's Horn." [2]
To be mixed wtih saffron and sugar candy, and taken
twice a day for six days in a glass of Rhenish wine.

[2] From *Bath*, by Edith Sitwell, by courtesy of the publisher, Peter
Smith.

Since Bath was in every way the prototype of the elegances, the culture and refinement of the Town, it is small wonder that very early in the eighteenth century it felt the need of a theater. In 1705 the first playhouse in the city was built on the site of the old Mineral Water Hospital at the top of hilly Parsonage Lane. It was a dreary place, small and badly ventilated, and given at times to the most amazing and inexplicable echoings. After a few years it was sold and the players presented their dramas at Simpson's Rooms, at the Globe or the George — both inns — or at a place in Kingsmead Street called simply " New Theatre." They performed the old favorites — *Othello* and the *Merchant,* Otway's *Ophelia,* Farquhar's *Constant Couple,* Mrs. Centlivre's *Gamester,* Steele's *Conscious Lovers* and Southern's *Oronooko.* Nightly in London one could see these same stately figures walking briefly in the light of a few candles, could listen to the same round, ringing speeches. But there was this difference. At Bath the strolling player was still a poor rogue, ill-clad and badly housed. His theater was a jerry-built affair, and he possessed none of those portable scenic effects, those magnificent trappings of royal might, which thrilled and awed the London audiences. Thus it is no surprise to read how some poor devil was forced so low by grim necessity that once in Bath he enacted " Alexander the Great in a paper cravat."

The passion for sumptuous costume was reaching such a height that the paper-cravatted Alexander was indeed a sorry figure. The clothes worn by the actors seldom bore any relation to the period of the drama; they were majestic in themselves and so served simply as one more factor in the genre of frank theatricality. In 1765 Garrick played Othello in a full suit of scarlet regimentals, gold-laced, a cocked hat, knee breeches and silk stockings which rendered his gouty legs quite conspicuous. His portrayal of Macbeth was made doubly memorable by his appearance in a court suit of sky blue and scarlet. But when, in John Home's *Tragedy of Douglas,* he essayed the harassed chieftain in the garb of a "modern Venetian gondolier," and elsewhere introduced a "Polish procession made up of white friars and other moveables, like a bishop, a *chœur des enfants,* etc.," the pamphleteers were loud in their contempt.

The famous actor Palmer and his son enlarged the theater at Bath during the season 1774–75, remodeling it and adding as the final embellishment of fashion some pillars in the Ionic style. Bath had in the last few years become so crowded that its one playhouse was thronged by the smartest and most critical of England's playgoers, and it was now the recognized place for a fashionable theatrical début. One of the most famous was that of young Henderson — "Mr. Courtney" he styled himself upon the playbill — whom the great Garrick had sent down to Palmer for *Hamlet.* Bath proved for young Mr. Henderson-Courtney an excellent school. He stepped from several seasons with the Palmers into stellar rôles in London. Furthermore, his own début at Bath having had for him the pleasantest of results, it was in that city that he sponsored the first successful appearance, in Vanbrugh's *Provok'd Husband*, of his " discovery." She was a tall, deep-breasted girl, the daughter of Roger Kemble and Sarah Ward, and already at twenty-three had been for several years the wife of one William Siddons, an actor in her father's company.

In 1761 Beau Nash died in Saw-Close in abject poverty. He had gambled away several fortunes at his own tables, and the friends who had won from him had not seemed anxious to gladden his last years with loans and little attentions. Five years later another of the city's most distinguished residents lay on his deathbed in a lodging-house in Pierrepont Street. His name was James Quin, and he had been called the greatest *Falstaff* ever to tread the boards. Shakily, in a darkening room, he wrote his last will and testament. " I give and bequeath to Thomas Gainsborough, limner, now living at Bath, fifty pounds." How gratefully the " limner " must have heard of his friend's bequest — Gainsborough, so busily painting the heads of the fashionable, so harassed by children and overrun with debts !

But the Beau's work lived on, although the gay town never seemed to pause long enough in its merrymaking to regret him. His energies had whipped Bath into a place of beauty, of comfortable inns, tolerably clean bathing-places, and shaded streets where one was reasonably safe from the depredations of footpads. He had even settled to some extent the incessant war which raged among the chair-bearers, regulating the tariff which they were permitted to charge, and putting to a stop the disgraceful practice which prevailed in London of "not letting customers out of the chair, though if it was raining they would open the top and let him or her — often an invalid — be exposed to the wet, until in despair the charge was met." [3]

Nash had given to Bath an enviable luster, a brilliance in which all sought to share. In consequence the city grew rich, for people came from far and near to taste its pleasures. Not a name of importance was omitted from the pages of its Visitors' Book. The brothers Wood, the architects, were kept busy building their perfect Palladian houses. The courtyards of the White Hart, the Bear or the Three Tuns clattered continually with the comings and goings of stage-coaches and post-chaises. Gill, the confectioner, provided in his shop a refuge for both constant and inconstant couples, and Scrace's livery stables furnished the fastest horses to aid eloping heiresses. It was the Bachelors' Elysium. They might subscribe a crown at any of the circulating libraries — Frederick's or Meyer's or Leak's. "Those evergreen trees of diabolical knowledge," Miss Lydia Languish's inimitable aunt would presently call them. At the *Chronicle* office the news, a short fourteen hours from London by courier, was al-

[3] From *Bath*, by Edith Sitwell. Courtesy of Peter Smith.

ways available. They could book places for the galas, gossip with friends over the waters at the Pump Rooms, and hear the newest scandal.

In *Humphrey Clinker* the irascible Dr. Smollett has painted the scene. Says Matthew Bramble: " Every upstart of fortune, harnessed in the trappings of the Mode, presents himself at Bath as in the very focus of observation. Clerks, factors from the East, loaded with the spoils of plundered provinces, planters, Negro drivers and hucksters from our American plantations, enriched they know not how; commissaries and contractors, who have fattened in two successive wars on the blood of the nation; brokers and jobbers of every kind; men of low birth and no breeding have found themselves translated into a state of affluence, unknown to former ages; and it is no wonder that their brains should be intoxicated with pride, vanity and presumption. Even the wives and daughters of low tradesmen, who, like shovel-nosed sharks, prey on the blubber of these uncouth whales of fortune, are affected with the same rage of displaying their importance, and the slightest indisposition serves them for a pretext to insist on being conveyed to Bath, where they may hobble country dances and cotillions among lordlings, squires, counsellors and clergy."

Bath carried to perfection the " art of doing nothing without being bored." By the year 1770 the city had acquired a resident population of unquestioned prestige, which seemed to have forgotten completely that as recently as the reign of the first George a Jacobite arsenal had been planted at Bath, and an uprising planned there. Lord Chesterfield maintained an establishment in Pierrepont Street, where not many years later the presence of Admiral Viscount Nelson made a perpetual show for the sightseers. There was Horace Walpole, residing elegantly in Chapel Course, and Viscount Clare, whom Oliver Goldsmith once visited. The Royal residence at West Gate, hard by the showrooms of Josiah Wedgwood, was kept by Her Royal Highness the brusque and eccentric Princess Amelia, author of those pathetic verses beginning:

> Unthinking, idle, wild and young,
> I laughed and danced and talked and sung.

Dr. Johnson lived at 4, Edgar Buildings; the Lexicographer was now the happy recipient of two hundred pounds a year from Lord Bute, which some people said had been secured for him by Thomas Sheridan. At 8 Gay Street there was Mrs. Piozzi — at that time still the wife of Thrale, the wealthy brewer. There was the aunt of Lord Ferrers, the notorious rake and murderer — Selina, Countess of Huntingdon, herself an ardent disciple of John Wesley. "The St. Theresa of the Methodists," Horace Walpole dubbed her. Besides Gainsborough the world of fashionable art was represented by Sir Thomas Lawrence. There was Priestley, the discoverer of oxygen, and at Prior Park the fortunate visitor went to dine with that Ralph Allen whom Fielding immortalized as Squire Allworthy. At Kingston House the Duke and Duchess of Kingston

entertained; in Liliput Alley dwelt a famous person-
age named Sally Lunn; and at 5 Pierrepont Street
lived Thomas Linley and his talented family. Near
them was the home of Thomas Sheridan — a grizzled,
choleric old man, very reminiscent of Sir Anthony
Absolute — of his daughters Alicia and Elizabeth, and
of his sons, Charles Francis and the handsome Richard.

CHAPTER TWO

Sirens and Perfect Syllables

LIKE so many of England's men of genius, Dick
Sheridan was Irish. His family line was long and,
although not particularly distinguished, nevertheless
contained the names of several personages who served
as satisfactory ancestors. Some of his forebears had
followed the Stuart fortunes and lost both their lives
and their estates ; others had been schoolmasters, poor
in purse, but rich in those treasures of the mind concerning which the poets had so feelingly sung. Dr.
Thomas Sheridan, his paternal grandfather, had been
a friend of the great Swift. The two old men had sat
sipping rum punches through many an interminable
evening of Olympian conversation. Thomas Sheridan's only fault, according to Swift, was " a wife and
four children." The friendship of the two men was
of long duration, and although there were times when
each spoke contemptuously of the other, the bond between them was very strong.

The Sheridans resided at Quilcagh House, which
had been restored to the family by Tom's marriage to
Elizabeth, daughter of the wealthy Charles MacFadden. To Quilcagh Swift came frequently. There, under his friend's noisy but hospitable roof, he wrote the

only two works which he ever signed — the *Drapier Letters* and *Gulliver's Travels*. The Dean had exacted from Thomas Sheridan a promise to tell him if ever he noticed any signs of avarice appearing in his friend; yet when Sheridan fulfilled his end of the bargain Swift quarreled violently with him, and they never spoke to each other again.

But when Swift's beloved Stella lay dying in 1727 she offered Tom Sheridan a legacy, which he stoutly refused. For, like his dazzling grandson, old Thomas Sheridan possessed a high, Quixotic sense of honor — and a propensity for being taken in by clever swindlers. His life is a foreshadowing on a modest scale of what Richard Brinsley Sheridan's would be sixty and seventy years later. There was the same never-ceasing struggle with duns and bailiffs, for his wife's fortune was soon spent and debts piled up faster than Thomas could pay them. There was the same love of practical jokes and foolery, the same lack of punctuality, the same disregard of all mundane things like bills and letters and dinner engagements. Above all, the same wit, the same sparkling and infectious gaiety.

Tom Sheridan had a son, also named Thomas, who was to be the playwright's father. Swift was his teacher as a young boy; later like any " gentleman's " son he continued his education at Westminster. But young Tom was not planning to follow his father and end his days as an impecunious schoolmaster with a flock of sniveling, ill-nourished children. In 1743 the rôle of Richard III was enacted at the Smock Alley

Theatre in Dublin by a "Young Gentleman," behind which phrase Tom was concealing his identity. For two years he remained nameless on the playbill; then he emerged and in his proper person took his place as Master of the Royal Theatre. A few years of moderate success here and Tom Sheridan would cross the sea to play Horatio in Rowe's *Fair Penitent* at Covent Garden, and the title rôle in *Tancred* at Drury Lane.

In London Tom Sheridan became involved in the first of those two theatrical mishaps with which his career is darkened. It concerned a beautiful young actress named Miss Bellamy, whose charms aroused the unwelcome attentions of a group of young rowdies. The gentlemen stormed the beauty's dressing-room, and Tom, who had played so many valiant heroes on the stage, leaped at once to her defense. A fight ensued. Chairs were smashed, heads were broken, the management pleaded and protested. Tom Sheridan found himself the victim of a mob. But there was one spectator in the audience that night whose sympathies were with the young actor. She was Miss Frances Anne Chamberlaine, and she was later to become Tom's wife and the mother of his children, as well as one of the most notable writers of her day.

Later Tom played with Peg Woffington, whom he remembered at the close of his life as " a most willing bitch, artful, dissembling, lewd and malicious. A very captivating woman, and one who never failed to get a great influence over all the men that lived with her."

That Mistress Woffington herself had no higher opinion of her own character is evidenced by what she once told Tom Sheridan when the two were discussing a possible mode of life for the lady's young sister. "There are two things which she should never become, by my advice — a whore and an actress, for I have sufficiently experienced the inconveniences of both these ways of life myself."

Sheridan and Miss Chamberlaine met; they became friends. He heard from her lips stories of her father, the eccentric Archdeacon of Glendalough, who abhorred female education so violently that he could barely be persuaded to have his daughters taught their letters. He read some of her verses and found them deeply moving. And in the spring of 1747 they were married and settled at No. 12, Dorset Street, in Dublin.

There in September of 1751 their son, Richard Brinsley, was born. There were other Sheridan children — Alicia and Charles Francis and Eliza — and Tom was very busy with his management of the Smock Alley Theatre. Until 1754 all went well. Then the second misfortune occurred, and the Sheridans were compelled to leave Dublin.

This time a man was the protagonist. He was a young actor named Digges, and he was appearing as Alcanor in Tom Sheridan's production of *Mahomet,* by Voltaire. In the course of the play Digges strode downstage toward the footlights and raised his arms to heaven:

Mrs Elizabeth Sheridan

Engraved by H. Meyer from a Drawing by Ozias Humphry, R.A.

ELIZABETH LINLEY SHERIDAN
From the drawing by Ozias Humphry

If, ye powers divine,
Ye mark the movements of this nether world
And bring them to account, crush, crush these vipers,
Who, singled out by the community
To guard their rights, shall for a grasp of ore
Or paltry office sell them to the foe.

Mr. Digges was speaking to a group of Irishmen.
For centuries they had felt themselves cowed and humiliated by an alien government which ruled them
from London and rarely troubled to cross the sea and
view conditions at first hand. There had been several
abortive attempts to drive out the English, but their
immediate results had been only the shedding of enormous quantities of blood and the enactment of still
more repressive measures. The audience rose in their
seats now and demanded frantically that Digges repeat
his lines. He did; such an overwhelming tribute to his
talents could not leave him unmoved. There was, an
instant afterward, pandemonium. Men leaped upon
the stage, shouting and raging and smashing the scenery. The candles in their tin shields were menaced.
Presently one candle was kicked aside, and before help
came Tom Sheridan's theater had burned to the
ground. History follows a definite pattern in the
Sheridan family. A little more than sixty years later
Drury Lane, in which his son had invested the earnings
of a lifetime, would also be consumed by fire.

Tom was now without a theater, without any means
of supporting his family. After weeks of despair, he
decided to set out once again for London. There at

least were a few theaters where he might try his luck. And the London public was admittedly the most cultured and critical in the world. Tom departed for the metropolis. Shortly after his arrival he began a season with Rich at Covent Garden.

But critical as the London public was, it still failed sufficiently to appreciate Thomas Sheridan. He and Rich quarreled constantly — over costumes, over the selection of rôles; and when Rich even questioned the proper shading of a line Tom quitted the stage of Covent Garden forever. Rich had unthinkingly touched the Irishman's vulnerable spot. For Thomas Sheridan, erstwhile pupil of Dean Swift, had his own ideas on declamation and elocution. When he saw that the world was not prepared to welcome them, he set out, single-handed, to teach the world.

Saving the world by rhetoric was a stupendous task. In his newly created rôle of educator extraordinary Thomas Sheridan wrote and published *The Art of Speaking,* and settled himself to wait for disciples. London accepted him as another in that long line of eccentrics which crowds the eighteenth century — that roster which includes Lady Hester Stanhope, who died in Syria, the Chevalier D'Eon, and Soubise, the Negro page of the Duchess of Queensberry, who was still alive at the close of the century. Samuel Foote, the supreme opportunist, wrote a comedy about him which he called *The Orators,* and it enjoyed a moderately successful run. But Thomas Sheridan persisted; he even contemplated a series of lecture tours for the following year.

His family was still living in Dublin. Money was scarce; there was never a time when the Sheridans were entirely free from dread of the bailiffs. Mrs. Sheridan, she who had been Frances Chamberlaine and had written pretty little verses and even a pamphlet on the state of the Dublin theater, took up her pen again — this time for the purpose of earning money. It was the day when the novel was burgeoning. A story filled three volumes, and a " good " novel — one, that is, with an easily discernible moral and a lofty didactic tone — might influence the lives of thousands of readers. Frances Sheridan applied herself diligently to the composition of such a work.

In 1761 she published *Sydney Biddulph,* of whose affecting chapters Dr. Johnson later told her, " I know not, madam, that you have a right upon moral principles to make your readers suffer so much." She dedicated it to Samuel Richardson, on whose advice it had been undertaken, and it was published anonymously. *Sydney Biddulph* was an overnight success. With her coffers replenished and her heart pleasantly warmed by praise from such distinguished men as Lord North and the Lexicographer, Mrs. Sheridan left for London to be near her husband. She left Dick and Alicia in Dublin in the care of Mr. Samuel Whyte, who kept a school in Grafton Street — " A Seminary for the In-struction of Youth" — which the two children attended.[1]

Tom Sheridan was overjoyed to welcome his wife. He talked to her in long swelling sentences of the work upon which he had embarked, and referred with pleasure to the successful lectures he had delivered at Oxford and Cambridge, during the course of which both universities had conferred upon him the degree of Master of Arts. She met his friends. The Lexicographer, who had read her novel; Mrs. Cholmondely and Mrs. Catherine Macaulay; Samuel Richardson, the author of *Pamela,* who praised her as a fellow craftsman, and David Garrick, who brought her life once again into contact with the theater. Tom must have been somewhat amazed at the ease with which this circle of the élite widened to include his wife. Frances had always been clever, to be sure. A bit of a bluestocking, perhaps. But to hear her " work " discussed so seriously by these superior persons, to be compelled to admit that *Sydney Biddulph* was not an isolated phenomenon but one which might recur again and yet again, gave the rhetorician pause. So far he had done very little toward saving the world by the application of logic to elocution. But Frances Sheridan had, for the moment at least, unquestionably saved the family.

Frances Sheridan enjoyed writing. What she wrote did not matter. Her pen was extremely facile and

[1] Another of Samuel Whyte's pupils, and a fellow-classmate of Richard Sheridan, was Thomas Moore, " the Minstrel Boy."

could produce pamphlets, essays and even dramas, as well as fiction. A few years after *Sydney Biddulph's* success the vogue of the Eastern romances began. Frances Sheridan read them; she determined to write one of her own. She called it *The Tale of Nourjahad,* and crammed it to its last page with beautiful sirens and tall palm trees, with necklaces and necromancers. It was even more popular than its predecessor, and when her bright-haired son Richard was a man past middle life *Nourjahad* was dramatized and produced at Drury Lane.

Perhaps it was the great Garrick who first suggested that this versatile woman try her hand at writing plays. Certainly it was not Tom. He had severed his connection with the stage. It was a dying institution where no one pronounced his consonants correctly, and Tom was well rid of it. And the plays were, if such a thing were possible, even worse than the actors, — silly, mawkish, artificial things. It was surely not worth the effort required to write one.

Yet Frances Sheridan found play-writing the most thrilling of all the forms of creation she had tried. To see one's written pages printed and bound was a keen, sweet pain. But when the characters one had evoked from within oneself took form, when they moved and spoke and suffered upon a lighted stage — that was an indescribable rapture. Like seeing one's children alive and grown before one's eyes, someone suggested. Perhaps, she mused, but in her heart she knew it was not so. One shared children — there was always, somewhere, a father. But these people she had created were *hers*. They belonged to a part of her life which neither Tom Sheridan nor the children she had borne him could ever hope to share. None of the children, of course, save Richard.

So Frances Sheridan wrote plays: *The Discovery* and *The Dupe;* and of the former David Garrick said that it was " one of the best comedies that ever I read." He produced it and acted in it at Drury Lane in 1763. She wrote and saw produced a comedy called *A Journey to Bath,* and it is not very difficult to see in this play the germ of her son Richard's *Rivals.* At least to recognize in Lady Tryfort the first sketch, faint but unmistakable, of the magnificent Mrs. Malaprop. For from the very first the theater strummed in young Richard's blood. Not his father's theater, a lifeless world of inflection and stilted gesture, but his mother's, where people were created and situations were tailored to their measure. It is no wonder that he wrote plays. The wonder is that Richard Brinsley Sheridan ever did anything else.

CHAPTER THREE

Puppet Promenade

HE WHO was destined to be the most brilliant sophisticate, the keenest wit of his day, was at school a dull and mediocre pupil. Later he soared so surely to the top; at school he lagged miserably behind. Already in 1759 Mr. Samuel Whyte of Grafton Street in Dublin had earned his immortality by declaring that the eight-year-old lad who nodded in his school-room was " a most impenetrable dunce." Three years later he was making the same impression upon the masters at Harrow.

Among his classmates were boys who would become the leaders of another generation. There was the future Sir William Jones; there was the boy who, as Dr. Parr, " the Latinist of tombs," [1] was to teach Cicero and Vergil to a young girl marked by fate for great unhappiness — Anne Isabella Milbanke, the future Lady Byron. There was Nathaniel Brassey Halhed, with whom Sheridan later collaborated. There was Lord Robert Spencer — he would set the fashion for those short skirtless coats called " spencers " by declaring

---

[1] Parr specialized in epitaphs. He wrote one for Samuel Johnson and one for Elizabeth Linley Sheridan.

that he could make the public wear anything, no matter how absurd and unbecoming it might be. And there was that young Robinson who gained his fame as husband of the exquisite " Perdita " Robinson, sometime mistress to Charles James Fox and to His Royal Highness Prince " Florizel " of Wales.

Harrow at that time was reminiscent of a village school. Its setting was definitely rustic, with its school buildings and adjacent boarding-houses lost completely behind tall, wide-branching trees. Young Dick thoroughly enjoyed the quiet beauty of its lawns and river-banks, but he was very lonely amidst all this pastoral charm. Harrow was a gentleman's school ; and the young gentlemen were not willing to accept or welcome the player's son. He was excluded from their games and friendships. They derided his origins. They laughed at his clothes, which were far from elegant since Tom Sheridan's elocution lessons had fallen off ; for it took a deal of scraping and pinching to keep four children clothed and fed. Dick's heart burned, but he managed to keep his temper. Only a few weeks more of Greek prose and jeers in the corridors. Then came holidays, and they were compensation enough for all the miseries of term. Sometimes he remained at Harrow after the other boys had gone, and all the lovely green solitude became his to cherish and to enjoy. He shied stones into the water, he read, he sat in a flowering glade and laboriously wrote some verses in his copy-book. It was for such moments of remembered bliss that he loved the country around

Harrow all his life. And sometimes he journeyed for his holidays to Richmond, to the home of Mr. Aikenhead, " the splendid West Indian."

In 1818, two years after Sheridan's death, when his friend Thomas Moore was collecting material for his very biased and distorted *Life* of the dramatist, Parr, an old and very feeble man, wrote to him reminiscently of Sheridan the boy: " With the aid of a scribe I sit down to fulfill my promise about Mr. Sheridan. There was little in his boyhood worth communication. He was inferior to many of his fellows in the ordinary business of a school, and I do not remember any one incident in which he distinguished himself by Latin or English composition, in prose or in verse." It was true that Sheridan, light-hearted, mischievous and gay, never received his masters' approbation for his knowledge of the classical authors. Yet of those many endless pages of Greek and Latin, so painfully construed, so stumblingly translated, something remained. Thirty years later, in the House of Commons, Sheridan was able to correct Lord Belgrave when he misquoted a line of Demosthenes in reference to Philip of Macedon.

Four years had rounded into completeness; and while Richard remained at Harrow, striving to live up to the traditions of the school and failing woefully, his father experienced another of his major financial reverses. The family found itself penniless. They fled to France to escape the sheriff's officer; after weeks of wandering they settled in Blois. There, in their haven under the plane trees, Frances Sheridan died on September 26, 1766. Her son Richard, who had adored her, was then fifteen.

He was lonelier than ever now, and so shocked by what had happened to his brave and clever mother that he failed at first to comprehend the tragedy. To his uncle Chamberlaine, his guardian in his father's absence and possesser of a purse much ampler than Tom Sheridan's, he wrote:

> DEAR UNCLE:
>
> It is now almost a week since Mr. Somner [2] [*sic*] told me the melancholy news of my poor mother's death, and as Mr. Somner has not heard what time my Father will be home, he desires me to write to you about mourning. I have wrote to Riley who with your orders will make me a suit of Black. I should be obliged if you would let me know what time you expect my Father. You will excuse the shortness of my letter as the subject is disagreeable.
>
> From your aff't nephew,
R. B. SHERIDAN
>
> P. S. I must also have a new hat with a Crape and black stokins [*sic*] and buckles. I should be glad of them on Saturday.

Poor Dick! The subject was " disagreeable " indeed! Choked by his grief and by a sense of loss which the years would not very much lighten, school became increasingly intolerable, and Richard pleaded to be free of it. Yet his harassed father remained in France.

---

[2] That was Mr. Sumner, of all the masters perhaps the closest to young Dick.

There was still the matter of those debts and the sheriff's officer. One year passed, and another. Monotonous and uneventful day followed day. The seasons marched by in painted sequence, and Richard construed his Greek and committed to memory the dates of the English kings. At last, in 1769, Thomas Sheridan returned to England. He published his *Matured Plan of Education for Young Nobility and Gentry,* paid off his creditors, and sent for his son.

Richard was to leave Harrow. His boxes and books were packed and waiting for the carter. His brief farewells were made. "Goodbye, sir," to Dr. Sumner. "Goodbye," a little more fervently, to Parr. He ran across the sparkling grass and up a flight of worn oak stairs. Halhed's room. His friend was waiting.

"Goodbye, Nat." It was the same word, yet its sad finality was clear to him for the first time. He and Nathaniel Halhed had found each other only a few months ago. Now they stood shaking hands —

"Goodbye, Dick Sheridan."

"You'll come to London, Nat? You promise?"

"Soon. Quite soon. In no time at all we shall meet in London."

Their clasped hands clung warmly. The days they had shared were past. When they met again each would have had some new experience of which the other knew nothing. So much they had planned together, these two. But now it was all so far away. Nathaniel might never come to London. Thomas Sheridan might be forced to take his family away again. No one knew.

[45]

Only what had happened was real — and that was all past. What had happened, and this tiny fragment of time which they still shared. A room with sunlight checkering the floor, an ormulu clock ticking in a corner, and two boys realizing that they had written FINIS to a chapter.

Tom Sheridan had taken lodgings in Frith Street, near Soho. There in a candle-lit twilight the little family met again. Tom clasped his boy to his heart and wept to see that he had grown, that presently he would be a boy no longer. Richard saw his brother, Charles Francis, and the two sisters, Eliza and Alicia. They were all so different from when they had last been together. Childhood was over. While he had been away at Harrow they had all been growing up. And once again he had the feeling he had known when he parted from Halhed. The moment passes. Everything fades and crumbles away. For such a little time it is ours to enjoy that we scarcely realize we have it until it is gone. Later, when he was older and no longer felt the clarity of the emotion, he was able to put it into words.

Charles and Richard soon made the acquaintance of a Mr. Lewis Ker, Irish like themselves and once a physician, who agreed to instruct them in matters of their own selection. Ker was a portentous bore as well as a poor teacher, but neither Richard nor his brother cared particularly. They had had their fill of school. Besides, Richard had met Angelo, the fencing-master, and in return for lessons in rhetoric which he gave Angelo's son the father was teaching him to handle the foils. This was sheer and undiluted delight. A leap, a turn of the wrist, a lunge . . . and there was your adversary, unarmed, defenseless! Dick applied himself diligently, and Angelo beamed his approbation.

Things at home could be dull, too, Richard discovered after a few weeks. Almost as dull as at school. His father talked constantly of the sad plight of the English stage and of the glories of the day to come, when his system of declamation would have been universally adopted. Sometimes he spoke of Frances Anne Sheridan, his dear wife, and tears clouded his voice. Richard, too, wept whenever his mother's name was mentioned. She seemed somehow to be receding from him. When he was alone he could call her quite distinctly to his side; but when his father recalled her death on that quiet autumn day in Blois he might almost have been describing the passing of a stranger.

Money was scarce, as it so frequently was with the Sheridans, and the household practiced some rigorous economies. The girls turned and refurbished old gowns. Candles were always being snuffed out to preserve their last scrap of brightness. And the pleasures of the table were temporarily postponed. But occasionally there was a gala evening. A few weeks after Richard's arrival Tom took his sons to a concert. The performers were two members of the gifted Linley family — Elizabeth Anne, then aged fifteen, and her sister Mary, eleven. The girls played uncommonly well, and Elizabeth possessed a voice of rare purity.

She was herself remarkably beautiful. Already gentlemen from one end of England to the other sighed and languished at her feet. Charles Sheridan was captivated at once. Dick, too, felt the power of her grace and of her charm, but he was not in love with her, he assured his brother. Not yet.

Dick was just turned eighteen and he was in London, the hub of the universe, for the first time. He and Charles explored it tirelessly. The sprawling metropolis, noisy and dirty and huge, seemed to them a cheerless and inhospitable place — and one of strange fascination. Its streets were narrow and winding, badly paved and at night so badly lit that thieves walked abroad boldly and even stopped now and then for a word with the watch! That was one of London's charms. The strangers who jostled him so rudely, whose loud voices rang in his ears — each one might be a potential purse-filcher or footpad.

Vice was everywhere. It smiled from the curtained windows of a sedan-chair. It leaned excitedly over long green gambling-tables. It whispered in the verdant *allées* at Vauxhall Gardens and Ranelagh, where one might enjoy Mr. Handel's music and a glass of wine as well as the romantic promise of the setting. And it conversed openly, in the most well-bred accents, in the lobbies of Parliament. The rake, the bawd, the bully and the cheat walked beside Charles Francis Sheridan and his handsome young brother. There was no way of telling whether that man in the street in his tight silk smallclothes, starched ruffles and correctly tied wig was a coiner, a seducer of young ladies, or a gentleman's gentleman taking an afternoon's airing in the Park. Everyone in the teeming city set himself consciously to ape the denizens of the smart world, the people of fashion. They were Fortune's favorites. They were London, the Town itself. And young Richard Sheridan soon decided that London was the world.

He watched them as he walked. He heard a phrase, he caught an inflection. A gesture of the hand, a quirk of the eyebrow, a slight sneering smile. His mind opened to receive and store them all. He heard how the valets and footmen copied their master's swagger as well as his debts. He saw young ladies walking by in their bright panniered skirts. Bits of their talk floated back to him; it was silly, empty of meaning. He heard the gossips at work; he caught the idiom of scandal. Everything that he heard or saw stayed with him. And later when he wrote his plays he had but to open the doors of his mind and the pent figures, released at last, moved and spoke and played their parts again.

Tom Sheridan had made friends in London. Some were men who, like himself, sought to secure a living by amusing or instructing the ladies and gentlemen of fashion. These were the underfed authors who besought my Lord Thingummy's indulgence, and would his Lordship permit them to dedicate to him their latest volume of whatever-it-was — and favor them with twenty pounds? The men who cringed and fawned and waited endlessly in the antechambers of the great for a nod of recognition and a few careless shillings. The men who wrote plays and produced them and acted in them.

Young Dick heard them talk, and he was thrilled as well as awed. While the candle-flames swam in the dark mahogany depths of the sideboard, while the claret and the rock-punch circulated and the drawn curtains shut out the night noises of London, the little room rocked with the tides of conversation. Mr. Garrick, in the deep voice which shook the tapers, spoke of the theater. And on the nights of the great man's absence George Colman [3] and the others spoke of Mr. Garrick. They told stories of his niggardliness and his talents and his love of show. One of these had been a favorite of the late James Quin. It seemed that Garrick, setting out one night to play a benefit, returned to his home a few minutes later, and refused to go on with his performance. He had been frightened, Quin used to say, when he had encountered in a dark alley the ghost of a shilling. . . .

Here again, as in the streets of London, one could amass vast treasuries of knowledge simply by keeping one's ears open and one's lips sealed. There was the craft of the writer, for example. Goldsmith and Johnson and old Richardson freely discussed their plots and their finely turned phrases. They laid bare a character's anguish with the emotionless calm of stockbrok-

[3] In 1766 Colman had collaborated with Garrick in writing *The Clandestine Marriage*, one of the most successful comedies of manners until it was overshadowed by Sheridan's plays.

ELIZABETH LINLEY SHERIDAN as St. Cecilia

From the painting by Reynolds

ers talking over the latest on the Exchange. Listening, Dick Sheridan realized that here were men not unlike himself. Older, of course. More world-weary, more disillusioned. Yet when he grew a bit bolder and placed himself in the forefront of their notice they smiled at his sallies. They found him witty; a bright and engaging talker. And Richard was overjoyed, for he knew that to the man who talked wittily and well no door could long remain closed.

His father's friends spoke also of politics. They stripped from Lord This and His Grace of That all their panoplies of office, and revealed the naked men. And what mean and unbeautiful creatures they were! Cold, avaricious, unscrupulous. Repeatedly these men had been guilty of nepotism, of tampering with the elections, of abusing the public trust in a hundred different ways. But the eighteenth century, although it was alive to the crimes of its men in office, did not condemn them. It was well aware how frail was human flesh, and how fiercely it could be tempted. When men called So-and-So a scoundrel and a rogue there was a hint of envy in their voices. " There," they said, " but for the grace of God, go I." . . .

It was an age of strange contrasts, of a brutal realism which walked hand-in-hand with the most exaggerated sentimentality. The emotions of the novel-reading and play-going public were always very near the surface. The most sophisticated Man of the World was not ashamed to weep at the mention of Virtue seduced, of Honor debauched and cast aside. The orators could with a few deftly rounded periods " dissolve a gallery of strong men in an ocean of tears." Tears were actually an essential feature of a debate. Burke wept unreservedly when Fox spoke to the House in his praise, in 1790. Fox himself was an inveterate weeper; one night while he watched Mrs. Siddons from a stage-box at Drury Lane his unchecked tears bedewed all the instruments of the orchestra. Emotions were violent and unrestrained. While they lasted they were terrible in their fury. But soon they passed like a swift summer shower; the world was calm once more. Scandal and corruption reigned, and one accepted them with a philosophic calm. Politics was admittedly a filthy business. What more logical, the eighteenth century reasoned, than that those who concerned themselves with politics must become filthy too?

Meanwhile Richard Sheridan listened and learned the Politicians' Primer. A political career was the way of all ways in which to achieve distinction. When you became a figure in the political world you automatically became rich. That was as simple as a proposition in Euclid. The Party Leader equals the Man of Means. But in order to win your first election you must have the money necessary to purchase votes. Then, having been duly " returned " from Blank — you substituted here the name of the borough of your choice — you proceeded to line your pockets. Not *too* openly. You were chary of being caught, careful not to offend public taste. But a sufficient number of successful elections could make a rich man out of a poor man. That, too, was axiomatic.

Richard therefore found himself desiring something more than the publication of the pretty little trifles he was forever scribbling. He liked to project himself into the future — not too far distant, he hoped — when he would be " Mr. Sheridan of the House." To that " Mr. Sheridan " a world was possible of attainment which Richard Brinsley Sheridan the simple citizen could never hope to enter.

Thus it happened that in 1769, his very first year in London, Dick began to occupy himself with the political world. He read the vitriolic letters in which *Junius* condemned that arch turncoat, the Duke of Grafton. His Grace was a man whom there indeed were few to praise. " In manner and person," wrote a biographer only ten years after Grafton's death, " he was equally disagreeable; his countenance being heavy and saturnine, and his deportment haughty, sullen and repulsive." Everybody in the London of those years devoured *Junius*. Men accosted each other outside White's or Brooks' with that gentleman's latest diatribe clutched in their hands.

" Have you seen it? " they shouted eagerly. " Scarce three hours old! "

" What the plague! Not another, so soon! "

The paper was snatched from hand to hand. Its cutting phrases wrapped themselves delightfully about one's tongue. A demned satisfying fellow, that *Junius!* That is, if you were of his political complexion.

Sheridan did more than read *Junius*. He set himself the task of answering that man of mystery whose identity no one in London knew. He tried his apprentice hand at a kind of writing which is not at all easy. Like the Dean of St. Patrick's who had once taught Tom Sheridan his letters, Tom's son produced his first serious compositions in the field of political satire. He also found himself composing an occasional lyric or song. These lacked something of Tom Moore's lilt and melody, but they possessed a strength and an authenticity of passion which Moore's tinsel stanzas never had. In Sheridan's songs one finds the true Restoration note sounding again after nearly a century of silence:

> Dry be that tear, my gentlest love,[4]
>   Be hushed that struggling sigh.
> Nor seasons, days, nor fate shall prove
>   More fixed, more true than I.
> Hushed be that sigh, be dry that tear,
> Cease, brooding doubt, cease, anxious fear;
>   Dry be that tear.
>
> Ask'st thou how long my love will stay
>   When all that's new is past?
> How long, ah Delia, can I say
>   How long my life may last? [5]
> Dry be that tear, be hushed that sigh,
> At least I'll love thee till I die!
>   Hushed be that sigh!

[4] *To Elizabeth Linley.*
[5] This idea, originally borrowed from Hume, Sheridan uses again and again.

CHAPTER FOUR

Infant Passion to Disclose

NATHANIEL HALHED came down at last to London. They met again, two tall young men full of bright visions and impalpable dreams. They talked excitedly and discovered that both were interested in literary careers — though with this difference: Sheridan desired, in addition to the world of letters, a more ample horizon; for Halhed, scholar and student, letters would always be sufficient.

They were two youths approaching manhood in an age of avid " classical " interests. Everyone who was anyone had read in the original Greek his Theocritus, his Hesiod and his Sophocles, and had pored over Vergil and Titus Livius in Latin. Ordinary fox-hunting, hard-drinking squires were absorbed in the past of antiquity. Gentlemen peppered their correspondence and their conversation with quotations from the standard classical authors. The times began to resemble those humane days at the dawn of the Renaissance, of which Master Rabelais had remarked that every washerwoman in France could write out her washing-bill in Greek.

They read and they reread Hesiod. More than that,

they retained their fondness for him after he had been " rendered suitably " into English. Thus translations flourished. Not a few of these simply interpreted the author's "spirit," and behind the screen of a name which time had made famous some poor hack was at long last able to break into print. Members of the aristocracy who lacked original ideas of their own could dip indiscriminately into the fountains of the past and bring to light whatever caught their fancy. It was sure of a publisher and of a public.

Sheridan and Halhed, meeting again, talked the moon to bed. Write they must. "Translations" in the current mode were easiest, and surest of success. Yet what to translate? Before them stretched a long, dim file, the classics of the past.

The *Songs* of Horace? Theocritus? Halhed rejected both. They were too common, he said. He wanted someone obscure and therefore intriguing. It was at length decided that Dick continue writing his verses; Halhed would on return to Oxford unearth some unknown author and they could fit the verses to him. Surely no one would recognize their old ruin then!

And so during the next months Dick Sheridan wrote verses. Halhed hunted the elusive "someone." But the songs were the kind which would fit any frame. Sheridan thoroughly enjoyed writing them. One of them is a rough draft of a song which later, in *The Duenna,* achieved a lasting success. It is an interesting reworking of George Wither's famous " *Shall I, wasting in despair,"* and reveals again how close was Sheridan's kinship to the poets of the Restoration.

> I ne'er could any lustre see
> In eyes that would not look on me.
> I ne'er saw nectar on a lip
> But where my own did hope to sip.
> Has the maid who seeks my heart
> Cheeks of rose untouched by art?
> I will yield the colours true
> When yielding blushes aid their hue.
> Is her hand so soft and pure?
> I must press it to be sure:
> Nor can I be certain then
> Till it, grateful, press again.
> Must I with attentive eye
> Watch her heaving bosom sigh?
> I will do so — when I see
> That heaving bosom sigh for me.

From this time dates one of his earliest poems on courtship, which was printed as late as 1800 in *The Festival of Love — a Collection of Cytherean Poems.* Robert Burns was also included in that volume, and another poet whose name appears startlingly out of place in Cytherea's galley. His name was William Wordsworth.

> I gave my love a budding rose
> My infant passion to disclose.
> And looking in her radiant eye
> I thought to read my destiny.
> She breathed upon it — it became
> Mature in form, no more the same
> As when with timid tears oppressed
> I placed the rosebud on her breast

Again she breathed in sportive play,
And wafted all the leaves away.
And thus she cried: " Your vows of love
As passing and as light will prove
As this dispersed and faded flower.
One sigh expanded it to bloom,
Another sigh, and it was gone,
Nor lived one transient fleeting hour."

In 1771 the Sheridan family left London for Bath. Tom was again feeling the pinch of circumstance, and he had heard that living was cheap in the watering-place of Fashion. There was also a theater in Bath. Surely it could furnish some employment for the talents of Thomas Sheridan? For weeks Frith Street hummed with the bustle of their impending departure. So much to pack — the girls' dresses, the silver plate, the prodigious manuscript of Tom Sheridan's pronouncing dictionary of the English language, which would preserve for all time the true and correct usages of the mother tongue. There was another manuscript traveling to Bath, but of its existence the Sheridan family was completely unaware. It was Dick's songs and charming stanzas for the *Epistles of Aristænetus: A Paraphrase,* upon which he and Nathaniel Halhed were hard at work.

The two collaborators were once again asunder. Halhed had gone to Oxford. He spent his time there struggling with debts and despair, and thoughts of suicide. These last were completely in the literary tradition of the day — in the school of the " graveyard

[58]

poets " and in the manner of that tortured young chap, Werther, who was just beginning to get himself talked about. Of late Halhed had occupied himself with his writings and disdainfully neglected his studies. The hours which he did not devote to his work on Aristænetus with Richard Sheridan he spent in the composition of terse paraphrases from other classical authors.

Actions and those alone can truly date
The period of our fluctuating fate;
The test of Merit, and of Life the test,
For *they've* lived *longest* who have lived the *best*.

This same Aristænetus who haunted the young collaborators' dreams had been himself more a translator than an author. A second-rate Sophist, he had written highly seasoned, erotic prose paragraphs, most of which were based on ideas already ancient when the clever Greek copied them down. The young men worked diligently over their poetic paraphrases. They polished the original text, and Sheridan strove mightily to give his work that lightness of touch which appears so careless and which takes so long to achieve. They signed the preface *H. S.*, the initials of both, and with a good deal of trepidation the manuscript was at last dispatched to a publisher. They had included in their collection "two or three epistles . . . which shelter themselves under the name of Aristænetus without any other title to his protection."

When *The Love Epistles* had gone off to seek their fortune in the world of letters, Richard found himself

suddenly with nothing to do. He was bored. For all
its parade of celebrities, Bath was not half so exciting
as he had imagined it. The weather was unseason-
able, hot one day, cheerless and cold the next. He
could find nothing whatever to do with his time. For
until he was certain how *Aristænetus* fared Dick was
resolved not to set pen to paper. He read over again
the letters from Oxford which Halhed signed *L. Y. D.*
— meaning Lazy Young Dog! In one of them he
caught a familiar name, and the spark of his interest
flickered and burned brighter. Linley . . . Linley
. . . now where . . .? Surely, young Dick frowned,
surely he had seen that name before.

In a moment he had recalled her. Elizabeth Linley,
whose beauty was white and clear as a tall gold-
crowned candle burning in a church. She whose voice
was so thrilling and sweet it seemed impossible for the
human throat to encompass such celestial sounds.
Elizabeth Linley, the "Maid of Bath."[1] He remembered the night he had seen her in London. The white
dress, the cloudy soft hair, the columnar throat arching in a succession of perfect octaves. And now this
paragon had touched Halhed's life as well as his own.
The beauty whose concerts were the rage of all England had appeared twice or thrice at Oxford, to wreak
untold havoc among the young gentlemen sequestered
there. Halhed had heard her sing; he was now her
slave. "I am petrified," he confided in a letter to

---

[1] She was so called in Samuel Foote's comedy based on the story of her
engagement to Mr. Long.

Sheridan. "My very faculties are annihilated with wonder; my conception could not form such a power of voice, such melody, such a soft yet so audible a tone." He called her the *Venus de Baiis,* and openly admitted that he loved her and that he had never loved before.

Nat's letter was disturbing. In love? Nat, the student, the cynic? In love, Dick mused, and wondered a little about the passion he had described so glibly and had never experienced. Not long afterwards he received another letter, and its contents agitated him even more than Halhed's. The wax broke, fine and powdery, and Richard read without crediting them the words of a certain Mr. Wilkie. This man — this Wilkie — blessed, thrice-blessed Wilkie! He was willing to accept for publication *The Love Epistles of Aristænetus.*

These same Linleys whose ravishing daughter Elizabeth was the toast of England were the Sheridans' neighbors in Bath. Nine children, all burning with a fierce, unearthly beauty, all incredibly gifted. And each one doomed to an early death. The gods had loved the Linleys well; only one of Thomas' and Maria's children lived to reach forty.

There were nine of them, and so it was only natural that those who saw them should at once recall the Muses. Elizabeth was the oldest. Her brother Thomas was two years younger, and aged sixteen at this time. He was first violin in the celebrated Bath concerts conducted by his father. Mozart, born in the same year, had pronounced him a prodigy and predicted that his star would ascend to the zenith of the musical firmament. His star, already paling into darkness. . . . There was Mary, who was a less perfect copy of her sister — less beautiful, less accomplished, but equally unfortunate. There was Sam, most beautiful of all these beautiful young people. They called him "Apollo," and Gainsborough and Lawrence tried many times to recapture on canvas the evanescent and spiritual quality of his face. There was Maria, who at ten died like a young white cygnet — singing. There was Ozias, named for Ozias Humphry, the twins, Jane and Charlotte, and William, the baby, whose cheeks were already too flushed, whose eyes were too feverishly bright.

Dr. Thomas Linley was himself an excellent musician and composer. His children learned to sing and play as soon as they were old enough to walk; the nursery walls rocked with cantatas and perfect choral harmonies. "We are all geniuses here, sir," little Tom Linley had artlessly informed the visitor who had come upon the young musicians practicing Bach and eating bread-and-jam, — "Every one of us." As geniuses they belonged to the entire country, and no Linley could remember a day when he had not performed in public. It was their mother, actually, who saw that their accomplishments were put to some honest and practical use. She traveled with them, watching hawk-eyed over the " concourse of sweet sounds " as it moved from theater to theater, from Edinburgh to Dublin to London, and back again to Bath. Maria Linley knew well the value of money. Her family earned a great deal, but the thin, tight-lipped woman whose smiles were so rare, whose voice in that household of sweet voices was harsh and unlovely, never knew what it meant to be satisfied. There was always another engagement somewhere for them to play. And at her stern insisting they played it. She had, besides " Queen Elizabeth," four beautiful and gifted girls. They would all marry well, Maria Linley was grimly determined. She would see to that.

Despite their popularity and great success, the Linley family was none too secure socially. They were, after all, paid performers — professionals. Eighteenth-century society drew back from any transaction which smacked even remotely of " trade." Money was as essential to a man as a heart or a liver. But actually to earn money put one immediately in the class of a domestic servant or a fishmonger. Necessary as individuals, to be sure, but definitely not to be cultivated.

And so Maria Linley watched Elizabeth growing daily more beautiful, more desirable. She scanned eagerly the faces of the gentlemen who sent her flowers and extravagant verses. Somewhere there must be the proper man for Elizabeth; wealthy, mature, and well-connected. When she ceased to be the " ravishing Miss Linley " Elizabeth must step at once into the Great World.

The Sheridan children and the young Linleys had struck up a friendship soon after the former's arrival in Bath. Tom Sheridan disapproved. He was inclined to look down his nose at his neighbors. Now that Tom had severed his connection with the theater he had grown quite patronizing toward actors and other " players." He felt that Linley exploited his children. A thing, Tom would tell you, thumping the table and raising his left arm in the conventional gesture, which he had never done and therefore could not countenance. Such a never-ceasing pother there was at Linley's. Coming and going in a post-chaise, like traveling gentry, and the grenadier of a mother in her bottle-green cloak watching the servants, taking in the boxes with the precious violins and flageolets, and those crowds of children, in one all-embracing glance.

But in the autumn of 1771 Thomas Sheridan himself set off on a trip. With the manuscript of *Captain O'Blunder* stowed away among his shirts and flowered-silk waistcoats he left for Dublin. The complete title of his play was *Captain O'Blunder* or *The Brave Irishman,* and although it never appeared in print it was a great favorite on the stage. With Tom away the household in Bath relaxed. The girls read as they pleased. They walked abroad in the thin November sunshine, two and two, like the animals in the Ark. Alicia Sheridan arm-in-arm with Elizabeth Linley, and Betsey Sheridan following with Elizabeth's sister Mary, whom everyone called Poll.

[64]

Richard watched them set off every afternoon on those strolls which would take them down Pierrepont Street and into the Parade, and past the Pump Rooms to the confectioner Gill's heavenly-smelling shop. He heard their voices fading sweetly away into the distance. Were they talking of him? It would be pleasant to think so. Quite a few people in England were speaking of him now, for a few months earlier Mr. Wilkie at No. 71 St. Paul's Churchyard had published *The Love Epistles of Aristænetus* — " translated from Greek into English metre," said the title-page. To the surprise of the two authors, the reviewers had actually noticed the book in their columns. A few of them saw behind those two initials *H. S.* the imposing figure of the Great Lexicographer. But that was because of Halhed's pompous paragraphs. Surely no one could have believed that those light, deft lyrics which gave the text its charm could have come from the pen of Samuel Johnson.

The Love Epistles having found the public disposed to lend a kindly ear, the two collaborators determined to try again. Many miles stretched between Bath and Oxford, and they worked together mostly by letter. Once again the subject was classical. Halhed's original idea seems to have been a burlesque, called *Jupiter,* which he forwarded to Richard in 1770, but it was later abandoned for the story of Ixion and Amphitryon.[2] There his contribution to the work ended. For the

[2] Never produced.

handling and the treatment of the theme and the robust dialogue are all Sheridan's.

Young Dick liked the device of the play within a play. Historically it had long been popular. There were Beaumont and Fletcher's *Knight of the Burning Pestle,* and Buckingham's *The Rehearsal,* to mention only two. It would not be long before people would be heading that list with Richard Sheridan's *The Critic. Ixion* is also a play within a play; it is feeble and inchoate, and for a comedy it is at times not funny at all. Yet it is unmistakably Sheridan's own. He is already beginning to emerge as a Style.

Now Maria Linley admitted that she had found the paragon who was to marry her daughter. His name was Walter Long. He was a country squire of excellent family, wealthy, mature, and hopelessly ensnared. He had been Miss Linley's admirer for years. Therefore it was not to be deemed presumptuous, he wrote, that he now ventured to address her parents. His letter impressed Mrs. Linley favorably. She was certain that she would take the same pleasure in meeting the man himself.

Mrs. Linley prided herself on the fact that nothing which concerned either her children or her household escaped her unremitting scrutiny. It was said that she made friends with each farthing before she parted with it; certainly she counted every piece of butter, every heel of bread, which passed through her house. Great would have been her amazement to learn that Elizabeth was in love — and with a married man! His name was Mathews, and from the time when Elizabeth had been a great-eyed, adorable child he had been her family's friend. For more than a year now he had been her secret love.

Even as a child she had been very fond of the lean, sardonic man who fondled her upon his knee and fed her sweetmeats. Men called him " Captain," though what were his military connections no one seemed to know precisely. Somewhere he had a wife. It was an easy matter to forget her existence completely as time went on, for nobody ever saw Mrs. Mathews, and her name rarely passed her husband's lips. He was a strange man. His eyes were dark and brooding, and sometimes their depths were stirred by wild gleamings, like marsh-fire. He had periods of black silence. From these he would shake himself, rail bitterly at his friends and curse his enemies, and then sink back once more into apathy. Elizabeth could remember how always he had terrified her — yet at the same time drawn her inexplicably to him.

Sometimes she was sure that he was a spirit of evil who had captured her soul and would ultimately destroy her. Lately as she had grown in breath-taking beauty, as he had watched other men flock to her with gifts and proposals of marriage, Mathews had begun to make threats. Veiled at first, these had recently become more and more unmistakable. No man should possess her, since he could not. She belonged to him in a union far more sacred than any earthly bond. Let her but attempt to escape him, and a bullet would extinguish her golden beauty as one snuffs out a candle flame. Elizabeth had seen his pistols. Long and sleek and black, reposing coldly together in a velvet-lined box. There were two of them, he told her with a twisted smile. One for her and one to put to rest his own passion, since without her life would be a hollow and meaningless inanity.

She had never revealed to her parents the terrible attraction which was consuming her. Thomas Linley noted that she moved like a girl in a trance. Her voice was as rich and pellucid as ever, and on the stage she was her old radiant self. But after the concert was over and the musicians had put away their instruments, a change came over her. When she flirted at parties or stepped through the figures of a quadrille her movements were jerky and stiff, like those of an automaton. There was a fixity in her glance, an exaggeration in her lovely color, which closed like an icy hand upon her father's heart. What was happening to this beautiful singing bird of theirs, he asked his wife. Something dreadful, he was certain; something malign. But Maria shook her head and laughed his fears to scorn. Elizabeth had been reading too many novels. Let Tom take her books away from her, and Maria would warrant that in a month she'd be cured without doctor or physic. Those novels — they'd make anybody sick. . . .

She produced Walter Long's correct letter and showed it to her husband. Surely Tom agreed that a proper marriage was the best thing in the world for

Elizabeth? Why did young girls moon and grow green and distracted? Because their heads were full of romantic nonsense. And what, she demanded, was the best way to cure this foolishness? Why, marriage, of course! What did Tom say to that?

"Whatever you say, my dear," he replied. And though in his heart he wondered whether a marriage to some stodgy country gentleman was precisely what his bright bird required to make her happy again, he promised Maria that he would speak to Elizabeth.

CHAPTER FIVE

Elopement à Trois

E LIZABETH LINLEY'S engagement to Walter
Long of Wiltshire was announced, and in the house
next door a young man knew too late that he loved
her. Charles Francis Sheridan, that pompous and
correct youth, indulged in the brooding melancholy
which the eighteenth century had come to associate
with thwarted or unrequited love. His home was a
horrible place from which he longed to flee. Lissy and
Betsey chattered all day of Eliza, so soon to become a
bride. Tom Sheridan was up and down between Dublin and London, and Dick — as an author and a playwright, what time had he for a brother's misery?

Dick was occupied now in writing something entirely different from the translations and the farce
which had heretofore engrossed him. It was called
Hernan's Miscellany, and it was a weekly serial after
the inimitable Richard Steele. Its protagonist, a wit
and a frequenter of the " Grecian " coffee-house, was
patterned after that uncle of Dick Sheridan's to whom
as a heartsick and bereaved boy he had written from
Harrow demanding " black stokins," the amiable and

eccentric Richard Chamberlaine. The minor characters of the *Miscellany*, chiefly the wooden-legged Rudliche, are all excellently drawn and seem to point ahead
to Lawrence Sterne as well as back to the *Spectator*. "I
will sit down and write for the good of the People," he
begins the book, " for (said I to myself, pulling off my
spectacles and drinking the remainder of my six penn'
worth) it cannot be but the people must be sick of these
same rascally Politics." Rudliche has an opinion on
every subject under heaven. " The first two Georges,"
he remarks, " though excellent in every other respect,
must be regarded as antidotes to learning." Richard
Sheridan wrote carefully and slowly. He polished and
erased and amended, and developed the fluent style
one has come to associate with him. As he himself
declared in *Clio's Protest*,[1] in a distich which the critics
have never stopped quoting:

> You write with ease to show your breeding,
> But *easy writing's* vile *hard reading.*

And Elizabeth Linley? Mathews was at the moment absent from Bath. At the insistence of her parents, after days of querulous tears and complaints and
short-lived reconciliations, she had consented to become Mrs. Long. Now she waited in a very obvious
apprehension for Mathews' return and for the cataclysm which must inevitably follow.

[1] Miles Peter Andrews, a young dandy and friend of David Garrick,
published some doggerel about the lovely ladies of Bath and signed his
poem *Clio*. The *Protest* is Sheridan's reply, but the couplet quoted above
is the best thing it contains.

A season passed. Elizabeth's terror had brought her to the verge of a complete breakdown. At last, after superhuman effort on her part, she was able to accomplish what Captain Mathews demanded. Fearing for her life, the distracted girl pleaded with her parents to break off her engagement; finally Thomas and Maria could hold out against her no longer. Her father consented to write to her fiancé. As for Mr. Long, he was still happy that he had almost become the beauty's husband. Grateful perhaps for thoughts of those blissful hours which now would never be his, he made over a sum of money in his will to his former fiancée. Upon his death several months later Elizabeth Linley found herself an heiress.

How the gossip-writers seized upon the story! With what gleeful relish did they tell and retell the romantic tale of the lovely young girl whose aged admirer had been so " kindly," so " considerate." The implication was there for all to read. The breath of scandal had never before blown across Elizabeth's path; now she was surrounded by a miasma of the foulest and most lurid lies. Men spoke about her in tap-rooms and coffee-houses, and every newspaper or gazette carried some barbed paragraph with her name. Worst of all, the playwright Foote grasped the opportunity afforded by the moment and produced a comedy called *The Maid of Bath*. Mercilessly it satirized the Linley-Long betrothal, and ridiculed Maria Linley as the mercenary *Mrs. Linnet*. Elizabeth saw her reputation vanishing like dew before the sun. Already receipts at her concerts had fallen off alarmingly. Unless the public soon discovered a new victim to persecute, she might be forced to retire.

During all this time Dick Sheridan was scarcely aware of the unfortunate circumstances in which his charming neighbor found herself. He knew that his brother still continued to worship her. Occasionally he would see Betsey, after nightfall, slipping through the hedge with something square and white in her hand which Dick recognized as another of Charles' sententious letters. He himself probably never gave Elizabeth Linley a thought. She was a beautiful girl and some harsh things were being said of her, but doubtless she deserved them. Zounds! Dick was, after all, something of a man of the world. Gossip might magnify Miss Linley's fault, but surely the stories had some slight basis in fact? He who was to be her champion before the world, who was to incur for her sake an almost mortal wound — he felt himself exceedingly bored by the Linleys and their troubles.

And now the orchestra of events mounted to its concluding crescendo. Charles Francis Sheridan realized that his passion for the unhappy girl next door was hopeless. " Very well, then," said Charles, " since I cannot have that which is my world, the world no longer delights me and I will renounce it." He spent the best part of a day making his adieux in the long letter which custom demanded, under the circumstances. Betsey, romping with the poodle in the windy sunshine, was summoned and given the missive to bear to the lady.

Then the disconsolate lover, mounted upon a hack from Scrace's Livery Stables, rode slowly from view.

Charles took his sorrow to a farmhouse on the outskirts of Bath. Here in a white-walled hermitage he lingered until the following April. He watched the ducks paddling in their pond, he saw the hedges wither and the frost breathe its doom upon the garden. Nature mourned. So did he.

But while Charles nursed his anguish in the country, his brother Richard was at last becoming interested in the lovely Elizabeth. He accompanied them sometimes when she and his sisters walked along the Parade and stared into the rows of tempting shop windows, or hurried through the Gardens to call upon the mother and sister of that gallant soldier, Major John André. He gave her books to read; occasionally when she opened one a paper fell out on which Dick had scribbled a few tentative verses for her approval. Almost every day he crossed the dead garden and walked into the Linley's house.

The scandal-mongers had not yet had their fill of Elizabeth Linley. Her concert engagements were becoming farcical. She sang to empty, echoing halls, and sometimes people hissed her as she slipped out to her chair — a tall, agitated girl wrapped in a black cloak. The strain upon her was growing too great. She was ill; she slept fitfully; long, tortured sobs shook her at the first harsh word. Someone had started a rumor about herself and Captain Mathews and its echoes were reverberating from all sides. Her feeling for the Captain had changed. The affection which had tempered her fear of him was dead. Her revulsion had deepened; with it had grown the dreadful apathy in which she moved. She was doomed, Elizabeth decided. There was no escape from those cruel, unpitying faces which hemmed her round. And now for the first time a little worm wriggled across her mind. If, she thought, if I should die . . . ?

Her parents would lose in her more than a daughter. She was a potential source of income. In the long nights during which she stared at the ceiling with cracking eyeballs Elizabeth thought of suicide. She determined to recompense her father for what she was about to do. There was old Mr. Long's money. It would belong to her father when she was gone; that might make it a little easier for him to bear the loss of her voice.

But Thomas Linley was not sleeping well either. A pall seemed to hang over his house. He could feel its weight upon him, smothering him, as he tossed in his bed at night. Elizabeth . . . Something unspeakable was threatening his golden girl. One night he heard her sobbing in her room at the end of the hall, and overriding the protests of his wife he seized a candle and hurried through the chill darkness to her side.

"Papa!" She flung herself upon him. He could feel her slender body shake against his tightening arms; he could sense the reality of her terror.

"Tell me — "

Sitting on his daughter's narrow bed while the candle's point flickered and paled against the encroachment of the dawn, Tom Linley heard the whole dreadful story. Mathews . . . it was too horrible! She must swear to her papa never to see him again.

At that Elizabeth's sobs broke out afresh. What was she saying now? Tom Linley, leaning forward, could scarcely credit her words. Mathews had threatened to kill her! . . . Monstrous! The man was mad!

"God help us!" prayed distracted Thomas Linley. "God have pity on us all!"

In the morning Elizabeth awoke to sunshine and a wonderful feeling of peace. She sipped her chocolate, dandled the baby, and dressed Charlotte and Jane for church. The family departed, and in the music-room she sat down before the pianoforte, practicing an aria. The tall doors to the garden opened and Mathews appeared. His eyes were bright with hatred; she screamed when she saw in his hand the long black barrel of a pistol.

"Your father," he hissed at her, "has just called upon me. He told me that you would not see me. That I must not force myself upon you. Force myself, he said. Tell me that it is not true, my jewel. Say it. I am waiting."

Elizabeth looked at him. Her voice was frozen in her throat.

"Your father was mistaken then, was he not, my

life? And I may continue to see you? Of course I may!"

In the hall someone stirred. Mathews, with one last look at her, put up his pistol and closed the garden windows quietly behind him. A moment later the parlor-maid, bringing in a fresh scuttle of coals for the grate, found Miss Elizabeth leaning against the piano-forte, sobbing hysterically.

It was the end. Her father had tried to help her, but she was past all redemption. Mathews would never give her up. The only way she could ever escape him was to die. And by my own hand, she thought. It will not hurt so much if I kill myself.

Upstairs in her room she sat before her little inlaid writing-desk and made out her will. "To my beloved father Thomas Linley I give and bequeath — ." Her hand did not tremble as she shook sand over her signature. Her mother kept a bottle of laudanum in the press. It was a sovereign remedy against the tooth-ache, which troubled Maria exceedingly. Elizabeth brought it out and placed it before her on the desk. She would say her prayers and commend her unquiet soul to God. Then the drink, and that deep, encompassing sleep from which there was never any waking.

A door slammed downstairs and someone was moving closer. Elizabeth raised the bottle to her lips. It was the vilest stuff she had ever tasted, but it was release. . . .

"Miss Linley! In God's name put down your hand!"

Richard Sheridan. She saw him through thick and blurring tears.

" No! " she moaned. " No — "

The bottle crashed against the wall as he struck her hand away. There was an odor in the room, pervasive, unmistakable.

It took him hours to quiet the hysterical girl. At first Elizabeth refused to tell him anything — how much of the drug she had swallowed, what had led her to the brink of such folly. At last her fingers, tense in his, relaxed. She stopped crying. Richard set her in an armchair by the window and pulled up a hassock for her feet. She was to sit there, without moving, while he fetched the doctor.

" No! Please, Mr. Sheridan! " She wrung her hands ; once again he heard her sobbing. She wanted no one . . . she was afraid.

A long moment passed. Then she looked up at Richard. Tears still winked upon her lashes, but her face was calm. There was something she must say to Mr. Sheridan, if only he would listen. And for the second time in less than twenty-four hours Elizabeth Linley laid bare her soul.

He listened, his eyes blazing with anger, wonder and disbelief crowding through his heart. When she had finished her whispered story anger alone remained. The pity he had felt for this lovely helpless girl had disappeared. In its place flamed a fierce desire to stand at her side, to outwit the devil who tortured her.

Her eyes were closing. Softly Richard moved from

the room and hurried for the doctor. But Elizabeth was not asleep. She lay with her head against the striped damask of the chair and smiled a little. For some unaccountable reason she felt safe — almost as though Mathews had already ceased to plague her. She knew that she had found a champion.

Dr. Harrington, a kind and fatherly man, listened intently while Richard told him what had occurred, and promised to keep it a secret. When the Linleys and their children returned from church they were told that Elizabeth was not well and must keep to her bed at least a week, that nothing must be permitted to trouble her.

Her mother nodded sagely. The vapors. Or else 'twas the spring. Young people were taken suddenly like this when the spring stirred. Elizabeth would be right as a trivet directly the weather settled.

The days lengthened. Tiny curled buds appeared on the oak trees, and the willows along the Avon's edge were a blur of smoky green. And Elizabeth Linley was still pale and thin, and there were huge black shadows under her eyes. Mathews had written that he would still gain his " point "; nothing that she or anyone else could do would deter him. Once again she stared at the ceiling through sleepless hours, and a new idea came to her.

Flight. That was it — actual escape. She would leave Bath and seek refuge in France, in a convent where the good sisters would shield her from Mathews and guard her until such time as the danger of his madness had passed. She fell asleep and dreamed of black-robed women walking in pairs down a garden path, and in her sleep she heard church bells ringing.

It was impossible for her to run away alone. How could she sleep unchaperoned at wayside ordinaries, and command horses at the posting stations? For a journey a man was indispensable. But who — ? Her brother Tom was a child; he had never been away from home without their father. Mr. Sheridan, on the other hand, had promised to help her, and he was a man. She would ask Mr. Sheridan to go with her to France. Not as a lover, because love for Richard Sheridan was furthest from her mind. But simply because he was kind, and because with him she felt so wonderfully secure. In 1773, when they were already married, she wrote to him explaining this very circumstance: "You are sensible that when I left Bath I had not an idea of you but as a friend. It was not your person that gained my affection. No, Sheridan, it was that delicacy, that tender compassion . . . that was the motive which induced me to love you."

She consulted with Richard. Neither he nor she saw anything fastastic in the situation. He was delighted with the prospect of a trip to the continent, and impatiently he went about planning all the details of this " elopement " straight from the pages of Beaumarchais. A fortnight more . . . then ten days . . . a week. . . . Jove! Was it possible that tomorrow

[81]

was Wednesday? For Wednesday, March 18th, was the breathlessly awaited day.

Her sister, father, and brother Tom were to appear that Wednesday evening at one of the Bath concerts. It was the first to be held since Captain Wade, Beau Nash's successor as Master of Ceremonies, had been presented by the citizens of Bath with a gold medal saluting him in a Latin inscription as " arbiter of elegant affairs." Mary, in white with a trailing blue sash, would sing their father's florid aria, *No Flower that Blows*. While she was dressing to accompany them Elizabeth suddenly felt a return of her " vapors " and was forced to lie down. Maria Linley dosed her liberally with sal volatile, stuck a warming-pan against her feet and a smelling-bottle into her hand, and hurried off to the concert beside her impatient husband. The servants went up to bed; the house was quiet. Elizabeth put on her cloak with its deep quilted hood. After she had slipped noiselessly down the stairs and unlatched the front door she stooped a moment and put on her shoes. The night was cold and black. There was no moon, and the stars seemed remote and disapproving. How would it all end, thought Elizabeth? Would they ever reach France? Should she turn back now while there was still time? Near the hedge loomed two darker shapes. Sedan chairs. From one of them stepped Richard.

" Miss Linley! Are you all right? " She nodded and he went on rapidly. " The luggage — 'tis all bestowed in the other chair. Will you enter? "

She sat beside him in the darkness. The chairs moved off. They were on their way to London, to France — to Freedom!

Their road took them through Savernake Forest and on over Hounslow Heath, which they crossed without once being halted by a gentleman in a black crape mask. The stars melted into a brightening sky. Cocks were crowing and dogs barking, and in some of the little thatch-roofed villages through which they passed men in soiled smocks with pitchforks slung across their shoulders stared after them in sleepy curiosity.

"Gad's life, Miss Linley, what a lovely morning!" exclaimed Richard.

Sunshine and clean, sweet air. And off there in the distance — London!

The travelers, stiff and hungry, breakfasted at a bake-shop. Miss Linley desired a place where she could rest until it was time for them to go on. The Sheridans had a kinsman named Ewarts who lived in London, Dick recalled. It was not above a mile or so away. To his astonished relative he introduced the drowsy girl beside him as " a wealthy young heiress." They were en route to France, he added, where they would be united. Ewarts beamed upon them both. How romantic it all was! Devoted young couple, stern parents, and a post-chaise hurrying throught the night. It was, Mr. Ewarts declared, a glorious thing to be young.

After a few hours the pair grew restless. An eternity remained until the coach left for Dover. This time Sheridan took Miss Linley to call upon " a respectable brandy merchant in the City " — that Mr. Field who was the godfather of Charles Lamb. They spent part of the evening with him, gossiping and playing cards. Years later, in memory perhaps of that evening's hospitality, Sheridan presented Field with a pass to Drury Lane — which the merchant promptly turned over to his godson.

In London the party was joined by a chaperon, an elderly female of so repellent an aspect that one knew instantly that she was virtuous. Thus having guaranteed the platonic nature of the affair, the elopement *à trois* crossed the Channel and stepped at last upon the soil of France.

But somewhere on the way to Lille, where the convent was in which Miss Linley would find peace, a change came over her young protector. The high and noble feelings which had led him to accompany her from Bath seemed to have blown away with the stiff salt winds of the Channel. He caught himself wishing that his " elopement " were not merely a form, but an actual flight of two loving hearts toward happiness. And the chaperon, whose presence was to be a pledge to the world of their good intentions, became simply an infernal nuisance.

The sea air had clarified Elizabeth's emotional disorders as well, and by the time they reached Calais the two young people had made up their minds that for the sake of appearances they must go through the form of a marriage. Apparently to the clear and logical minds of the Frenchmen who observed them a chaperoned elopement was an anomaly, a contradiction in terms.

In the little windy seaport town a French priest performed the ceremony and they continued on their way to Lille, Mr. and Mrs. Richard Brinsley Sheridan. A wistful pathos hung over the unfamiliar landscape. Each realized that their days together were numbered. Soon they must separate, until such a time as Richard was of age or could support a wife, — a time, the young husband decided grimly, as remote as the millennium. They kissed and clung to each other at the thought of parting, and the tears of both fell without restraint. There was no longer any pretense, any dissembling. They loved each other, they had just been married — and Fate was about to force them asunder.

Instead of the convent upon which they had at first agreed, they planned to spend their time in Lille at the home of the cultivated Dr. Dolman. Here the strange circumstances of their nominal marriage were explained, and not only credited but respected. A week passed, a fortnight. How was their absence being received at home, each wondered. In secret, for neither one would confess to the other how many times a day his thoughts turned to Bath, where two infuriated old men raged and a scandal was brewing to set all England by the ears.

CHAPTER SIX

While Reason's Blind

SHERIDAN had left a note for Elizabeth's father wherein he set forth the reasons for their flight and explained the somewhat improbable manner in which they proposed to travel. But Dr. Linley did not believe a word. " Poppycock! " he bellowed, and swore that he would pursue the elopers and rescue his daughter from that impudent young rogue. The newspapers pounced upon another story concerning the lovely Maid of Bath. Their columns attacked Elizabeth Linley's morals and tore to shreds what remained of her character. The dramatist Foote, who had turned to such advantage her engagement to Mr. Long, now wrote a comedy about her elopement. He called it *A Trip to Calais,* and it held up to leering laughter that marriage ceremony in Calais " which they will tell you is but the outward shape and semblance of a marriage." Worst of all, Captain Mathews was raving hysterically about the lady and printing items in all the papers about the gentleman.

In the *Bath Chronicle* of April 9th, the following appeared:

Mr. R. Sh . . . having attempted in a letter left behind
him for that purpose to account for his scandalous method
of running away from this Place, by insinuations, derogating
my character and that of a young Lady, innocent as far as
relates to my knowledge; since which he has neither taken
notice of my letters, or even informed his own family of the
place where he has hid himself — I can no longer think he
deserves the treatment of a gentleman, and shall therefore
trouble to post him as a L . . . and a treacherous S . . .

THOMAS MATHEWS

Dr. Linley meanwhile waxed furious at the concert
engagements which his daughter's absence prevented
him from filling. He set off for France to find her and
bring her back. His feelings as a father had been
wounded. But when he thought of the money Elizabeth's stay in France was costing him his face grew
purple and he roared to the postillion to whip up his
damned beasts. It was taking the irate Doctor longer
than he had anticipated to find the young lovers;
it was almost the end of April before he burst in
upon them in the parlor of Dr. Dolman's house in
Lille.

The news he brought was far from reassuring.
Elizabeth's name was being dragged in the mud by
every inky-fingered hack who could write a paragraph.
As for Sheridan — he had been publicly slandered,
had he not? There was one course open to him, and
one alone. That is, if he were a gentleman and not the
treacherous what's-its-name Mathews had branded
him. Sheridan might remain in France if he chose.
For his part, Dr. Linley cared not the veriest fig. But

above the young man's protestations he shouted that Elizabeth was returning to England with him.

" She is *my daughter,* sir, and she will go with *me!*"

They returned to England. In their elopement they had been accompanied by an elderly female chaperon; they came back now from their " honeymoon abroad " with the bride's angry father.

In London they separated. Elizabeth and Dr. Linley continued on to Bath where she was to resume her interrupted career as the talented and beautiful songbird, *Miss Elizabeth Linley* — and damn the gossips! Richard would remain in London. There were certain matters between himself and Captain Mathews which, as his father-in-law had pointed out, could be settled in only one way. Furthermore he must set out to find himself a career.

> Let all the learned say what they can,
> 'Tis ready money makes the man!

He was a married man. If ever he intended to claim his wife he must be prepared to keep her. He had determined that Elizabeth would never sing again in public and accept payment for her singing. She should be Mrs. Sheridan, and not Elizabeth Linley.

Beneath the unrelenting eye of Thomas Linley the lovers said farewell.

" Oh, Richard, Richard! " sobbed Elizabeth.

Feebly he tried to console her. He would come for her presently. . . . The words mocked him; he realized only too well that he might never be able to claim Elizabeth, and he grew cold with fear. They clasped each other closer.

The postillion cracked his whip. Dr. Linley demanded testily how much longer she proposed to keep them waiting. Elizabeth stumbled to her seat and the coach moved forward. Suddenly she leaned from the window.

"Wait, Richard!" she called. "Richard!"

But he had turned and was hurrying up the street. The coach bounced and rattled its way over the cobblestones.

Richard walked back to his lodgings. Despair sat like lead upon his heart. The world was black and bitter. Sundered from his wife, slandered by a villain from whom he must presently demand satisfaction, without funds, without friends — there was not the slightest ray to penetrate the clouds.

He did not sleep at all that night. Having thus put himself into the proper frame of mind he rose, dressed in his best, and called upon Captain Mathews in Crutched Friars. That gentleman was still abed. So suddenly roused, he seemed unable at first to comprehend what his visitor was saying. After several threats and arguments had passed between them, Mathews finally agreed to retract his statements in the *Chronicle,* and Sheridan departed, feeling that he had accomplished one of the many tasks to which he had set himself.

But Mathews' promises were worthless. Only one

thing remained. He must challenge his defamer to a duel.

On May 4th he and Ewarts met Mathews and his second, Knight, at the appointed place — the Ring near Rotten Row. Mathews appeared upset and unwilling to fight. He suggested that they move to Hyde Park Corner; when that had been vetoed he urged a postponement of their meeting. At this Sheridan became furious. They must fight! They had agreed to fight, and fight they would. They did, several hours later, by candle-light in an upper room of the Cask Tavern, at the confluence of Bedford and Henrietta Streets. Dick disarmed his adversary and Mathews, on his knees, begged for his life. He would publish a retraction. This time he swore it.

Two days later the *Bath Chronicle* carried his statement: " Being convinced that the expressions I made use of to Mr. Sheridan's disadvantage were the effects of passion and misrepresentation, I retract what I have said to his disadvantage, and particularly beg his pardon for my advertisement in the *Bath Chronicle*."

The Captain now retired to his home in Wales. Dick had routed him successfully — for the moment. He returned to live at his father's house in Bath, a cheaper and more convenient arrangement than maintaining a residence in London. He knew that in Bath he would be afforded an occasional glimpse of Elizabeth. Marriage between them was still a remote improbability, but in the long summer twilights they could walk beside the Avon in the deep shade of the willow trees, and read aloud the verses with which each lamented the other's enforced absence. Some of Sheridan's are especially puerile and sentimental.

> Near Avon's ridgy bank there grows
> A willow of no vulgar size:
> That tree first heard poor Sylvio's woes,
> And heard how bright were Laura's eyes.

In most of these stanzas he is *Sylvio*, although the lady is not always *Laura*.

> Shall my Eliza to the birds and trees
> Alone communicate her tuneful lays?
> Shall breathe her rhyme to the unmindful breeze,
> And be content with Echo's idle praise?
>
> Oh, let your Sylvio share, my gentlest love,
> Let Sylvio share each line that you rehearse.
> Or will he hate flowers, elms, sweet birds and groves,
> Which shall inspire the too unsocial verse.

The last two lines of the above contain a series which he later expressed much more ably in Tilburina's speech in *The Critic*:

> The striped carnation, and the guarded rose,
> The vulgar wallflower, and smart gillyflower,
> The polyanthus mean, the dapper daisy,
> Sweet William and sweet marjoram — and all
> The tribe of single and of double pinks!
> Now, too, the feathered warblers tune their notes
> Around, and charm the listening grove. The lark!
> The linnet! chaffinch! bullfinch! goldfinch! greenfinch!
> But oh! to me no joy they can afford!

[92]

No rose, nor wallflower, nor smart gillyflower,
Nor polyanthus mean, nor dapper daisy,
Nor William sweet, nor marjoram — nor lark,
Linnet, nor all the finches of the grove!

The Bath gardens blazed with the blooming of the roses. It was full summer now. Larks sang in the mornings, and in the deep green forest the nightingales enriched the midnight with their music. Charles Sheridan missed the country these first days of summer. The thatch of the tight little farmhouse must be fragrant with tiny new flowers. Bath seemed to him, recently returned to its streets and to its noises, a cold and heartless spot.

By Midsummer Day the warm weather had arrived in earnest. And before June was over Richard Sheridan learned that Mathews was back again; his brief security was over. A new duel was soon arranged, for the Captain had never been entirely satisfied with the outcome of that first meeting in the inn bedroom, and was anxious to try his hand again. Accordingly, at three o'clock in the morning of July 1st, Sheridan and Captain Paumier met Mathews and Mr. Barnett at the White Hart Inn. Here they climbed into post-chaises and drove toward a sky streaked with salmon and gold until they reached Kingsdown. The carriages pulled up along the roadside; there they would await the result.

The struggle was brief. Sheridan tripped and fell, and heard his sword splinter against the concealed armor his opponent was wearing. Mathews still possessed a weapon and he used it viciously. The postillions rushed from their boxes and with the help of Paumier they dragged the wounded man into one of the carriages. Mathews leaped into the other. Before Dick's bleeding had been stanched the Captain was rocketing down the long white road to France.

Richard, gasping and moaning, soaked in blood and covered with dirt, was a terrifying sight as he lolled beside Paumier in the swaying chaise. Impossible to get him back to Bath without a surgeon. "We shall have to stop somewhere along the way," thought his agonized second, "whilst his wounds are dressed and he rests." He yelled to the coachman to pull up at the first house he spied.

It was a small, unprepossessing farmhouse. The peasant who occupied it smelled rather definitely of sweat and manure. He clucked his surprise at the strangers, but he helped Paumier as well as he could to make Richard comfortable. Later in the day another post-chaise stopped before the rustic's door. It brought Lee and Ditcher, the eminent medicos who had been summoned from Bath by Richard's coachman. They dressed the wounds, bled the patient — he was already weakened by the loss of blood — and pronounced him well enough to return home. The doctors then rolled off in their chaise and Richard and Paumier followed close behind them. Left alone, the humble son of the soil stared at the money which Paumier had given him, and scratched his head. Such a pother! The sick gentleman, and those two doctors with their gold canes and their snuff-boxes. . . . But the day had paid him well. It recompensed him even more when, years later, he sold to visitors " relics " of the hero's agony. Particularly the blood-soaked frame which was supposed to have enclosed Elizabeth Linley's miniature and which, their guide explained with relish, her lover had worn over his poor wounded heart. . . .

At first Mathews' conduct in the affair at Kingsdown earned for him complete social ostracism. But he did not remain in Coventry long. The years passed. The *cause célèbre* of yesterday was the commonplace of today. The Captain returned to Bath, and after a while not a head turned when he passed in the streets. In 1821 he died there — a gentleman of the " military " type who played phenomenal whist and still retained an eye for a pretty face. He had survived his famous adversary by five years.

The gazettes were delighted with the story of the duel at Kingsdown. Between her concerts to the enraptured youth at Oxford, Elizabeth read their lurid paragraphs and felt her heart dissolve. Her husband was wounded. . . . She must fly to him at once.

" Wounded, madam? " her father roared. " Fly, ma'am? We have engagements, ma'am. And nothing has happened to cancel them — *nothing*, I say! You'll oblige me by ceasing to act as though you've taken leave of your senses — or your senses of you! "

Tom Sheridan, in Bath, was irate also. The situation had now become frankly melodramatic. The two young lovers parted by their obdurate fathers pouring their sufferings into verses, sighing their longings on the midnight breeze. Dick would give up that girl, swore Tom. He would not, swore Richard. Very well then, his father would take matters into his own hands, and the sooner the better. Like young Romeo, of whom he thought so frequently these days, Dick was banished; packed off to a farm near Waltham Abbey to read for the Bar. Let him at least use his enforced exile to some purpose, thundered his parent. His son did. He wrote those songs which later were sung so successfully in *The Duenna*.

> Could I her faults remember
> Forgetting every charm,
> Soon would impartial reason
> The tyrant love disarm;
> But when enraged I number
> Each failing of her mind,
> Love still suggests her beauty
> And sees — while Reason's blind.

The Law was not particularly attractive to Richard Sheridan. But then, what was? He had very little use for the red coat and the gold braid of the Army, even if Tom had been willing to buy him a commission. And to take orders and secure a living in the Church was like condemning oneself to a neuter existence — "neither life nor death, but something in-between" — since a clergyman was not of this world, surely, yet had not attained to any other. He wanted

to write plays and win fame, to cut a figure in the world
of politics and to win fortune and position. But how?
The trees and the quietly folding hills at Waltham
remained silent.

Charles, that correct young man, had got himself an
under-secretaryship to Stockholm. And here was
Richard still reading Blackstone and Coke! Yet the
Law might be that wedge with which he was to force
the door of political security. In one of his earliest
legal writings appears the adumbration of an argument which he later made to Burke. Its thought is
singularly profound for so young a man. " An un-
natural Power given to anyone, though by the general
consent, is not the less a Tyranny. The hardest restraint is that succeeding generations have always
been in some degree bound by the actions of their
ignorant ancestors; and they have always promised
for Posterity. *Therefore* every man is born in a state
of *absolute* slavery, for even though he may assist in
the modes of Government he must submit to its Principle. . . . Am I not born to an Allegiance which I
can in no ways shake off? — is it in my Power solemnly to renounce the Government and go to live in
a Desert or change it? We should be *born* subjects to
none but the Government, and be received as *citizens,*
if we choose it, at an age of maturity. A man is suffered to change his Religion — Dissenters will leave a
Bishop. I do not nor can[not] consider myself as a
free Being."

He worried about Mathews, who still lived, unpun-

ished, to spread his stories and vilify the name of
Sheridan. Dick wrote out a long and laborious account of the second duel at Kingsdown and persuaded
Captain Paumier, his second, to sign it. And so it
stood — his story against Mathews' — for all the
world to read.

CHAPTER SEVEN

The Wonderful Year

IT WAS 1773. Richard Sheridan and his lovely bride were still sundered by parental opposition. His letters to her were becoming more and more frantic as months passed without a sight of her. Rumors had her betrothed to Lord This and Mr. That. Was it true? The poor girl wrote that she was his and his alone — but there was small comfort in reading words which were almost a fortnight old when they reached him. He upbraided her constantly, scolding her when she wrote as well as when, heartsick and bewildered, she neglected to answer him.

Elizabeth was in London now, whither her father had brought her to sing in the Oratorios. She went to balls and routs and *conversaziones*, and gossip reported how she had danced all evening with one ardent gentleman and then permitted another to escort her to her chair. Heartless flirt! thought her husband. Presently he stopped writing to her.

AT THE
THEATRE ROYAL
Tomorrow, Wednesday, March 3, 1773
Will Be Performed
JUDAS MACCABÆUS

SHERIDAN OF DRURY LANE

An Oratorio
Composed by Mr. Handel
The Principal Vocal Parts By
Miss Linley
Mrs. Weichsel
Miss Mary Linley
Mr. Norris
And Mr. Parry

When had she last heard from Sheridan? Elizabeth wondered, while fear grew like an icicle in her heart. Perhaps her father was right when he called Richard a worthless rogue, a ne'er-do-well. Perhaps she should incline a more sympathetic ear to the protestations of those gentlemen who clustered about her, undistinguishable in their satin coats and ruffles, who sent her bouquets in starched white-paper petticoats and pomanders filled with scent. Their faces blurred together whenever she thought of them. But Richard — dear Richard! There was his bright smile and the long, level glance of his eyes. She sobbed as she wrote to him. " Believe me, I am incapable of loving any man. There are insurmountable obstacles to prevent our ever being united, even supposing I ever could be induced to believe in you." That was a thrust, pitiful and ineffectual, at all those days when she had waited breathlessly for a letter. " Know that before I left Bath, after I had refused Sir T. C[larges] [1] and other gentlemen of fortune on your account . . . in the an-

---

[1] Sir Thomas Clarges was one of the most persistent of Elizabeth's suitors, and the one of whom Richard was most jealous.

guish of my soul . . . I vowed in the most solemn manner upon my knees before my parents that I would never be yours by my own consent. . . . My father took advantage of my distress . . . and prevailed on me to promise to marry the first man (whose character was unexceptionable) that offered." There was such a man in London, she continued. Not young, still he was a worthy gentleman, for although he knew that Elizabeth could never love him, " he is more in earnest than ever." He had also given his promise to Dr. Linley not to touch her fortune, " and you may be assured," she added artlessly, " this will have just weight with him." It was useless, therefore, for Richard to write to her again.

To this period of doubt and turmoil belong the following song, also from *The Duenna* — the repository, in fact, of all the verses written during Richard's courtship.

O had my love ne'er smiled on me,
   I had ne'er known such anguish:
But think how false, how cruel, she
   To bid me cease to languish.
To bid me hope her hand to gain, ·
   Breathe on a flame, half-perished.
And then, with cold and fixed disdain,
   To kill the hope she cherished.

Not worse his fate who on a wreck
   That drove as winds did blow it,
Silent had left the shattered deck
   To find a grave below it;

Then land was cried: no more resigned
He glowed with joy to hear it,
Not worse his fate, his woe, to find
The wreck must sink ere near it.

It is typical of all Sheridan's songs of the period:
rather charming beginning; a weak and inept conclusion.

Elizabeth's letter sent Dick hurrying to London.
He would see her before it was too late! He told his
father that he intended to pursue his legal studies further at the Middle Temple, and Tom Sheridan consented to his departure. And now to the already familiar story in which Richard Sheridan and Elizabeth
Linley moved — the story of two young and loving
hearts separated by a pair of angry fathers — there
was added another element straight from the romances. The hero disguised himself in order that he
might be near the heroine. Returning from the theater
where nightly she sang so exquisitely the graceful intricacies of Handel's music, Miss Linley was driven
by a certain hackney-coachman whose bearing, whose
manner, were strangely familiar. Was it possible?
Could it be that under the bulky greatcoat there beat
the enraptured heart of her Richard? She sat in the
carriage, her hands clasped tightly under her cloak,
while the tired horse picked his way through dark
streets and the coachman's back loomed solidly on
the box before her. At last they stopped before her
house.

"Goodnight, miss," said the coachman. His hand

barely brushed against hers in the darkness. "Good-night, my dearest love."

"Richard!" Suddenly the night seemed to glow with his name. "You came to me!"

"Hush, my love." He kissed her hand. "Good-night, my Eliza."

He climbed upon his box and disappeared. The night had swallowed Richard in his too-large great-coat, with the shiny black hat on his head and the long black whip coiled snakily in his hand. "Come back, Richard!" called Elizabeth, but the street was eyeless and secretive where they had stood together. She walked up the steps and into the house. Everything was the same. Curtains drawn, candles lit, her father's slippers on the hearth. Yet she had spoken to Richard and that had changed everything. The icicles in her heart were dissolving. She was happy again, confident that the blackness would break and the sun shine upon them soon.

Still living the pages of his romance, the hero now secured the services of an intermediary to negotiate between himself and the stern father of the heroine. The go-between was Ewarts, his kinsman. The two men met — the blustering and irascible Dr. Linley, and Ewarts who dusted snuff from his ruffles and pre-sented in low tones the case of his young relative. At length their conferences were concluded — and more successfully than Richard had dared to hope. Perhaps Dr. Linley, for all his sound and fury, had a secret fondness in his heart for the young man his daughter had married. Perhaps he desired to see love triumphant, as it always was in the romances. Or perhaps he was growing tired of the whole affair. He had held out as long as possible; now he must yield, and face the loss of Elizabeth's voice — and of Elizabeth — with what equanimity he could muster.

Whatever the reason, yield he did. He imposed one or two conditions, however, to which the young man readily agreed. Sheridan must promise not to touch a certain stipulated portion of that twelve hundred pounds which old Mr. Long had bequeathed to Elizabeth, and which she had dutifully given to her father. Elizabeth herself, who was earning a fortune yearly with her music, must promise never to sing in public for money again. That was her husband's condition. She must have hated to give up a life she loved and the singing which was the breath of that life to her; nevertheless Elizabeth complied. She accepted with a tender smile those verses with which Richard had graced the occasion:

To Eliza on Ceasing to Sing

Does my Eliza cease to sing,
Or tires my love to touch the string?
Behold, she knows with equal skill
To grace the Muse's nobler will.
Hear but her voice! amazed you swear
The soul of music centers there.
Read but her voice, and you'll confess
Her song did raise your wonder less.

Nor did Richard ever change his mind, for eighteen months later, when George III offered him the post of Director of Oratorios, he refused, thinking that Elizabeth might be asked to perform in one of them, and that the position had been tendered him only because of her. At the same time he declined for her an offer of three thousand two hundred pounds to sing at the Pantheon.

Now at last the two men were satisfied; the "insurmountable obstacles" had been removed. On Tuesday, April 13, 1774, Elizabeth Linley and Richard Brinsley Sheridan were married for the second time, in Marylebone Church. It was a double wedding, the other couple being the faithful Ewarts and the young heiress with whom he had recently eloped.

One wind blew chillingly across their happiness. Tom Sheridan, in Ireland at the time of his son's marriage, heard the news in an apoplectic fury. Not until three years had passed did Richard and his father meet and speak together again.

On April 15th the *Morning Post* apprised its readers: " Mr. Sheridan, a student of the Temple, is at last firmly united to Miss Linley, the celebrated Maid of Bath, on Tuesday last."

The rapturous pair departed for East Burnham, where they were to spend their honeymoon. Later, when Elizabeth was dead and the dream of those long-forgotten days had dissolved forever, Richard Sheridan looked back to East Burnham as to a place sacred

[105]

and apart. Here was every ingredient to make a poem, and every inspiration to make a poet. The little cottage in its quiet rustic setting; the lengthening spring twilights when the air grew swiftly chill and a single star gleamed in a sky which was the color of aquamarines; the snapping of logs in the fireplace after midnight, when the world was still and an occasional mouse scuttled through the wainscoting; the murmur of the bees returning to the vine outside their bedchamber; and always, above every other sound, the sound of Elizabeth singing.

April passed, and May, and in June Dr. Linley came with Mary to visit the lovers. Thomas Linley owned himself satisfied with his daughter's marriage. One could not spend an hour under the same roof with Elizabeth Sheridan and not feel the warmth of her happiness, the all-pervading radiance of her love. On July 8, 1774, Elizabeth sang at Oxford when Lord North was installed as Chancellor of the University. His election to this office nine months earlier had greatly pleased His Majesty, who regarded it " a compliment to me, and a credit to that ancient seat of learning."

The glorious summer at East Burnham was passing. Soon autumn would be crisp in the air; they must be settled without delay in London. He must make his fortune. He must take his place with his lovely bride, in Society.

They took a house in Orchard Street, Portman Square, furnished it with a charming correctness, engaged servants. And almost instantly they were in debt. The never-ending game between Sheridan and his creditors had started. The young people gave parties, to which an increasing number of the Great World came. Bills came too, and these Richard tore across, or tucked out of sight somewhere in his crowded desk; sometimes he used their blank backs to scribble verses. "Godlike in giving," Tom Moore wrote of him after his death. " But the devil to pay."

The nest of linnets from which Elizabeth had flown was shaken now by black and tragic storms. In August, 1778, Tom, the Linleys' marvelous boy — he for whom Mozart had painted so glowing a future — was drowned in the Duke of Ancaster's private lake. He was then just turned twenty-two. For a while it seemed as though his shattered parents would never smile again. His sister Elizabeth was moved to write the simplest and most poignant of all her lyrics.

ON MY BROTHER'S VIOLIN

Sweet instrument of him for whom I mourn,
    Tuneful companion of my Lycid's hours,
How liest thou now, neglected and forlorn,
    What skilful hand shall now call forth thy powers?

Ah, none like his can reach those liquid notes,
    So soft, so sweet, so eloquently clear.
To lie beyond the touch, and gently float.
    In dying modulations on the ear.

That hectic and consuming fire whose spark all Thomas Linley's children bore burned now in Samuel, the dead boy's junior by one scant year.[2] Fevers scorched him; he wasted away in that "galloping consumption" which was the scourge of the young. Watching helplessly, his parents tried all the little futile things which medicine prescribed without knowing why. They bathed his forehead with Eau de Cologne and sealed the windows in his bedroom with putty, lest the dangerous night air intrude. The Linleys had a pretty servant-maid who sat sometimes beside the bedside of the sick boy and gossiped with him. Her name was Emma Lyon. Years later as Lady Hamilton she became the talk of the world.

Mary Linley had married. She was Mrs. Tickell, and like her adored sister wife to a writer who had his way to make in the world. Tickell possessed a nice wit and a considerable talent; he had, too, a more than considerable desire to "puff" for his distinguished brother-in-law. He turned his hand with no apparent difficulty to all kinds of writing — political things for Fox, the *Camp* in 1778, the burlesque *Carnival of Venice* in 1781. He even produced part of that all-embracing satire, *The Rolliad*. Like Sheridan, Tickell was extravagant, impetuous, witty, sentimental. It was no wonder at all that between the two men a very firm friendship should develop. This was especially fortunate since Elizabeth Sheridan and Mary Tickell were closer to each other than sisters usually are. They saw each other constantly. When they were

---

[2] The Linleys all died young; Jane at 39; Mary (Mrs. Tickell) before she was 30; Elizabeth Sheridan at 37; Thomas at 22; Samuel at 21.

apart they wrote long, affectionate and minutely detailed letters in a particular " little language " of their own invention.

Before she was thirty Mary Tickell died of that disease which would also cause her sister Elizabeth's untimely end. A prolonged " cure " at the Hot Wells failed to check the progress of her malady. Until her own death Elizabeth constantly wore the miniature of Mary which Cosway had painted, and she herself wrote Mary's epitaph:

> To charm with heavenly sound a mortal ear,
> A sample of the joys we may attain,
> God lent awhile a warbling cherub here,
> But missed her song, and snatched her back again.

Five years later Elizabeth Sheridan was laid to rest beside her sister in the vault of the Cathedral at Wells.

Life in Orchard Street was thoroughly delightful. Elizabeth was sitting for her portrait to Sir Joshua Reynolds who headed the Royal Academy — although His Majesty much preferred the work of Benjamin West.[3] Lovelier than ever in those months following her marriage, Sir Joshua painted her as St. Cecilia, with the two musical Coote children, their neighbors, grouped beside her as listening cherubs.

Reynolds was not the only denizen of the world of fashion whose carriage stopped at the Sheridans' door. Very frequently they were honored by a visit from

[3] For thirty years George III bought two pictures annually from West, at five hundred pounds apiece.

Her Grace of Devonshire. Georgiana, the beautiful, the legendary, was at that time seventeen, and but a few months married to William Cavendish, the cold and cynical Duke. Already she was a creature of whims, of conflicts and contradictions. History has called her a rake and a gambler and has made much of that curious *ménage à trois* which she maintained later with her husband and the latter's mistress, her friend Lady Elisabeth Foster. Yet the fact that she was also a woman of keen perceptions and of no small literary talent is evidenced by a perusal of the recently discovered Devonshire House manuscripts. In these pages the reader is privileged to meet not only Georgiana but her circle as well in a succession of cleverly drawn portraits. She and her sister, Lady Bessborough, were to influence greatly the lives of their young protégées, the Sheridans.

Best of all, Richard was writing. Essays occupied him at first in 1775. He was attempting to find a style that was his own — not cynical like Lord Chesterfield's, which he disliked, not ponderous and stilted like that of Dr. Johnson, with whom he disagreed. The first faint rumblings of the American War were beginning to roll across the Atlantic, and though the Crown's arms had triumphed momentarily at Lexington, Sheridan felt dubious of their ability to attain either an ultimate or a lasting victory. Justice was dying, he believed; liberty was dead. It was in this vein that he replied to the Lexicographer's *Taxation No Tyranny,* in which Johnson had written: " To be born a subject means a tacit consent to the established government." " If," Sheridan answered him, " by our birth we give a tacit bond of acquiescence to that form of government under which we were born, there never would have been one alteration of the first modes of Government — there never would have been a Revolution in England."

A somewhat similar idea he expressed in his dedication to George III of a long poem entitled *On the General Fast.* " The truth, Sire, which every schoolboy in political knowledge could confirm, is simply that the American War, founded in injustice and carried on by folly, must end in irretrievable disgrace, or in absolute destruction. The idea, Sire, of conquering a people, in arms and arts confessedly our equals, in every virtue undoubtedly our superiors, savours too much of folly, or something worse than folly, to have been promulgated by any genius less than those very contemptible ones which at present surround and disgrace the throne." In the *Ode* Richard continued his championship of the rebels:

> There was a time, to Britain dear,
> (Its memory let our sons revere)
>   When Western Climes were ours.
> When Albion's thunders through the world
> In the red lightning's rage were hurled
>   And awed the tyrant powers.
>
> But now, alas! So changed the time,
> (Detested thought that mars my rhyme!)
>   Debauchery holds the helm.

[111]

Rank impotence and dire disease
Waft Britain's flota o'er the seas,
    And curse the sinking realm.

But sing, my Muse, in worthier strains
Th' heroic souls who glad the plains
    Where Freedom loves to dwell.
Putnam and Washington and Lee,
Arnold and brave Montgomery,[4]
    The faithful page shall swell.

Ships must be mann'd and armies bought,
For murderous views — O curse the thought!
    And curse each German plan,
Which deals at large in human blood,
And stabs the brave and stabs the good,
    At eighteen pounds per man!

What were His Majesty's thoughts on reading this dedication and the fervent stanzas which accompanied it we may only surmise. For it is no secret that George felt very strongly on the subject of the rebellious colonies. From his earliest childhood he had been trained to regard very seriously the first duty of kingship — which is to rule — and that divinity which encompasses the person of the monarch. George wanted to be a king; his ministers had long ago decided that he could never be more than a constitutional ruler. He looked upon the American colonists as directly insubordinate to the royal person. They were " wicked and disappointed men " whose " outrageous licentiousness " must be subdued at once.

[4] He fell before Quebec.

[112]

Richard was writing. One of the things which occupied him after the completion of his *Ode* was a fairy operetta entitled *King Arthur*. It was an amusing little trifle and mildly successful; one of the reasons for that success being the presence in the cast of Miss Therese De Camp, a tiny dark-eyed child who danced divinely. Miss De Camp with her twinkling toes and her round white arms weaves in and out of the Sheridan story. Not long afterwards she was to appear before Richard's great friend, His Royal Highness the Prince of Wales, and his mistress Mrs. Fitzherbert. When she was a mature woman, a little stout but still graceful, she watched her husband Charles Kemble and her daughter Fanny walk many times across the stage at Covent Garden as characters in Sheridan's plays.

To this same period belongs also a dull and humorless composition called *A Drama of Devils,* in which appeared for the first time the lovely song beginning, " Dry be that tear."

1775 was a wonderful year for Richard Sheridan. It found him obscure, the veriest nobody. At its close he was a social lion, and there was in Great Britain no hamlet so small that the echoes of his fame had not reached it.

On Tuesday, January 17, 1775, the lights at Covent Garden shone upon the first performance of a comedy called *The Rivals*. It was a dismal, a shuddering failure. After only two performances, both enlivened by catcalls from the gallery and hoots and jeers from the pit, the play was withdrawn. Harris, the manager, scurried frantically about London for a new cast. The youthful author, who refused to permit himself to become discouraged by the play's reception, tied his head up in wet towels and retired to his closet " to remove those imperfections in the first representation which were too obvious to escape reprehension and too numerous to admit of a hasty correction," he tells us in his *Preface* to the published play. He expunged, he altered, he rewrote. After ten exhausting days the revised text was completed and once again the sputtering footlights around the stage at Covent Garden lit up Act I, Scene i, A Street in Bath. When the final curtain descended the audience was wild with delight. *The Rivals* was a sensation; its author was a success.

The reason for its failure at its first performance was simple. The English theater was experiencing a reaction away from the *comédie larmoyante* of Diderot and his school; plays which were dull and bloodless, without an animating spark or a touch of reality. The reaction had started with the production of Oliver Goldsmith's *She Stoops to Conquer,* which, although well received by the critics, met with a definite opposition from certain lovers of tradition. Horace Walpole wrote to Lady Ossory, March 16, 1773 : " Stoops ! Indeed, so she does ! She is draggled up to the knees and has trudged all the way from Southwark Fair ! " But in the next few years the style of Goldsmith was accepted. Sheridan's first draft of *The Rivals* had been too long, the critics caviled; it was too artificial and much too verbose. Rewriting it he destroyed many of the dull places, but the characters of Julia and Falkland, those sentimental " excrescences " on the pure form of the comedy, he retained. For although Sheridan laughs at them occasionally he secretly admires them — with their florid speeches and the exasperating complexity of their emotions.

Across *The Rivals* there blows a new and vitalizing breeze. Jack Absolute and his choleric father are the stock father-and-son of romance. As for the plot — " He knew he had a good plot for the theatre, because it always had been a good plot in the theatre. He gave the public what the public always had wanted and therefore what the public always will want." [5] But in the characters of Bob Acres and the swaggering Sir Lucius O'Trigger, Sheridan has found something fresh and original. As for Mrs. Malaprop, she is magnificent, and while the type she represents may not be unique either in the drama or in fiction, she is unquestionably that type's most perfect example. No writer since has produced a character that can outshine her. The manuscript of his mother's *A Journey to Bath,* which rests now in the British Museum, provided the general idea for the character of Mrs. Malaprop and for some of her lines. In Frances Sheridan's sketch Mrs. Tryfort says: " My Lord Stewkley is so embel-

[5] *Plays by Richard Brinsley Sheridan,* edited and with an Introduction by Clayton Hamilton.

lished . . . if you were to hear him describe the contagious countries!" Richard employed that last phrase: "I would have her instructed in geometry," Mrs. Malaprop remarks, "that she might know something of the contagious countries." His mother referred to Lord Stewkley as "a progeny, a perfect progeny," which her son amplified into: "I would by no means wish a daughter of mine to be a progeny of learning."

The scene of Richard's play was Bath, the pretty town he knew and loved so well. *The Rivals* has caught every single facet of life in Bath. The circulating libraries, the scheming servants who ape their masters' follies, the restrictions against dueling — "We wear no swords here," Sir Lucius tells the timorous Bob Acres, "but you understand me." It was essentially an English play, yet audiences must have recognized its characters as universal, transcending all bounds of nationality, for soon after its production it was a favorite on the continent. There was a German version called *Julia und Acres*, and when the playwright Kotzebue was a little boy attending a Minorite cloister he once appeared in it.

When *The Rivals* was withdrawn after its first two disastrous performances Elizabeth Sheridan was pleased. She had regarded as peculiar Richard's stubborn refusal to allow her to pay some of their debts by resuming her singing. Dick insisted that he could earn more than enough for them by writing plays! From Slough, where she was visiting, Elizabeth wrote

after the play's opening: " My dear Dick, I am delighted. I always knew it was impossible you could
make anything by writing plays; so now there is nothing for it but my beginning to sing publickly again, and
we shall have as much money as we like."

Dick hardly noticed that letter. He stuck it away
somewhere — he never bothered much about what became of letters or bills — and returned to his manuscript, which was almost ready for its second appearance.

When *The Rivals* reopened on January 28th the rôle
of Sir Lucius O'Trigger was played by an Irishman
named Laurence Clinch, who rolled his r's, cocked his
head at the ladies, swaggered and roared and tickled
the spectators immeasurably. Mr. Lee, his predecessor in the part, had feared so to offend both the Irish
and the audience that he had stumbled through his
lines. But Sheridan had not intended in the character
of Sir Lucius to provoke the country of his birth. " It is
not without pleasure," he continues in the Preface already quoted, " that I catch at an opportunity of justi-
fying myself from the charge of intending any national
reflection in the character of Sir Lucius O'Trigger. If
any gentlemen opposed the piece from that idea, I
thank them sincerely for their opposition; and if the
condemnation of this comedy . . . could have added
one spark to the decaying flame of national attachment to the country supposed to be reflected on, I
should have been happy in its fate, and might . . .
have boasted that it had done more real service in its

[117]

failure than the successful morality of a thousand novels will ever effect."

Clinch loved the part and the audience applauded him madly. He had made the play, Dick realized. Not long afterward Clinch had a benefit and Richard gratefully wrote for him, in forty-eight hours, the rollicking farce, St. Patrick's Day, or The Scheming Lieutenant.

1775. Annus Mirabilis. First The Rivals, and then on May 2nd St. Patrick's Day, to convince the critics that here was an authentic talent, not merely another bright young man. Spring and summer went by almost unobserved while he scribbled down his verses and lyrics for The Duenna, for which Dr. Linley was to provide the score. The Duenna opened to a packed house on November 21st and was a tremendous success. It ran for seventy-five nights, bettering by ten the run of John Gay's Beggar's Opera, which had been regarded for nearly half a century as the finest comic opera ever produced. Richard and his father-in-law had done their work superbly. The music and the text were completely one, and it was impossible to dissociate one from the other. Technically it is the best constructed of all Sheridan's plays, yet today only the lovely songs which he wrote for it have survived. Mrs. Green, who had created the rôle of Mrs. Malaprop, played the Duenna; Isaac Mendoza was enacted by the celebrated Mr. Quick, who had been Dr. Rosy in St. Patrick's Day and Bob Acres in The Rivals.

Four days before the première of *The Duenna* Elizabeth Sheridan had given birth to a son, whom the young parents, gesturing deferentially toward both grandfathers, named Thomas. Perhaps it was the birth of his grandson which softened Tom Sheridan's heart; perhaps it was the success his son had achieved in the theater and the rumors which the old man heard everywhere that Richard was soon to buy out the great Garrick and become manager of the greatest theater in England, the Theatre Royal, Drury Lane. Tom Sheridan, prototype of Sir Anthony Absolute, relented. He accepted Elizabeth to his bosom as his daughter-in-law, he kissed the baby's wrinkled face, and spoke civilly to Thomas Linley — like himself that baby's grandfather. There was peace in Orchard Street. There was, sang Richard's jubilant heart, peace in all the world!

There was also in Orchard Street a brief respite from the debts which normally plagued the householder. Richard had made an arrangement whereby he shared in the sale of the music from *The Duenna*. Since there was not a band in the Kingdom or a concert orchestra which did not play its airs, or a young girl learning to vocalize who did not " execute " its love-songs, Dick was for the first time in his life enjoying the heady feeling of prosperity. He spent his money. That, he discovered, gave him an even headier feeling than merely possessing it. New clothes for himself and Elizabeth; new liveries for the servants; a carriage and pair; wine for the cellars and elaborate dishes for their crowded tables. He was introduced to Dr. Johnson, who was lavish in his praise of the young man's talents — almost as lavish as he had been of the young man's mother's. The Doctor agreed to sponsor Sheridan for the Literary Club which met in St. James Street and to which flocked the choicest spirits of the day. Less than a year later Sheridan had been duly elected, and was privileged to meet Gibbon and Burke and Fox, his political mentor. Dr. Johnson must, therefore, be regarded as the man who started Sheridan upon his political career.

In another sense his life began that year. The ladies of the Great World were lionizing him at last. In his gorgeous new clothes he attended the Duchess of Devonshire's ball, and there made the acquaintance of the lovely and famous Mrs. Crewe, the " Amoret " with whom his name was later to be coupled. He has described her vividly in those verses which he presented to her with a copy of his *School for Scandal:*

> Adorning fashion, unadorned by dress,
> Simple from taste and not from carelessness,
> Discreet in gesture, in deportment mild,
> Not stiff with prudence, or uncouthly wild;
> No state has Amoret; no studied mien;
> She frowns no goddess, and she moves no queen;
> The softer charm that in her manner lies,
> Is framed to captivate, yet not surprise;
> It justly suits th' expression of her face —
> 'Tis less than Dignity, and more than Grace.

1775 was a wonderful year. A year of tremendous intellectual activity, of vigorous political growth.

Titanic figures strode across it. Some had already attained the heights they were to reach; to others destiny lay as yet unrevealed. Forces and movements which were to mature generations later slumbered in the womb of 1775.

Charles James Fox, having received from Lord North the following communication: " Sir: His Majesty has thought proper to order a new Commission of the Treasury to be made, in which I do not see your name," quitted politics for eight years. On January 18, 1775, Walpole noted: " This week came accounts of very riotous proceedings at Boston, where the mob broke into the ships that had brought teas, and threw three hundred and forty chests into the sea." William Pitt, the younger, aged fifteen, a thin, pale boy, was recovering from a breakdown at Pembroke Hall; in ten years he would be England's Prime Minister. George, Prince of Wales, and the Duke of York his brother, were being reared in strict seclusion by Dr. Markham of Westminster, who neither spared the rod nor spoiled the child. And in Ireland the Hon. Arthur Wellesley had reached the age of five.

Priestley was investigating oxygen, and an energetic Scotsman named James Watt was entertaining some fantastic and impractical notions about steam. Dr. Arne and Dr. Linley composed their pretty melodies and the nation continued to sing them. Gainsborough, the " limner " of Bath, was painting the portraits of the fashionable. The mantle of Hogarth had descended upon Thomas Rowlandson, whose caricatures were every bit as bitter and brutally descriptive of his time as had been those of the master. The Great Lexicographer was an old man — sixty-five — but his mind was still functioning as actively as ever. He was the Dean of Letters, the unchallenged arbiter in every matter that concerned the mind. Otherwise the literary scene was at the moment bare. Goldsmith had died recently. William Wordsworth was a little child of four, toddling among his flowers; his sister Dorothy, whose exquisite journals later inspired Keats and Southey, was just three. Chatterton, his " marvelous boy," had taken his tragic talents to the grave not many years before. Southey and Coleridge were babies, Gray had just died, and Cowper was writing his uninspired stanzas from a quiet haven in the country. A youth named Samuel Rogers, whose table and whose generous purse would later sustain hundreds of artists, was being educated in 1775 in the comfortable ways of the Banker.

In 1775 Edward Gibbon joined that Literary Club which Dr. Johnson and Sir Joshua Reynolds had founded a decade earlier. Charles James Fox was also honored by admission to the Club in the same year. David Garrick was still in control at Drury Lane. The Wedgwood factories in Staffordshire were working full blast to produce the exquisite pottery in which everyone took such delight. And on March 23, 1775, Edmund Burke had spoken for three hours on Conciliation with the American Colonies.

Life itself had not altered appreciably since the pre-

[122]

vious century. It was still England's cheapest, most abundant commodity. Houses had not changed much, in fact, since the days of Elizabeth. They were still badly ventilated and improperly heated, and although candlelight was soft and flattering it was very much of a strain on the eyes. London was crowded with dirty, verminous slums in which disease bred and vice and crime flourished. Although he would stoutly have denied the allegation, the rich man in St. James's was directly responsible for, as he was affected by, the miserable slum dweller in Billingsgate. Dirt was frankly to be seen everywhere. In matters of hygiene, at least, little advancement had been made since the day when Samuel Pepys, discovering that bathing gave him a cold, straightway gave up his bath.

In her political structure England boasted the possession of certain fundamental democratic principles; yet upon close examination they proved to be woefully lacking. Universal male suffrage was still a Utopian dream which would not be realized for half a century. Catholics and " dissenters " were likewise denied the privilege of the ballot; a privilege which was in reality more shadowy than substantial. For the system that obtained in Parliamentary elections was rotten. Men were " returned " from places which had no other existence beside their names. Owing to shifts in population their erstwhile voters had long departed, but the " pocket borough " sent its representatives to Commons just the same.

The first faint mutterings of what would later become the thunder of the Industrial Revolution were already discernible in various inventions which would take the workers from their homes into factories. Men were being driven from their lands as the estates of the great spread out, absorbing farms and pastures for hunting parks and game preserves. Education was still the privilege of the rich. The rigidly exclusive system of the " public school " managed to keep out the sons of the poor. Thus the rustic and the indigent slum dweller alike preserved their illiteracy — so quaint and charming in the pages of a novel, in actuality so threatening to the progress of the country.

CHAPTER EIGHT

School for Scandal

ON JUNE 10, 1776, David Garrick played his last rôle on the stage of Drury Lane — Don Felix in Mrs. Centlivre's *The Wonder*. He was sixty years old; he had achieved his fortune, and he was growing tired. For several months he had been negotiating with young Sheridan to have him take over the management of the theater. Before the first of July all the arrangements had been completed, and thanks to the more than considerable assistance of Dr. James Ford of Albemarle Street, Court physician and man of means, Richard found himself in possession of Garrick's theater.

The intricate and involved manner in which Sheridan acquired his control of Drury Lane, the toppling structure of mortgage piled on mortgage, of notes and unpaid bills, makes extraordinary telling. Up to June, 1776, the ownership of the theater's patent had been divided between the retiring manager David Garrick, and Mr. Willoughby Lacy, who had in the past thirty years trebled the value of the property. It was estimated now at £70,000, with a return of ten percent on the investment. Garrick demanded to be paid

£35,000 for his half-share of the patent, and at this price it was finally purchased by a syndicate composed of Sheridan, Dr. Linley, and the affluent Dr. Ford. The latter contributed £15,000 to the purchase of Garrick's half-share. Linley gave £10,000, which he borrowed in the City at four percent. As for Richard, he raised his £10,000 by offering a mortgage to Ford, and by mortgaging two annuities he held to Garrick's solicitors, Wallis and Troward. Lacy at first refused to part with his share. But when a year had passed and Drury Lane under its new management was flourishing so visibly that he felt he could better Garrick's price, he offered his half to the syndicate. The price paid was " something exceeding forty-five thousand pounds." Every plank in the theater was mortgaged now; the roof was snowed under by debts. Yet the value of the property on which Sheridan was to lose so much kept on increasing. During the next twelve years it reached £130,000.

Richard was not satisfied for long. He wanted to be Drury Lane's sole owner. In order to accomplish this and absorb the shares of his father-in-law and Dr. Ford he sank deeper and deeper into the quagmire of debt and financial involvement. By 1780 he had acquired complete possession. His wife kept all his accounts, read plays, interviewed and soothed ruffled actors who were dissatisfied with their rôles or their salaries — or both. Richard paid off old debts so that, with the receipts as security, he might borrow still more. He was trying to enter Parliament, and it cost a thundering amount to swing an election. But he owned his theater, and he loved it. Without realizing it, he had erected a Colossus which would bestride his world completely, and would eventually destroy him.

To be manager of a theater like Drury Lane was to be arbiter of the taste of millions. What was performed at Drury Lane sooner or later found its way into the provinces; sometimes the fact that a play had enjoyed a Drury Lane production was its only virtue. Yet it was enough. It was the hallmark of quality and distinction. Bearing this in mind, Richard Sheridan determined that under his ægis the standards of the venerable institution would be raised. He would offer the public only works of merit and refinement.

That implied, necessarily, a certain amount of expurgation and revision of the classics, since the elegant tastes of the eighteenth century were very easily shocked by the franker speech of the past. Sheridan set to work upon the Restoration dramatists. On February 24, 1777, he had ready for production a milder and less salty version of Vanbrugh's *Relapse,* the title altered to *A Trip to Scarborough.* He has begun here to laugh at the ladies of fashion — those creatures of paint and whalebone, of plumes and perfume.

> Were they designed to be, when put together,
> Made up like shuttlecocks, of cork and feather?
> Their pale-faced grandmammas appeared with grace
> When dawning blushes rose upon the face;
> No blushes now their once-loved stations seek,

The foe is in possession of the cheek.
No heads of old too high for feathered state,
Hindered the fair to pass the lowest gate;
A church to enter now they must be bent,
If ever they should try th' experiment.

A Trip to Scarborough played ninety-nine performances and realized almost fifteen hundred pounds.
One of the reasons for its long run was unquestionably the appearance as Amanda of Mary Robinson —
so much better known as " Perdita," the beautiful, the
exquisite. Gossip was thick around London that
Sheridan was at work upon a new comedy which
would be funnier than his *Rivals*. It was to open at
Drury Lane next week, next month — who could
tell?

The manager, a bit more prosperous now, had
moved his household to Great Queen Street, near the
Freemasons' Tavern, where he continued to reside
until his election to Parliament nearly three years
later. He was working very hard on the comedy which
all London was awaiting, but he would drop it occasionally to dabble with two others which never reached
beyond the fragmentary stage — *The Statesman* and
The Foresters. He also wrote the prologue to the
dour Miss Hannah More's *Fatal Falsehood*, which he
produced at Drury Lane, and an epitaph on the passing of Brooks. He had been the owner of Brooks'
Club, a man who had watched unmoved while fortunes
came and went across his tables, and had then lent
money at exorbitant rates to the losers.

[128]

Alas! that Brooks, returned to dust
    Should pay at length the debt that we,
Adverse to parchment, mortgage, trust,
    Shall pay when forced, as well as he.

And die so poor, too! He whose trade
    Such profits cleared by draught and deed.
Though pigeons called him Murmuring Brooks,
    And dipped their bills in him at need.

At length his last conveyance see,
    Each witness mournful as a brother.
To think that this world's mortgagee
    Must suffer judgment in another.

Where no appeals to court can rest,
    Reversing a supreme decree;
But each decision stands expressed
    A final precedent *in re*.

The play was ready at last. On May 8, 1777, *The School for Scandal* was produced at Drury Lane — an opening that was a sensation. A minor playwright named Reynolds recorded for posterity, as he was walking past the pit-passage about nine o'clock of that memorable night: " I heard such a tremendous noise over my head that, fearing the theater was proceeding to fall about it, I ran for my life; but found the next morning that the noise did not arise from the falling of the house, but from the falling of the screen in the fourth act, so violent and tumultuous were the applause and laughter."

Also present, in a stage-box, was Sheridan's rival

the dramatist Cumberland, whose tragedy *The Battle of Hastings* was currently curdling audiences at Covent Garden. He is said to have reproved his children who were convulsed by the falling of that same screen. " There is nothing to laugh at, my little angels. You should not laugh! " he kept enjoining them, adding finally, " Keep still, you little dunces! " When the story was told to Sheridan he said, " It was rather ungrateful of Cumberland to have scolded his children for laughing at my comedy. When I went to see his tragedy I laughed from beginning to end."

Two years later Sheridan revenged himself upon Cumberland when he satirized him in *The Critic,* or *A Tragedy Rehearsed.*

Richard Sheridan had been before the public as a dramatist only two years, yet he had written the greatest comedy in the English language, and one of the greatest comedies in the repertory of the theater. Shakespeare had never tried his hand at the comedy of manners. Hence we can compare Sheridan in this field only to Congreve, and while Congreve's plays are more intense and possess a slight undercurrent of tragedy, the wit and brilliance of Sheridan's writing is ageless and untarnishable. The idea of a " scandalous college " was not a new one with Sheridan; he had himself known what it meant to be exposed to the pitiless tongues of the gossips. His experiences in Bath and the scandals connected with his marriage may have furnished him with the background of his play.

The Honble Chas James Fox

CHARLES JAMES FOX

Dick Sheridan was twenty-five now. He had matured since writing *The Rivals*, and since he had reached that maturity while living in the Great World he had sacrificed humor for wit; his writing had lost some of the warmth and humanity with which the earlier play abounded. *The School for Scandal* is a brilliant play. It is sharp and dazzling, like a diamond, and like a diamond the fires at its heart are cold.

When he was an old man Charles Lamb used to say that one of the compensations of age was that he could remember *The School for Scandal* in all its pristine glory. Certainly no cast has ever played it as it was played by the actors whom Dick Sheridan assembled for that first production. Indeed, his unerring sense of the theater is shown by the fact that he created his characters to fit the peculiarities and potentialities of his actors. He was once asked why, since Maria married Charles Surface at the end of the play, he had never written a love scene between the two young people. " That," said Sheridan, " is because neither Miss Hopkins nor Mr. Smith are capable of making love charmingly or convincingly." As for Joseph Surface, Sheridan could have had no one else in his mind when he wrote the part except John Palmer, the actor who played it. Once after shamming an illness, Mr. Palmer returned to the theater and became very humble and repentant in Sheridan's presence. He put his hand upon his heart, raised his eyes to heaven, and said in a *tremolo* voice, " My dear Mr. Sheridan, if you could but know what I feel at this moment —

here!" Sheridan looked at him quizzically. "Why, Jack!" he exclaimed. "You forget that I *wrote* it!"

The beautiful Mrs. Abington, who had delighted audiences as Miss Hoyden in *A Trip to Scarborough*, played Lady Teazle. She was winning and witty and gay; a country miss whom a few short months of marriage and contact with the Town had changed into a lady of quality.

On the 30th of October, 1779, Sheridan produced the last of his great plays. It was the satire, *The Critic*, and in form it harked back to the time-honored device of the play-within-a-play, which the Duke of Buckingham had used in *The Rehearsal*, and Beaumont and Fletcher before him in *The Knight of the Burning Pestle*. So popular did Sheridan's play become that it drove *The Rehearsal* off the stage. Produced just after his twenty-eighth birthday, it signalized the young author's retirement from the field of dramatic composition. Not until two decades have passed, in 1799, will Sheridan attempt another play — his adaptation from Kotzebue of *Pizarro*.

Besides being perfect satire, *The Critic* contained a few topical allusions to the great and the near great. Don Whiskerandos was John James Hamilton, afterward Marquis of Abercorn. Puff's remark, "A soliloquy always to the pit, if you please," was intended as a slap at "Glorious" John Kemble, darling of the groundlings. As for the *Spanish Armada*, the drama which Mr. Puff wrote and which Mr. Dangle was privileged to see rehearsed, that uproarious play was

[132]

meant to ridicule not only Cumberland's pompous tragedies but also the popular *Douglas* of John Home.

Mr. King, who had created Sir Peter Teazle, played Mr. Puff. Mr. Palmer was cast in the rôle of Sneer, a correct one for his Surfaceish talents. Puff is the most discerning of all Sheridan's characters. Since he is not a person at all but merely the personification of an abstract quality which now goes by his name — "puffing" — he speaks for the author; wisely, wittily and well.

People are always discovering that Sheridan's plots are not original, that his characters and situations are "stock." Certainly he belongs to a long line of literary borrowers, but he was one of the few of these of whom it could be said that he touched nothing which he did not adorn. Already in the *Preface* to *The Rivals* he has anticipated the charge of plagiarism: ". . . on subjects on which the mind has been much informed, invention is slow of exerting itself. Faded ideas float in the fancy like half-forgotten dreams; and the imagination in its fullest enjoyments becomes suspicious of its offspring, and doubts whether it has created or adopted." And in *The Critic* Puff speaks in defense of his creator: "All that can be said is that two people happened to hit on the same thought and Shakespeare made use of it first — that's all!"

His fame as a dramatist and his not inconsiderable fortune still failed to satisfy Richard Sheridan. He yearned to sit among the politicos; the songs and the jests of the nation interested him no longer, since he was eager now to pass upon its laws. His wife's charm and beauty, his own wit and the thrill of his success had opened to him the houses of the great. Everywhere he encountered men of wealth and undisputed position, any of whom might become his patron and sponsor his candidacy for office. Without a patron a man was as helpless as without his legs. A patron was even more essential to a successful career than either intellect or ability. In fact, if the patron were sufficiently important, one could lose oneself completely in his shadow — and rise to prominence just the same.

Despite all the predictions which had foretold its end before another year, the war with America continued. Every day its unpopularity increased. As early as 1774 Edmund Burke had made his great speech on American taxation, in which he had solemnly warned his hearers " to reflect how you are to govern a people who think they ought to be free and think they are not." Fox too had urged a similar point: " The Americans will become useful subjects, if you use them with that temper and lenity which you ought to do." Three years later Lord Chatham, a feeble old man of seventy, electrified the House with a return of his old fire. " You cannot conquer the Americans! " he thundered. " You talk of your powerful forces to disperse their army — I might as well talk of driving them before me with this cane." Now came news of the shocking defeat at Saratoga of

"Gentleman Johnny" Burgoyne. The misfeasances in the conduct of the war of Lord George Germain and the other muddled ministers were rapidly approaching an open scandal. Charles James Fox warned Germain, now Secretary of State for the Colonies, that Burgoyne should not be blamed at all, but that the reason for his defeat " must be sought nearer home."

The average Englishman had come to regard the war as another example of the King's German pig-headedness — like the celebrated case of John Wilkes which everyone refused to forget. He knew by heart most of the ringing phrases of the Declaration of Independence, with which those beggars in America had flung down the gage to old George. Every reformer attacking Lord North's Government on whatever ground was sure of a hearing so long as he styled himself a " friend of Washington " or a " true American."

Sheridan had long admired the rebellious colonists. Soon after his introduction to Charles James Fox and Richard Burke he agreed to edit a paper called *The Englishman*, in which pro-American views and criticisms of the existing government were boldly stated. In this work he was assisted for a time by his brother-in-law Tickell and by John Townshend. The paper appeared each Wednesday and Saturday from March 3, 1777, to June 2 of the same year. In the third issue Sheridan, writing against Germain and North, found himself objecting also to Gibbon, who had recently accepted a minor post in the Government. " Some gentlemen, as Mr. Gibbon, for instance — while in private they indulge their opinion pretty freely, will yet, in their zeal for the public good, even condescend to accept a place in order to give colour to their confidence in the wisdom of the Government."

The Englishman perished, but its editor continued working toward that great day when he would take his seat in Parliament. It came at last on September 12, 1780. It had cost him well over a thousand pounds; he had exhausted himself making speeches to the electors, and it had required the combined efforts of the Duchess of Devonshire and her father and Lord Monckton, brother of Lady Cork. But Richard Brinsley Sheridan was now " the member from Stafford." He had been launched upon a public career which would continue without interruption for more than thirty years.

Four months after his entrance into the House of Commons died the man who had, by retiring, made possible most of Richard Sheridan's success as a theatrical producer. David Garrick, the great, the golden-voiced. He who had lived a thousand men's lives in the life-span of one man died in January, 1781. Sheridan was deeply grieved. As a tribute to the man and the actor he wrote his *Monody on the Death of David Garrick,* which was recited from the stage at Drury Lane by Mrs. Yates as the Tragic Muse. Sheridan's *Monody* was a gesture of friendship. It does not compare with Oliver Goldsmith's *Retaliation,* written several years before Garrick's death, and containing " epitaphs " for Burke, John Douglas, and

[136]

Reynolds as well as for Garrick. Goldsmith most critically summarizes the actor's character:

> Here lies David Garrick, describe me who can
> An abridgement of all that was pleasant in man.
> As an actor, confessed without rival to shine;
> As a wit, if not first, in the very first line;
> Yet with talents like these, and an excellent heart,
> The man had his failings, a dupe to his art.
> Like an ill-judging beauty, his colours he spread,
> And beplastered with rouge his own natural red.
> On the stage he was natural, simple, affecting;
> 'Twas only that when he was off he was acting.

CHAPTER NINE

Member from Stafford

O N OCTOBER 31, 1780, Parliament convened. The new members included three young men marked by destiny's finger. Richard Brinsley Sheridan, aged twenty-nine, from Stafford, William Wilberforce, twenty-one, from Hull, and William Pitt, twenty-one, from Appleby. The nation was still aroused over the "No Popery!" issue. The mad Lord Gordon, whom Horace Walpole designated the "lunatic apostle," had whipped into a maniacal hysteria a mob which rioted through London, burning and looting embassy chapels and completely terrorizing the metropolis for eight horrible days. The question of Catholic Emancipation, not to be settled for half a century, would surely not be raised in the present term.

Politically Sheridan might be styled a New Whig. He belonged to that party which, under the guidance of Charles James Fox, was to change from Whig into Liberal. Before he had taken his seat in the House Sheridan and Fox had presided on February 2, 1780, over a mass meeting in Westminster Hall to demand an annual Parliament and the establishment of universal suffrage. The meeting accomplished nothing, but it gave the young man a pleasant feeling to hear himself speak and to witness his effect upon an audience. He was, in other words, ripe for an oratorical career.

George III had now reached the age of forty-two; for twenty-two years he had been King. The popular enthusiasm he had aroused when he mounted the throne as the " first English-born and English-speaking Monarch of his line " had waned rapidly. One reason might have been the presence among his closest advisors of Lord Bute. The nation still recalled vividly the horrors of '45, and Scotsmen were consequently not likely to have the approval of the populace. Another reason was to be found in the character of George himself. A mild-mannered, genial man, he became when crossed an obstinate and unreasonable fool. His foreign policy lacked vision and possessed no insight whatever into the growing complexities of the age. Careful of his own privy purse and mathematically precise in the smallest detail, the King did not hesitate to demand the expenditure of tremendous sums on ventures doomed from the start to failure. His relationship with the members of his immediate family was always tense. Between the King and his brother, the Duke of Cumberland, there existed a definite hatred. His Royal Highness, George Frederick, Prince of Wales, came to feel for his father as he grew older an active and contemptuous dislike which the King blamed first on the influence of his brother, and then on the Prince's dissolute comrades. Among them he numbered Charles James Fox.

Destined to live out his great age a madman and a
political pawn scrambled over by Whigs and Tories,
George was in reality a figure of darkest tragedy. He
possessed courage and admired the pomp and outward
show of kingship. He attempted to set his subjects an
example of the simpler virtues — virtues which were
notably absent in his son and heir. On every side he
found himself thwarted and betrayed. The Constitution of his country prevented him from being a king.
Indeed, the contagious madness of revolutionary ideas
was outlawing kingship throughout the world. His
son's behavior froze his paternal feelings; he quarreled with his wife, he found his other children tire-
some. There was nothing at the end but a succession
of darkened rooms at Windsor, and an old man at a
harpsichord playing to the shadows the silvery music
of Handel.

But in 1780 George was still King. The bitter Regency crisis was more than a decade away. And Lord
North was still in control of the government.

Soon after he took his seat Fox brought Sheridan
into Brooks', the Whig stronghold. On November 11,
1780, the member from Stafford arose to deliver his
maiden speech, which was a bald protest against a petition to unseat him for bribery during the election.
This in a day when everyone's election to office was accomplished by the open purchase of votes and the
frank exercise of suasion! " He was heard with particular attention," recounts Woodfall, the reporter,

" and the House was uncommonly still while he was speaking." Apparently the petition was killed, for Sheridan retained his seat. He did not speak again during the session except in a vote of thanks to Lord Cornwallis.

But the following year the fledgling bird had found his wings. He made a speech on the Navy — Samuel Linley, his wife's brother, had died a member of its service. To the end of his political life the Navy was to remain a subject close to his heart. He even raised his voice in disagreement with Fox, when his friend and mentor proposed a clause to reduce the age under the Marriage Act. " If girls were allowed to marry at sixteen," declared Sheridan, who had always advocated the granting of greater freedom to women, " they would be abridged of that happy freedom of intercourse which modern custom has introduced between the youth of both sexes . . . and boys in a moment of passion . . . might be prevailed upon to make an imprudent or indecent match."

A few weeks later the House was treated to its first taste of the new member's wit. When Sheridan had finished speaking against the projected terms of a treaty between Great Britain and Holland, Pitt arose and sneeringly alluding to his " dramatic points," regretted that they were not kept intact for their " proper stage." Sheridan's instant reply gave to the future Prime Minister an appellation he long retained. " If ever I engage in the composition the honourable gentleman has alluded to," said young Dick, " I may be tempted . . . to attempt an improvement on one of Ben Jonson's characters, the character of the Angry Boy in the *Alchymist*."

In 1782 Lord North resigned. The King, although he disliked Rockingham personally, sent for him to form a ministry. Rockingham was the hope of Old and New Whig alike. Lord North and Lord Shelburne were men of small political stature, unimaginative and interested chiefly in personal aggrandizement. Rockingham was gentle and of a blameless reputation. He was rich enough to keep his fingers out of the public funds, and gentleman enough to refuse no one anything. He was the perfect instrument, and Burke's were the masterly hands which played upon him.

In the new ministry Sheridan was given the appointment of Under-Secretary of State. He was becoming vitally concerned over the question of Home Rule for Ireland, the country of his birth; he had not, however, forgotten America, and his voice was heard frequently pleading for peace with the " American Continent." Like many other Englishmen he felt that England's prestige abroad had suffered a serious diminution with the loss of her American colonies. He urged, therefore, that she attempt a more harmonious adjustment with those dependencies she still retained — Ireland, for example, and India, whose strong man, Warren Hastings, was already in disgrace.

Lord Rockingham continued in office for two years. After his death the King insisted on the formation of a " comprehensive ministry." But that, " like the

Peace of Utrecht and the Peace of God, passed all understanding." George stormed and cajoled by turns. He wheedled and he wept; he even threatened to return permanently to the Electorate of Hanover. And despite him, on April 2nd, the Coalition came in. Lord North was Secretary for the Home Department, Fox for Foreign Affairs. Edmund Burke was Paymaster of the Forces, Sheridan and Burke's son shared the Treasury between them, while Lord John Cavendish was Chancellor of the Exchequer. There is undoubtedly something humorous in the sight of Richard Sheridan, a man harassed to the end of his days by debts and possessing the vaguest notions about money, being intrusted with the office of the Treasury. Deservedly the Coalition was called a fraud, and deservedly it was reviled alike by the nation and the King. To His Majesty its mien was so dreadful that he is said to have prayed nightly for its dissolution. His prayers were granted. The Coalition Government collapsed, and with it went Richard Sheridan's Cabinet position.

A new figure was rising now. Politically he grew in importance every day; socially he was already the First Gentleman of the Kingdom. George Frederick, Prince of Wales, had in his early 'teens shaken off every restraint which the stern tutelage of Dr. Markham had sought to impose upon him. He set himself to the pursuit of the life of a man of pleasure, which consisted of gaming, drinking, women, and an inordinate concern for the cut of his coat. He became the friend of Fox, whose life had followed an identical pattern; at a ball at Devonshire House Sheridan was presented to him. That was the beginning of a friendship which was to outlast Fox's, yet Sheridan's ill-starred attachment to the Prince brought to the former only confusion and defeat. Sheridan, usually so perspicacious, was unable to distinguish between his allegiance to his party and his dogged championship of the royal reprobate.

In 1781 the King became alarmed because an actress named Mary Robinson threatened to make public some letters she had received from the royal heir. She was a charming girl, fragile and beautiful, and she had been educated by the pedantic Miss Hannah More. In 1778 she had appeared as Perdita in *The Winter's Tale*. The Prince saw her and eagerly sought her acquaintance. Trysts followed at Kew, where Florizel walked with Perdita under the arching trees and caressed her to the music of the fountains. The Prince presented his mistress with a bond for twenty thousand pounds to be paid when he reached his majority. His father, always fearful lest his son entangle himself permanently with some unsuitable female, finally bought the letters at a price much lower than Mrs. Robinson had originally demanded. Of the bond he remained ignorant until 1784, when Fox counseled the Prince to redeem it for a pension of five hundred pounds a year. But by this time Perdita had ceased to charm her corpulent swain. Fox was her lover now, and the pair romped up and down England, visiting Tunbridge and Epsom and taking the waters with the crowds at Bath. What more natural than that Fox should provide for the lady against the moment — remote yet inevitable — when her charms should have palled on him?

The Prince possessed all those qualities which the popular fancy demanded in a hero of romance. He was young and handsome, and although inclined to stoutness he moved with an assured grace. Very distant indeed were those days when his Royal Highness, gasping and sobbing, would be laced into his stays; when he would disgust his friends by his drinking and his bestiality.

> A noble nasty course he ran,
> Superbly filthy and fastidious.
> He was the world's First Gentleman,
> And made the appellation hideous.

Barely of age, the Prince rode well; he sang a sentimental ballad charmingly; he was an excellent shot and a pleasing talker. On a dance floor, under the lusters of the great chandeliers, his well-turned leg was exhibited nightly to great advantage. He reacted vigorously against the strictures of his early training, and although at the close of his life he had become vulgar and besotted he was never stupid, and was given at times to rare flashes of insight into the characters of his friends. But he had an itch for notoriety, a desire to " cut a figure," which proved his undoing as a man

HESTER JANE OGLE
Sheridan's second wife

and as a king. A poseur until the end, the Prince was incapable alike of " awkwardness and of speaking the truth."

His friendship with Fox brought him into very close contact with the Whig Party. They saw in the Prince a standard around which to rally. For the Prince, Fox and his Whigs were simply a collective tool for obtaining his own way. In the beginning the Whigs were to help settle the unpleasant business connected with his debts. Later, as the King grew worse and all Pitt's clever maneuvering could no longer put aside the question of a Regency, the Whigs were to get for him the outward panoplies of majesty. For like his father, whom he so little resembled, George Frederick, Prince of Wales, wanted desperately to rule his country.

We come now to a part of English history that is dark and brutal. It has all the fantastic and glittering unreality of one of those " Gothic " novels in which the eighteenth century took such peculiar delight. It is the story of Warren Hastings — " India's ablest proconsul " — of his exploits, his crimes, and his interminable trial, and of how Richard Brinsley Sheridan spoke at that trial and stepped forever into the pages of history.

In May, 1773, Charles James Fox had called upon the House to investigate Lord Clive's affairs in India, and had denounced the hero of Plassey as " the origin of all plunder, and the source of all robbery." Lord North, then Prime Minister, had found the whole affair tedious in the extreme, and had slept throughout the ensuing debate. It was unnaturally hot in those first days of May, and the younger members kept clamoring for a division. Clive was exonerated, but the affair had permanently tarnished his reputation; the following year he committed suicide. The discussion of his career in India and the commotion attendant upon the death of one who had served his country so signally accomplished one fact. It brought the question of India into compellingly close range, and kept it there for the next twenty years.

Eight years after Clive's death, in 1782, Philip Francis returned from India. He was Hastings' enemy, and he told incredible stories. Hastings must be recalled and his affairs subjected to public scrutiny. Unquestionably an investigation which had revealed nothing in the case of Clive would now prove how culpable the East India Company had become. Yet so firmly entrenched was the Company and so far-reaching was its influence that its investigators knew they must tread very cautiously indeed, lest they bruise some very important toes.[1]

The King advised circumspection. " The situation of the East India Company will require the utmost exertion of your wisdom to maintain and improve the valuable advantages derived from our Indian possessions, and to promote and secure the happiness of the native inhabitants of these provinces."

[1] It administered a revenue of more than seven million pounds sterling, commanded an army of some six thousand men and disposed of the lives and fortunes of thirty million people.

The number of Hastings' enemies grew every day. Burke regarded him as the very incarnation of the Fiend. Fox, the " People's Friend," referred to him as " the great Mr. Hastings, a man who, by disobeying the orders of his employers, had made himself so great as to be now able to mix in every question of state, and make every measure of government a personal point in which he had a share." Both Burke and Fox, the academician and the demagogue, were united in their hatred of the Indian system. It was patronage in its worst form; it was gross abuse of prerogative; it was a ruthless triumphing of force over justice.

For a month Fox held forth on Indian affairs. He spoke fervently and sincerely, and his sentiments rang like thunder. " Necessity is said to be the plea of tyranny. It is also the plea of freedom! . . . What is the end of all government? Certainly the happiness of the governed. . . . It is no violation of the right to abolish the authority that is abused!" He then brought in a bill which he hoped would permanently wreck the power of the East India Company. In this he had the unqualified support of Burke; yet seven years later Burke would be vehement in his opposition to Fox.

Sheridan, too, grew every day more enraged over the tales of an India ravished and despoiled. He trembled over the fate of Fox's bill, hoping to see his friend victorious. But the Lords defeated the bill by nineteen votes. And on the 22nd of December William Pitt, aged twenty-four, became England's Prime

Minister.[2] The King, not Fox, had scored the victory.

Said *The Rolliad:*

> Above the rest, majestically great,
> Behold the Infant Atlas of the State,
> The matchless miracle of modern days,
> In whom Britannia to the world displays
> A sight to make surrounding nations stare —
> A Kingdom trusted to a Schoolboy's care.

More and more Sheridan was associating himself with the fortunes of the Whig cause. " If Mr. Pitt succeeds," wrote the Duchess of Devonshire, whose sympathies too were with Fox and his " Fox-hounds," " he will have brought about an event which he himself, as well as every Englishman, will repent ever after — for if he and the King conquer the House of Commons he will destroy the consequence of that House and make the Government quite absolute." [3] But the Duchess and her friends alarmed themselves unduly. Pitt's India Bill, far less sweeping in effect than Fox's, nevertheless suffered a similar fate. The Lords rejected it on January 23rd. The affairs of India were precisely where they had been before, in the hands of the Company, and where its directors piously hoped they would continue to remain.

The contest between Pitt and Fox had not, however, been settled with the extinction of their bills. There was a new election, and Pitt had resolved that at all

---

[2] An office to which his father had attained twenty-six years earlier.
[3] Written to Lady Spencer, her mother, February 8, 1784.

costs the Whig leader must not be returned. He heard with great displeasure and not a little trepidation the stories concerning Fox's campaign. How Georgianna, Duchess of Devonshire, and her sister, Lady Harriet Duncannon, obtained votes for their candidate by selling kisses to the avid electors.[4] How there were processions and free drinks for all — a veritable Saturnalia in Westminster. How, horror of horrors, the Prince himself had in his friend's behalf descended among the rabble wearing Fox's brush and his laurel cockade. Instantly the Tories looked about for a siren of their own; the Party secured the services of Lady Salisbury, as beautiful and as high-born as the Duchess herself. But Georgianna loved the common people more. Her Ladyship found it extremely unpleasant to kiss every tailor's apprentice who presented himself. When the votes were counted, Fox had gained Westminster.

Fox's friends signalized his victory by a series of magnificent balls and parties. At one of these, given by the lovely " Amoret," His Royal Highness himself appeared — wearing Fox's colors, blue and buff. Fox's triumph was complete. But Pitt was still unwilling to own that he had been defeated. For several months he was able to prevent the member from Westminster from taking his seat, while he " investigated " the conduct of the election.

In hour-glasses all over the Kingdom the year 1784

---

[4] " The most beautiful portraits that ever appeared on a canvass," some contemporary wit remarked of them.

was slipping inexorably by. The affairs of India were no nearer settlement. The Company still maintained its undisputed sway; sent out its troops, and collected its revenues. Three years were yet to pass before Warren Hastings would be tried and the system revealed in all its infamy.

CHAPTER TEN

The Prince's Man

ELIZABETH SHERIDAN had been married eleven years. Her son Thomas, the boy who had been named for both his grandfathers, was ten years old. He was a bright and winning child; his teachers at fashionable Salt Hill found him an apt and engaging pupil. Elizabeth was still very much in love with her husband, whose Parliamentary career she followed with the combined feelings of pride, admiration and respect — altogether proper in so devoted a wife. Drury Lane continued to occupy her attentions, for in proportion as Richard's importance to the Whigs increased and he became a man of affairs, his interest in his theater waned. There was his father to assist her, of course, but somehow the execution of his ideas invariably fell short of their conception. He was more of a nuisance than an aid. He had grandiose ideas of his importance as a teacher and a director. The actors were constantly offending him for one reason or another, and he had never been satisfied with the salary Richard paid him. Elizabeth made peace between the company and her father-in-law — and the very next day it was all to do over again. Richard barely glanced at the plays she showed him, and every month her account-books grew more hopelessly muddled. She was busy, but Elizabeth recognized it as a treadmill existence. Whenever she paused to think its empty futility terrified her.

She was beset by terrors. Nameless, amorphous, they were nevertheless her constant companions. She feared for Richard and for herself. Of late the complex web about them was making her fearful of their life together.

Soon after their marriage the Sheridans had been accepted in the great houses of London. They danced at Carlton House, where His Royal Highness lived apart from his parents; they were guests of the Duke and Duchess of Devonshire, or of the Duke of Portland at Burlington House. Richard reveled in all the glitter and gaiety. The food was superlative. The jewels of the ladies glowed in the candlelight like stars; there was music and wine, and everyone seemed to appreciate the keenness of his wit. Elizabeth too received her share of attention. She had grown lovelier since her marriage. There was a compelling quality in her beauty which singled her out in a roomful of London's belles. Sometimes she sang the melodies of Dr. Arne or Mr. Handel, and the shock of the applause following on her last crystalline note revived for her the old days when she had been the Maid of Bath. At first she had been pleased and flattered by this easy intimacy with the great. It frightened her now because she saw its effect upon Richard.

Women pursued him. Mrs. Crewe, Her Grace of Devonshire, and her dark-eyed sister Lady Harriet Duncannon.[1] Scores of others whose very names spelled beauty hung upon his arm, demanded his presence beside them at dinner, flattered him, openly courted him. Elizabeth knew that any one of these women would gladly have consented to become her husband's mistress. What she did not know — and that ignorance was exquisite torture — was whether he still was faithful to her; and if he was, for how long.

For the beau monde had decreed that love was a fashionable game. As in the figures of a minuet, husbands and wives passed from one casual partner to another. Marriage was no longer a sacrament but a pleasantly maintained fiction, and as for fidelity . . . Egad, laughed the Great World, 'twas as out of fashion as Queen Elizabeth's stomacher! One must observe certain rules. There were niceties of behavior in the conduct of an amour, which must be followed, lest what was delightful and tantalizing gossip degenerate into a vulgar scandal, and the world be told what it merely suspected. All around her Elizabeth saw the game in progress. What frightened her was that she no longer found it shocking. Sooner or later, she knew, she must find herself playing at it too. . . .

There were Richard's debts to frighten her. The exact amount for which his creditors clamored she never knew, but it must be a staggering sum, for they spent

[1] Afterward the wife of Lord Bessborough.

money in such a never-dwindling stream. They had a house in Bruton Street, a flock of liveried servants, and there was Tom's school, to which the children of the great were sent. Richard, now a member of Brooks', found himself drawn to the tables. Even Elizabeth played whist and deplored her losses. " It is the abominable whist they make us play — twenty-one guineas last night and fifteen the night before." [2] They had bought another carriage and pair, for they were visiting at country houses now, and sometimes received separate invitations to Crewe Hall, Chatsworth — the Duke of Devonshire's estate — or Mr. Edward Bouverie's Delapré Abbey.

There was one scant consolation. As long as Richard remained a member of Parliament he could not be jailed for his debts, since to members was granted a special immunity to arrest on these grounds. But what if he should lose the next election . . .? Elizabeth, tossing sleepless on her bed, was certain she heard the bailiff's officer already beating upon her door.

There was trouble brewing with Ireland. Pitt had brought in a bill which aimed directly at a repression of Irish trade, since it demanded that Ireland yield to England all authority in matters of navigation and commerce. Although Wedgwood and other merchants protested loudly, Pitt and his colleagues continued to work for the bill's passage.

---

[2] Written to her husband from Crewe Hall in 1786.

The measure angered Sheridan. He raised his voice to swell the chorus of protesting voices through which Pitt moved with such bland unconcern. "There is not a single argument which can be used as an inducement to Great Britain to attempt to resume this power which does not equally apply as a motive to Ireland not to part with it; with this difference only, that fact and experience will justify the result of the one, but have afforded no pretense for the requisition from the other." [3] Shall Ireland's commerce be halted entirely? Pitt's acidulous smile seemed an affirmation. Yet Sheridan heard from his friend Stratford Canning how unbridled had been the enthusiasm of the Dublin Parliament over his speech.

The next subject to engage the orator's attention was the question of general taxation. The Whigs opposed violently Pitt's ideas on national finance, although their reasons for that opposition were no stronger than Pitt's reasons for supporting his views. National finance was in a very muddled state at the close of the eighteenth century. Economics, "that dismal science," had hardly been born. Since gentlemen were not supposed to know anything about making money, and since the most arrant dolt learned in his cradle how to run through a fortune, questions of the national debt, of a stable currency and a regulated tariff seldom arose in the House.

Of Pitt, George Ellis wrote in *The Rolliad:* [4]

[3] May 30, 1785.
[4] Circa 1785.

Pert without fire, without experience sage,
Young with more art than Shelburne gleaned from age;
Too proud from pilfered greatness to descend,
Too humble not to call Dundas his friend.
In solemn dignity and sullen state
This new Octavius rises to debate!
Mild and more mild he sees each placid row
Of Country Gentlemen with rapture glow.
He sees convulsed with sympathetic throbs
Apprentice Peers and Deputy Nabobs.
Nor Rum-Contractors think his speech too long,
While words like treacle trickle from his tongue! [5]

There were more balls than usual at Carlton House, for His Royal Highness' roving attentions were for the moment engaged, and the fortunate lady must be fêted. Her name was Maria Smythe Fitzherbert, and at twenty-nine she had been twice widowed. She possessed an income of two thousand pounds a year and a character so spotless that even Sheridan's *Mrs. Candour* could not have found a flaw. She lived alone in the almost rustic seclusion of Richmond Hill. There " Prinny " came to court her. He was three-and-twenty now, a shade heavier about the jowls and with a slightly thickened waistline. He found a lady beautiful and tempting enough to seduce an anchorite, yet endowed with principles more inflexible than granite. For Mrs. Fitzherbert would not join the procession of the Prince's mistresses. She was sensible of the honor His Royal Highness did her. She was very de-

---

[5] Because it was the work of many authors the *Rolliad* exhibits such a charming diversity of styles.

voted to His Royal Highness. But she was a devout
Catholic. Mrs. Fitzherbert, having been married
twice, enjoyed the connubial state. She would, she
told her gaping suitor, become his wife. And there
for a time the matter rested.

Thwarted, the Prince mooned like a schoolboy in
his first affair. The lady herself had left England for
a few months, but couriers from His Royal Highness
pursued her half across Europe, bringing her verses
and trinkets and the undying protestations of her
swain. Back in London the ballad-mongers set the
tale in rhyme and everywhere people sang with them
The Lass of Richmond Hill.

> I would crowns resign to call her mine,
> Sweet Lass of Richmond Hill.

But the Act of Settlement stated emphatically that
no one might inherit the crown if married to a Papist.
And equally emphatic was the Royal Marriages Act,
which declared null and void the union of a Prince
under twenty-five contracted without his father's consent. The Prince was distracted; he turned to Fox
for counsel. It has been said that Fox was anxious to
see Mrs. Fitzherbert married to the Prince, since he
realized what an asset the latter was to the Whig cause
and he knew that Mrs. Fitzherbert was necessary to
his continued good spirits. But a letter which Fox
wrote the Prince shortly after the lady's return to
England in 1785 seems to contradict such an assumption. "A mock marriage (for it can be no other) is

neither honourable for either of the parties, nor, with respect to Your Royal Highness, even safe." The Prince hastened to reassure his dear Charles. " Make yourself easy, my dear friend; believe me the world will now soon be convinced that there not only is but never was any ground for those reports which of late have been so explicitly circulated."

Ten days later, at six o'clock in the evening of December 15, 1785, a minister of the Church of England joined in marriage Maria Smythe Fitzherbert and the young man who would one day be George IV of England.

The blissful pair kept their union a secret. Even the Prince's closest friends knew nothing — a circumstance which was later to create unpleasantness for His Royal Highness and bring opprobrium down upon the lady's lovely head.

And so the chandeliers at Carlton House were lit each night and the dancers moved in pretty precision across the long gleaming floors. George and his radiant Maria sat together at the head of the banquet-tables; they applauded the musicians and pledged each other from the same wine-glass. Everyone gossiped about Mrs. Fitzherbert and the Prince, but the " delicacy " of the situation was most acute and no one dared shatter by a single word the fragile structure of the illusion.

No one dared, that is, until the question of the Prince's debts came up again in Parliament. His country had paid them once; there was some talk now as to why it should be asked a second time to assume His Highness' obligations. The Whigs had promised the royal heir payment. The Tories, on the other hand, saw no reason at all why the Prince should have incurred so vast an indebtedness — or why they should be required to settle it for him. At last some more daring soul ventured to inquire into the precise nature of His Highness' debts. Old Squire Rolle arose, determined on the performance of his duty. The word " marriage " was not mentioned, yet its silent specter was there to terrify the members. For it was only five years after Gordon's riots, and " No Popery! " was still a cry to rally the countryside.

Sheridan hurried to Mrs. Fitzherbert. The honor of his beloved Prince had been impugned; surely the lady herself would refute the base charges? But Mrs. Fitzherbert simply wept and wrung her hands. She threw herself upon the mercy of the gentlemen who had taken away her character. " They know I'm like a dog with a log tied around its neck! " she sobbed. " They must protect me! "

In the House of Commons, meanwhile, Fox was protesting to His Majesty and to His Majesty's ministers the " utter falsehood of the fact in question." He had advised the Prince against marriage. How was he to suspect that his advice had been rejected? Fox denied the calumny " *in toto* — in point of fact as well as of law." And he added that his words were directly authorized by the Prince.

Throughout all the hubbub in the House " Prinny "

maintained what the newspapers of another age would call " a discreet silence." All over London he heard Mrs. Fitzherbert's name mentioned in terms which left nothing to the imagination; in every ginshop one could buy a penny ballad on the Prince's marriage. Even the foreign press took up the story. The Prince neither affirmed his union to his friends nor denied it to his enemies. Maria waited for him to vindicate her in the scornful eyes of the nation. Fox waited for him to substantiate his ardent denunciation of his calumniators. And " Prinny " waited for the whole affair to blow over.

Fox had advised against marriage. Fox had defended him, confident that the thing was a lie. What more natural than to shove the blame for this awkward situation on Fox? Soon the Prince was wiping Maria's streaming eyes. " Only think, my love! Fox said we were not married! "

But Maria did not smile. She was beginning to understand, and the knowledge was far from pleasant. She refused to see the Prince unless he cleared her name, and that meant the dismissal of Fox, who had denied her marriage.

In his fashion Florizel loved Maria. He needed Fox, the only one among that political crew who cared a pennyworth for him and his prospects. Amity between the two must be restored — but how? At last came the brilliant idea. Through Sheridan, who was the Prince's man — and also Fox's. Sheridan must effect the peace.

This he did in an ingenious manner. Sheridan addressed the House in defense of the maligned Maria, " a lady to whom it was supposed the late Parliamentary allusions had been pointed, affirming that ignorance and vulgar folly alone could have persevered in attempting to detract from a character upon which truth could fix no just reproach, and which was in reality entitled to the truest and most general respect." A wise young man! Thus able at once to satisfy the lady by praising her as a wife and at the same time not to offend Mr. Fox by impugning his veracity.

The whole affair dies away on a note of music. Mrs. Fitzherbert, dressed in white and wearing the Prince's white roses, presides with her accustomed vivacity and grace at Lady Gideon's banquet. She dances with Fox and Sheridan and smiles sweetly on them both. Society has accepted her again and she is happy.[6]

Her happiness lasted ten years. But in 1795 His Royal Highness was prevailed upon by the King's ministers to contract a marriage of state, and he wedded Caroline of Brunswick. For a single year the unhappy couple kept up the pretense of a marriage; then they separated and the Prince returned to Maria's waiting arms. Which was after all both fitting and proper, for had not the Roman Catholic Church bidden her regard herself as his wife? And with her he remained until 1803, when Lady Hertford became her successor.

[6] About this time Gainsborough painted the Prince and Mrs. Fitzherbert embarking in a skiff accompanied by Elizabeth Sheridan and that angel of peace, her husband.

After he had become King, George denied to Mr. Croker the " absurd story of my supposed marriage." He was still an unblushing and unmitigated liar. But Maria Fitzherbert always recalled with a flutter of her heart how once she had been the bride of a Prince. When she was an old lady whose passionate youth belonged to a dead century she spoke to her confessor of her vanished glory. It was all gone — laughter and gaiety and friendship. Life was noisy now and very strange. Hardly anyone remembered when she had been " Queen of Hanover " — she who could never be Queen of England. And Mrs. Fitzherbert sighed, bowed her gray head over her folded hands, and finished her prayers.

CHAPTER ELEVEN

The Trial of Warren Hastings

NOW comes the trial of Warren Hastings, and with it Richard Sheridan's perfect moment as a public figure. For several years thunderous rumors of Hastings and an East Indian scandal have been crashing across England; momently, it has seemed, the storm must break. Yet the instant has always passed and the skies have blown clear again.

The syllables of Warren Hastings' name were on everybody's tongue. Vaguely people knew that he had been accused of dark and dreadful malefactions. What they were no one was certain. Whether or not Hastings was guilty depended on where you stood politically — whether you were Pitt's man or Fox's. But wasn't there any more to know about Hastings? Could anything at all be said in his favor? " H'm," said the average Englishman. " Let me see."

Himself a victim of the ruthless and aggressive East India system, Warren Hastings was about to be sacrificed to it, as Sheridan was later to be sacrificed to the Whig cause for which he had labored so long. Hastings was a leader, an executive, a military strate-

gist and a statesman.[1] He had reorganized completely
the chaotic native governments in the several Indian
states under his control; he had established their public credit. At the time when Burgoyne's surrender at
Saratoga was darkening the prestige of English arms,
Hastings had organized the epic march from Juma to
Surat; seven thousand native soldiers across eight
hundred miles of hostile country. He was the rescuer
of Madras and Bombay; the man who had prevented
France from regaining her old foothold in India; the
general who had successfully routed those native leaders who objected to the growing domination of the
British. All around him men gorged themselves on
plunder, yet Hastings returned to England a com-
paratively poor man — particularly when he was
judged by the standards of the " Nabobs." But Hastings had enemies at home who clamored for his impeachment. In 1782 Philip Francis had reported the
scandals connected with the despoiling of the two
Begums of Oude. They were accused of arming for
an insurrection. They were robbed, their servants
beaten and tortured; the two Princesses themselves
were exposed to cold and hunger and the rude treatment of the English soldiers. Hastings had acted in
the name of English justice? Let him now, in the
name of English justice, face a jury of his peers.

[1] Warren Hastings was a man for whom Nature had done much of
what the Stoic philosophy pretended. *Mens æqua in arduis* is the inscription under his picture in Government House in Calcutta, and never was there
a more appropriate motto."
— *Thomas Babington Macaulay to Macvey Napier,*
January 11, 1841

The story of the Begums of Oude deserves retelling for it is on a small stage the story of the East India Company in action. It is a story of chicanery and corruption which did not trouble to conceal themselves, of unjustifiable sadistic cruelty; it is also the story of two women of great rank set upon by enemies and utterly without defenses.

Oude was a wealthy and prosperous native state. By the terms of a treaty concluded in 1775 between the East India Company and the Nawab, the latter agreed to support a brigade of the Company's troops at a certain specified allowance. The Nawab was the son of the Bow Begum and the grandson of the Munny Begum. Two years later the Company had increased the allowance required. Unable to meet his obligations, the Nawab obtained from his mother access to his dead father's treasure. If he paid this year's sum would the Company promise not to raise the amount another time? The Company's Resident solemnly agreed; in 1778 came a demand for a greater " allowance." The Nawab's mother decided to take her problems to Mecca and set out with her retinue, but Warren Hastings ordered the Resident to " protect " the Princess, and the pilgrimage was summarily halted.

Matters remained unchanged for three years. The Nawab of Oude paid his tribute to the Company, and the Resident received it. Then, in 1781, Rajah Cheyt Singh of Benares rebelled. It was said that he was aided by Oude. Whether or not that is true, the Governor promptly disposed of the rebellion. Then

Warren Hastings made a second treaty with the Nawab, the terms of which were absolutely without mercy.

He quartered upon the hapless Princeling the body-guard of Middleton, the Resident. He revived the obsolete custom of *Jagirs*, or feudal estates, with the condition that the holders of these estates who had been guaranteed by the Company must be indemnified from the Nawab's exchequer. Although the Company's name was not mentioned in these documents, actually it was to receive one hundred thousand pounds. The Nawab's mother and grandmother lost not only their treasure but their lands as well.

The two unfortunate Princesses retired to their palace at Fyzabad where, it was rumored, they still possessed uncounted treasures. In January of 1782 the Nawab accompanied by Middleton attempted to break into the palace. The zenana where his mother and grandmother lived was guarded by two ancients who had been from childhood in their service. Middleton ordered them seized; they were starved and tortured until the Prince agreed to ransom them. The two Begums themselves fared not much better. At last, after days of insufficient food, of cold and wretchedness, they consented to pay Middleton an additional sum because of their alleged connection with Cheyt Singh's rebellion.

From the outset the Company had been the prime mover in the unsavory affair, fomenting trouble, punishing the innocent with the guilty. The Company

[168]

therefore, in the person of Warren Hastings, was now summoned to trial.

Prompted by the vengeful Francis, Edmund Burke acted to move charges against Hastings. Even Pitt, who at first had declared himself unequivocally for the Governor, now appeared to be wavering in his allegiance. Days, weeks, passed. The calendar stood at February 7, 1787. The House was in Committee with Mr. St. John presiding. It was just on midnight when Richard Brinsley Sheridan arose to speak; morning had come and London was awake once more before he concluded and sank exhausted to his chair. He had spoken without interruption for six hours. "When it was over," said Fox, " all that I had ever heard — all that I had ever read — when compared with it, dwindled into nothing and vanished like vapour before the sun."

Sheridan was thirty-six when he made his historical oration. His eyes were growing dull, his face heavy. He had been in Parliament seven years. Once, briefly, he had filled a Cabinet position — yet he was beginning to feel success eluding him. His creditors were pressing. Only until the next election could he consider himself safe from a debtors' prison. His social position was vague. The whole unstable structure might one day collapse about his ears; then he would find himself poor, friendless — and, worst of all, unpopular. It is not illogical to regard Sheridan's Begum oration as a deliberate bid for fame. His sure dramatic instinct had sensed at once the magnificent opportunity which the plight of the two Princesses afforded the orator who was at the same time an actor.

Burke considered Sheridan's oration as "the most astonishing effort of eloquence, argument, and wit united of which there is any record or tradition." It was, in fact, Richard Sheridan's supreme effort. He never attained to its splendid heights again.

Of the violation of the zenana he said: "Still he (Hastings) recurs to Mohammedanism for an excuse — as if there was something in the institution of Mohammed that made it meritorious in a Christian to be a savage; that rendered it criminal to treat the inhabitants of India with humanity or mercy; that even made it impious in a son *not* to plunder his mother. . . . What has become of that awful sanction which has proved the consolation of so many nations and the glory of our own?"

Of the activities of the prisoner during 1781: "Mr. Hastings at that time . . . said that he had only two resources — Benares and Oude. What was he to derive from these resources? Not the collection of a just revenue, not the voluntary contributions of a people attached to the Company from sincere motives of esteem and gratitude, but the exaction and extortion of pretended debts, and the plunder of the innocent. It was exactly like the malversation of a highwayman, who, in justification of his crimes, should say that he had only two resources — Bagshot or Hounslow!"

Of the treaty between the Nawab and the Company:
" Is there anything in Machiavel, any treachery upon
record, any perfidy among nations or individuals, any
cold Italian fraud you have ever known . . . com-
parable in any degree to a management thus black and
perfidious? "

When he spoke of the man Hastings his antitheses
and climaxes gleamed and scintillated. " His course
is one invariable deviation from rectitude. . . . He is
all shuffling, twisting, cold and little. . . . There is
nothing in him open and upright, simple or unmixed. . . . His crimes are the only great things
about him, and these are contrasted by the littleness
of his motives. . . . He affects to be a conqueror and
a law-giver, an Alexander and a Cæsar, but he is a
Dionysios and a Scapin. . . . He reasons in bombast,
prevaricates in metaphor, and quibbles in heroics."

For the East India Company and the system which
had produced both Warren Hastings and his crimes
Sheridan had only the most uncompromising criticism. The word " imperialism " had not yet been
coined, but England's empire-building policies were
already in practice, and Sheridan was fully cognizant
of all their potential evils. " It was in this manner
that nations have been extirpated for a sum of money,
whole tracts of country laid waste by fire and sword
to furnish investments; revolutions occasioned by an
affidavit; an army employed in executing an arrest;
towns besieged on a note of hand; a prince expelled
for the balance of an account; generals made auction-

[171]

eers; a truncheon contrasted with the implements of a counting-house; and the British Government exhibited in every part of Hindostan holding a bloody sceptre in one hand, and picking pockets with the other!"

Feelingly he dropped his voice when he mentioned the two women, "whose treasure was their treason. . . . Let the Committee picture to themselves any of the British Royal Family thus surrounded, assailed and forced to surrender their property and their servants, their bosom friends, at the point of a bayonet. To us at least who live in a land where every man's house is his sanctuary, where the arm of power dares not intrude, where the Constitution has erected an insuperable barrier to every encroachment or outrage, such an instance of violence cannot but appear monstrous and atrocious beyond all example or idea.

"Let the Commons of Great Britain," he demanded in his peroration, "set an example to the nations of stretching the strong arm of justice across the habitable globe in protection of injured innocence. . . . The omnipotence of a British Parliament will be demonstrated by extending protection to the helpless . . . and I move that the Committee, on hearing the evidence . . . are of the opinion . . . to impeach Warren Hastings, Esquire, of high crimes and misdemeanors."

The impeachment was decided upon and a committee was appointed, consisting of Burke, Sheridan, Fox, Grey, Windham and Sheridan's friend, Michael

Angelo Taylor. The proceedings lasted seven years
— at the rate of some twenty days a year. Hastings
was an embittered and broken man when the farce
finally ended and the House of Lords in 1795 found
him " not guilty." He was bankrupt. He besought
Pitt to reimburse him for the trial from the public
funds, but his plea was denied. At length, when he
was actually destitute, the Company he had served
so unselfishly granted him an annuity of four thousand
pounds for a term of years, with a large sum paid out
to him in advance. The annuity expired before Hastings' death in 1818. Once again he threw himself on
the Company's mercy, and once again he was not
refused.

Many years later the two men, accuser and accused,
found themselves face to face at Brighton, where they
were attending one of His Royal Highness' lavish parties. Sheridan shook Warren Hastings' hand and
begged the former Governor-General of India to believe that political necessity and that alone had " over-
charged the atmosphere and caused his fulminations."
Mr. Hastings, with that same ironic smile with which
he had faced his jurors, thanked the younger man; it
would be a great consolation to him, he admitted, if
Mr. Sheridan would publish that statement. But
Sheridan merely muttered something unintelligible
and hurried away.

Naturally the question of Sheridan's sincerity must
arise here. For sincere he undoubtedly was. But
when? When he clamored so vehemently for Has-

tings' blood — or when he attempted to cajole himself into a tired old man's favor? Had he been merely the blind tool of his Party, or had he honestly believed in Hastings' guilt [2] and changed his opinion with the passing years? Or is there the possibility that on both occasions he meant what he said? From what we know of Sheridan's temperament, of his fierce desire to excel in whatever rôle he attempted, the last assumption is not in the least unlikely.

The trial of Warren Hastings was held in Westminster Abbey. It was a brilliant social occasion, for everyone from the Great World attended, including the Prince and his guest, the Duke of Orleans. A ticket to the trial cost fifty guineas. Truly magnificent must have been the pageant of velvets and jewels and embroidered silks — the marshals, the heralds in gold and ermine, the hallowed walls hung with banners. And to this vivid tapestry the prisoner himself contributed no insignificant part. For Hastings appeared dressed in the finest of laces and silks, and as he knelt at the bar and solemnly invoked the protection of heaven against these his persecutors, the splendid diamond-studded sword he wore winked back at the spectators with a cold and malevolent brilliance.

One of the principal attractions at the trial was unquestionably Sheridan, whose Begum Oration before the Committee had made him once again the most talked-of man in England, as in the days of *The School*

[2] Cf. *Creevey Papers*, Vol. I, p. 59.

for Scandal's production. All his friends came to
hear him, and everyone these days was Sheridan's
friend. Mrs. Siddons attended, and so moved was she
by his dynamics that she fainted in her seat. Gainsborough came, and in the cavernous corridors of the
Abbey he caught the cold which was to prove fatal.
Elizabeth Sheridan, pale with joy, listened to her husband and to the people who cheered and applauded
him. And still his voice went on — ringing and clear
as when he had begun. " Even party prejudice has
been overcome by such a display of genius, of eloquence and goodness," she wrote to her sister-in-law.
" What must my feelings be you can only imagine."

The six-hour oration he had made before the Committee paled into nothingness; at the trial of Warren
Hastings Sheridan spoke on the two Begums of Oude
for four days! During one of these days he became
ill — probably from nervous exhaustion — but he was
able on the morrow to continue and to bring his arguments to the thundering crescendo which concluded
them.

Probably because all England was his audience now
Sheridan's second Begum Oration was more spectacu-
lar — and far less sincere — than the first. He wanted
the applause, the acclaim of the crowd. The best way
to secure it was to shower them with epigrams and to
dazzle them with wit. Underneath the glitter his
speech abounds in loose argument and showy rhetoric.
His hyberboles are ostentatious; he appeals frequently
to the emotions of his hearers and not to their intellect.

[175]

Yet on the whole his presentation is masterly. He tells a story grippingly, and when one strips aside the tinsel the soundness and logic of his thinking is often amazing.

He called the Elder Begum " a capricious woman that had a strange objection to being starved. They wanted to take away all her treasures . . . and her dislike to this . . . is called an act of feminine displeasure and caprice."

Then he turned to Hastings and declared him a " Commercial Caligula," but the former Governor-General listened with a thin slice of ironic smile.

Everyone knew that the Company and its representatives accepted " presents " of money, yet, said Sheridan, " It was thought the greatest infamy as well as the greatest danger in anyone native of India ever to reproach the English with having received money! "

" My Lords, I have closed the evidence! " The speaker's voice routed every echo sleeping in the Abbey's vaulted darkness. Everybody sat forward, faces still, nerves tense; the agony until the next words came was excruciating. Only the prisoner appeared composed. He smiled that smile which was at once ironic and insolently provoking, and idly fingered his diamond-studded sword. " I have no further comments. . . . I conjure your Lordships, for your own honour, for the honour of the nations, for the honour of human nature now entrusted to your care; that I, for the Commons of England speaking through us, claim this duty at your hands. They exhort you to it by everything that calls sublimely upon the heart of men, by the majesty of justice which this bold man had libeled, by the wide fame of your own renowned tribunal, by the sacred pledge which you swear in the solemn hour of decision, knowing that that decision will bring you the greatest reward that ever blessed the heart of man — the consciousness of having done the greatest act of mercy for the world that the earth has ever yet received from any hand but Heaven's.

"My Lords, I have done!" He stepped back a little and faltered. The waiting arms of Edmund Burke caught him as he fell.

There was no compass to the fame of Richard Sheridan. England, the Continent, rang with his name. When Thomas Sheridan returned to England in July of 1788 he was informed that his son was the nation's first subject. It must have gladdened his heart to learn that he, who had spent half a lifetime teaching a people how to pronounce its mother tongue, had sired the English Demosthenes. Thomas Sheridan had struggled hard, until now he was a recognized authority on English speech. Eight years earlier he had published the two volumes of his *General Dictionary of the English Language*. When he died at Margate shortly after his son's triumph — August 14, 1788 — he left the manuscript of a life of Swift. Entertaining and witty, yet far from complete, it was published four years later to accompany a new edition of Swift's works.

[177]

In his own day and among his own contemporaries Richard Sheridan had the singular pleasure of watching himself become a legend. He heard his speeches acclaimed as the most flawless in English. Men who had listened to him during those four epic days never tired of telling about it; every inflection he had employed was known, every nuance recorded.

Almost thirty years later, when after his death his friends and admirers were preparing eulogies and editing laudatory verses, the glory of the Begum Orations had not paled. They were still historic utterances. Lord Byron mentioned them in his *Monody on the Death of the Rt. Hon. Richard Brinsley Sheridan:*

> When the loud cry of trampled Hindostan
> Arose to Heaven in her appeal from Man,
> His was the thunder — his the avenging rod,
> The wrath, the delegated voice of God!
> Which shook the nations through his lips, and blazed
> Till vanquished senates trembled as they praised.

CHAPTER TWELVE

The King is Mad

IT HAD never been unusual for the nation to gossip about the Royal Family. The Duke of Cumberland had long been providing conversation; as they grew older and emerged from their seclusion into the public gaze, the Prince of Wales and his brother proved their uncle the merest novice at scandalizing the righteous and affording merriment to the ungodly. But never had the faintest cloud blown across the name of His Majesty, George III. Since those far-off days of his youth when as Prince he had almost wedded the beautiful Lady Sarah Lennox, the King had led a life entirely above reproach. He was a loving and devoted father; even his relations with the Queen were tranquil. Yet suddenly, in the year of Warren Hastings' trial, rumors sprang up from nowhere. In a twinkling everyone knew that the King was mad.

People recalled that his wet-nurse had been a lunatic, and medical science had for years declared that madness could be carried in mothers' milk. His Majesty was also afflicted with the gout. When, during May, 1788, his legs swelled alarmingly and he was heard to speak of abdication, his physicians said that the gout had settled in his head, and pronounced the outlook grave indeed.

Summer came. His Majesty went to Cheltenham to take the waters. His behavior became daily more frightening. He was content to sit embroidering with the ladies of the Queen's household, and one morning he horrified his courtiers by attempting to race with a horse from the royal stables. When Benjamin West called, the King lectured him for hours on the art of mixing colors — the while His Majesty mixed them with his feet.

A crisis was imminent, although Lord Salisbury made light of the King's malady and said that His Majesty had as much sense now as he had ever had. When he was informed that the King had almost set Queen Charlotte on fire by pushing a lighted candle into her face, Fox interrupted his tour of Italy and hurried home. If the King were really mad then a Regency must be declared at once. Pitt and his followers would, Fox knew, exert every effort to prevent the Prince being named Regent. The Queen was their tool as the Prince was Fox's; they were determined to advance her on the political chessboard in opposition to her son.

The poor old man sat in his rooms at Windsor dictating to his bewildered secretaries from the Bible and *Don Quixote* at the same time. He had always loved music. Now through endless hours — for day and night were become as one to him — the sound of his harpsichord echoed eerily through the empty corridors. He played Bach and Handel and little snatches of hymns which he remembered from his childhood. He prayed for himself and for the nation which was helpless without him. Then he returned to the harpsichord, and while his fingers stumbled across the keys he wept because he was alone and very frightened. For the Queen had gone with his dear children, and the Prince was at Carlton House, carousing with his friends.

On November 24th Fox and Mrs. Armistead, his mistress, returned from Italy. In his absence Sheridan's intimacy with the Prince had grown; it was strengthened by Mrs. Fitzherbert's openly avowed friendship, for she had still not forgiven Fox. Every day saw Sheridan at Carlton House. He had access to all the royal apartments. He was privileged to witness Prince Florizel being put to bed in a drunken stupor; he was present when the heir awoke and called grumblingly for his stays. Sheridan was unswervingly the Prince's man. To His Royal Highness, who broke hearts and promises with equal impunity, Sheridan gave an unflinching and selfless devotion, which was surely worthy of a better cause.

Among the Whigs there was great rejoicing. At any moment a Regency might be proclaimed. Since no one had any money and everyone was plagued with debts, the gentlemen at Brooks' planned excitedly for the future. What sinecures awaited them! The re-

ceivership of a Duchy; a fat Cabinet post; a coveted
Colonial appointment. . . . Even cards were forgotten. A game was afoot more thrilling than quadrille
and possessed of infinitely more possibilities than
whist. The Party's leaders gathered nightly at Devonshire House. The Duke of Portland, the Duke of
Devonshire, and Sir John Townshend — they were re-
serving the Chancellorship of the Exchequer for him
— quarreled over a proper distribution of the spoils.
Sheridan listened in a delirium of anticipation and
excitement. He had been promised a Cabinet position
with the advent of the Regency! The hand which held
his wine-glass trembled and he shut his eyes because
the glory of the days ahead was too bright to bear.
And he had not long to wait; any day now he might
awake to find himself miraculously possessed of both
wealth and position. He waited, however, eighteen
years, until 1806, before he became Treasurer of the
Navy.

Three days after Fox's return the King was removed
to Kew. The trees which lined the long straight
avenues were bare. A cold persistent rain was falling,
and on the wet brown branches the rooks sat, disconso-
lately flapping their wings. It was quiet at Kew. The
stillness was more somber than at Windsor, but His
Majesty's baffled physicians had decided that quiet
would restore his outraged nerves. Despite the ex-
cellence of their medical advice he continued to rave.
He mangled two of his attendants, though when the
frenzy passed he was simply a docile old man who

hummed to himself off-key and wanted pathetically to be amused. He played cards with his pages, and once he donned his new tie-wig and solemnly led his terrified apothecary through the figures of a minuet.

The rumors grew louder, and Pitt, who had tried so hard not to hear them, was forced at last to recognize the existence of the King's malady — if not its seriousness. Resignedly he called in the physicians. But the doctors themselves were unable to agree on the exact nature of the illness — depending on whether they were Whigs or Tories in addition to being doctors of medicine. Dr. Warren held one opinion, Dr. Addington another. He even consulted Dr. Willis, the clergyman-quack with the hypnotic eye. Pitt conferred with the men of science. Then he thanked them and politely dismissed them all. He had determined upon the course he would pursue.

Assuming that the King was mad, he was automatically rendered unfit to govern and his son must reign as Regent in his stead. But what, thought the Prime Minister, if His Majesty were not mad — merely ill? A Regent in that case was absolutely unnecessary. Furthermore, had the heir the *right* to the prerogatives of the throne during the disability of the ruler, or even to any of its privileges? Could such a right be enforced in the face of opposition by the Commons? Pitt was aware that certain jurists who had studied the British Constitution might decide that the Prince possessed a just claim upon his father's throne; they might even attempt to establish such a claim. The

Prime Minister wondered how wise it would be for the Prince or his supporters to try to coerce the Commons into appointing him Regent.

He appeared before the House and demanded a lengthy research into the historical precedents affecting the case. The result, said Sheridan, was " a little bad Latin and worse French," but every day the Prime Minister gained by his delay brought him nearer the time when the Tory physicians must pronounce the King " as sane as he ever was."

Queen Charlotte loved her eldest son. At the same time she distrusted him thoroughly; while for his advisers she felt only loathing and contempt, — Fox and those other wastrels who had spoken so vehemently against the war with America. . . . Who knew, thought the Queen, what trickery they were planning? Their sympathies with America were so vociferous they might even hope to create a republic in England, with their tool the Prince as its nominal head! Pitt, too, she feared. He was so cold, so inscrutable; it was impossible to know what his thoughts were behind his deferential manner.

Almost as fervently as her son, Queen Charlotte desired a Regency. But there must be a place somewhere in it for her, otherwise she would oppose it with all the guile and cunning at her command. For Charlotte loved petty intrigues almost as much as she loved those petty economies which were the delight of every true German housewife. It thrilled her to be the center of plots, to know she was being spied upon and to feel herself growing stronger, becoming a formidable rival to her son and a worthy opponent to Pitt. Charlotte engaged spies of her own, and set herself to confound her enemies.

On December 1st the Prince and the Duke of York drove through the wintry sunshine to Windsor where they demanded of their mother the privy purse and her jewels. The Queen refused; she screamed until the Princes bowed and withdrew. But it was open war now between His Royal Highness and his mother. Three days later Parliament convened and the Prince let it be known that he was " anxious " for the immediate formation of a Regency. But Pitt was not yet prepared to surrender to Florizel. He conferred with Her Majesty and his words must have been very encouraging, for when he left Charlotte was happier than she had been for weeks.

It was almost the middle of December and still the momentous question had not been settled. Once again the Prime Minister stilled the enquiries in the House by demanding a further investigation into legal precedents. An angry roar from the Whigs greeted his words. Burke jumped to his feet and shouted hysterically that if matters continued Pitt might well be accused of trying to place himself in competition for the Regency. It was the enraged Tories' turn to roar; they stamped their feet and shouted while the Whigs loudly applauded Burke. Pitt very shrewdly sensed that he had almost overplayed his hand. Delay had served its purpose. A new means of warfare must be employed now. He moved that the House sit in Committee on " the State of the Nation."

At Brooks' they were still discounting the roseate days ahead. There would be new peers, new titles — hands all around. A few Whigs were somewhat fearful of the Prince's promise to elevate his friends to high rank. The creation of a new nobility might not be the best thing for England; and Sheridan advised his royal master to curb his generous hand and wait six months before he appointed the lords of the bedchamber.

Meanwhile at Kew the old King wept and shrank cowering back from the implacable Dr. Willis, who had walked into the royal apartments brandishing a strait-jacket. He had been worse lately. His loud and uncontrolled weeping frightened the little Princesses in their nursery. The faces around him were strange, unrecognizable; he sensed their hostility, and he sobbed and prayed louder than ever. The burden of those prayers was always the same. For himself, that he might with God's help speedily recover. For his family. For his poor friendless people.

It was almost as though his addled brain perceived what forces were moving against him. Pitt had offered a plan to the House in Committee. Since the King was unable to transact public affairs, Parliament must decide on a means to remedy this deficiency in the legislature. Dismissing entirely the Prince's right, Pitt asked that Parliament be granted the power of

placing the Great Seal on all legislative acts. Fox protested, challenging Pitt's motives. In a fiery outburst
Burke supported him and affirmed his love for the
Constitution. Now from the Whig stronghold in
Devonshire House came the *Letter to Mr. Pitt* by
Richard Brinsley Sheridan.[1] It was a plea for a more
trusting attitude on both sides. It termed Pitt's plan
a scheme "for producing weakness . . . in every
branch of the administration of affairs." He deprecated leaving "the national safety and the welfare of
the nation in the hands of the present ministers"; he
relied on the nation's generosity in "this melancholy
crisis." The letter lacks Sheridan's force and the
clarity and vigor which usually distinguish his thinking. It sets the author upon a middle-of-the-road
course which he had hitherto eschewed and which he
never later followed.

The debate grew more envenomed. The long-
drawn suspense of waiting had stretched everyone's
nerves to breaking. At last, when the entire nation
had joined the exasperated Prince in despairing of its
ever happening, the Regency Bill was passed. Sheridan's Cabinet position was actually within his grasp.
He dined with the delegates who had come over from
Ireland to attend the bill's passing, and through a
happy evening he drank to them and to his future.
But the elusive moment had vanished before Sheridan
had even touched its promise. The Prime Minister
had not overplayed his hand at all.

---

[1] The authorship of this letter has been disputed.

[187]

On February 24, 1789, His Majesty George III was pronounced perfectly well. London was illuminated in his honor. Church-bells rang jubilantly; there were processions and endless speeches, and everyone who had the price of a glass toasted the King and his miraculous recovery. A public Thanksgiving was celebrated in St. Paul's for the restored monarch, and George drove through lanes of cheering people to hear a vested choir sing the hymns which he had muttered so incessantly at Kew. But those days were past now, and he promised himself that never again would he think of them. God had been merciful. He had spared him to his happy subjects. The King wiped his eyes, and on his knees gave thanks with the rest of England.

For Sheridan the King's recovery marks the beginning of his downward march. Since he and the other Whigs had acted during the Regency crisis as though they were definitely anti-monarchists, the King turned the light of his countenance away from them. The sun of the royal favor shone now upon the Tories, and mightily they flourished beneath it. Sheridan continued to work for the Prince and to support his cause, but when the next Regency crisis came up His Royal Highness had forgotten, and his favors were bestowed elsewhere.

CHAPTER THIRTEEN

Time of Torture

FOR the moment, Sheridan was thoroughly disgusted with politics. He still controlled Drury Lane, though for several years he had not spared it even the most perfunctory interest. Now he returned to his theater with a renewed zest. Several months after George III had resumed his seat upon the throne Sheridan produced the very successful farce *The Doctor and the Apothecary,* with music by the fashionable composer Stephen Storace. But the will-o'-the-wisp of that Cabinet post to which he had so nearly attained still dazzled him. Every other pleasure was as tasteless as Dead Sea fruit, and long before the close of 1789 Sheridan was again making speeches in the House of Commons, — on the Newspaper Duty Act, the Tobacco Regulations Bill, and the Scots Boroughs Reform Bill.

Strange and terrible forces were at work during 1789. The world was struggling with the birth-pangs of events whose true significance is only now being fully realized. Incredible stories blew across the Channel from France. The Bastille, impregnable stronghold of the Divine Right, had fallen. Blood ran

in the streets of Paris; heads were dropping everywhere; before the implacable fury of the mob both the
Church and the Law were equally powerless.

In England a group of enthusiastic young men
hailed the crimson streak which was appearing across
the skies of France as the dawn of a new epoch.
" Now the Great Age returns again! " rhapsodized the
poets — among them Wordsworth, who lived long
enough to regret these excesses of his hot-blooded
youth. America had given the world the Rights of
Man. Now the torch had begun to blaze in France.
Who could say, the Liberals asked each other excitedly, where next the magic sparks might appear?
But the Tories only shuddered and shook their heads.
The conflagration kindled in France presaged the end
of the world . . . of their world, the world of all right-
thinking men. For surely neither justice nor decency
could long survive that greatest of all terrors, the
frenzy of a people grown mad.[1]

One of the strangest of all the many strange things
which took place in that unpredictable year was the
volte-face of Edmund Burke. The champion of
America did not lift his voice in ecstasy over the tide
of events in France. Instead he moved over to the
other side. Fourteen years earlier he had pleaded for

---

[1] Wrote Schiller, also an exponent of the *status quo:*

> *Gefährlich ist's, den Leü zu wecken,*
> *Verderblich ist des Tigers Zahn;*
> *Jedoch der schreckliste der Schrecken,*
> *Dass ist Der Mensch in seinem Wahn.*
>
> *Das Lied von der Glocke*

the Rights of Man; now he regarded them as "chimerical and visionary," and his fears increased for the threatened Rights of Kings. He had always honored order, justice and tradition. The American Revolution, he felt, was fought to preserve the ancient rights of Englishmen everywhere, but the turmoil in France could result only in the absolute annihilation of all that civilization had ever achieved. He warned the world that "philosophic dogmas might become as much a Cause for Fanaticism as a dogma in Religion." He began to distrust the men who had for years been his closest companions — Sheridan, Fox and Grey. They were "men of feeling," idealists, romanticists. Burke, grown of a sudden so practical, found himself completely out of step with them, and he broke with them one by one.

Burke and Fox had always been more opposite than alike, although for a time they had shared the same political views. Burke's speeches were coldly logical and perfect, without flaw or emotion; it had always been easier to read them than to hear them delivered. Fox was an orator; Burke a writer on politics. Burke's change was a shock to his friends. But Oliver Goldsmith had anticipated it all nearly twenty years before, when he wrote an "epitaph" for him and included it in his *Retaliation*:

> Here lies our good Edmund, whose genius was such
> We scarcely can praise it, or blame it too much;
> Who, born for the Universe, narrowed his mind,
> And to Party gave up what was meant for Mankind.

Sheridan's breach with Burke occurred over the former's speech on the Army Estimates and the French Revolution.[2] Burke listened with impatient contempt to the dramatist's Jacobin arguments. When he rose to reply he had forever allied himself with Pitt and the principles of Toryism. France, he declared, had been " expunged out of the system of Europe." The doctrine of the Rights of Man he termed an " institute and digest of anarchy." Blackguards and men entirely lacking in principle were in control in France. The spirits of atheism and treason were abroad; let England beware lest their dread influence contaminate her own peaceful shores. Sheridan regarded the French Revolution as a concerted mass movement toward freedom, worthy of being placed beside similar movements in England and in America. He objected to the indiscriminate use of unsavory epithets by which Burke sought to discredit the patriotic motives of the leaders.[3] " To traduce the National Assembly was to libel the whole French nation." Every one of his hearers was familiar with the innate bravery and generosity of the French people; " a people," his voice rang out sternly, " whose only vice had been their Government."

But Burke was not to be softened. They were as wide apart now as they had once been closely allied. What possible kinship could Sheridan have with the man who had said in a speech at Bristol: " It is now

[2] February 9, 1790.
[3] Particularly Lafayette and Bailly.

[192]

sixteen or seventeen years since I saw the Queen of France, then the Dauphiness, at Versailles; and surely never lighted on this orb, which she seemed hardly to touch, a more delightful vision. I saw her just above the horizon, decorating and cheering the elevated sphere she just began to move in — glittering like the morning star, full of life, and splendour, and joy. Oh, what a revolution! and what a heart must I have to contemplate without emotion that elevation and that fall! . . . I thought ten thousand swords must have leaped from their scabbards to avenge even a look that threatened her with insult. But the age of chivalry is gone. That of sophisters, of economists and calculators, has succeeded; and the glory of Europe is extinguished forever."

Three times their friends attempted reconciliations between them, and each failed dismally of fruition.

Sheridan continued to plead for the cause of the Revolution. But gradually his voice dwindled and at last was heard no more. For daily on the horizon the shadow of the Corsican loomed larger and more ominous; and in that shadow Sheridan was convinced that neither freedom nor justice could endure, and that the Rights of Man must become hollow and meaningless.

The signs of that dire malady which had carried off Mary Tickell were beginning to appear in her sister. Elizabeth failed to realize their significance; stubbornly she refused to be warned. Her days and nights were spent in the usual round of pleasures. She danced and played cards, she drank tea and gossiped. No question now of the Maid of Bath's place in the Great World. Over the tea-cups her name was spoken more and more frequently. Unfounded but none the less exciting rumors whispered that His Royal Highness had looked upon his friend's wife and found her alluring, and her husband complacent.

The year when the Bastille crashed marked the ruin of Sheridan's domestic felicity. He received one day an anonymous letter hinting at his wife's indiscretions, and his reactions to it were astonishing in one so urbane and sophisticated. Richard Sheridan discovered that he was, after all, insanely and primitively jealous.

Whether or not Elizabeth Sheridan was guilty is still uncertain. At any rate, she had relaxed her once rigid standards; she could now condone a sin, even though she might not commit one. Certainly the letter she wrote to her only close woman friend, Mrs. Stratford Canning, is remarkably revealing:

I was very near coming to spend a week with you some little time ago, if I had not been afraid of my dear Sister Christian's [4] purity bringing me and my peccadillos into a scrape that I know she would have been sorry for. Seriously, I was coming, but I thought if I did that Sheridan would most probably pay me a visit, and then, if he should have asked me a question about the anonymous letter, I felt sure that your face at least would betray me, which, now that everything is blown over, would have been attended with very disagreeable

4 An affectionate nickname for Mrs. Canning.

consequences — and I therefore gave up a scheme which would have given us both, I hope, great pleasure.

It was said that Mrs. Sheridan's lover was Lord Edward Fitzgerald, later to become the husband of Pamela de Genlis. Exactly how much Mrs. Canning knew of the affair is doubtful, but her attitude toward Elizabeth seems to have changed after 1789. She never quite forgave her friend that moment's lapse into madness. . . . It caused Elizabeth hours of grief, for she had loved and admired Mrs. Canning, and she wanted desperately to be respected by her.

Richard, too, was unhappy. It tortured him to see Elizabeth so stricken. Ever since his fury over the anonymous letter had burned itself out his love for his wife had grown deeper. The old feeling of worship was gone. He loved her with a fierce and protective pity, since she was as frail and human as everyone else. Angrily he took her part, writing to Mrs. Canning:

> I wish exceedingly to speak to you about your friend and your answer to Mrs. B. [probably Mrs. Bouverie]. I am confident you do not know what her situation is, or what effect may arise . . . from the apprehension that the *Friend she loved best in the World* appears . . . to be chang'd towards her. She has not seen your letter to Mrs. B., and I would not for the world that she should. . . . You do not know the state she has been in, and how perilous and critical her state now is, or indeed you would upbraid yourself for harbouring one altered thought, or even abating in the least degree, the warmest zeal of Friendship.

Mrs. Canning unbent a little after Richard's plea; and the intimacy between the two women was resumed. But her friend's transgression continued to obsess her; when Elizabeth lay dying she could not refrain from making one last allusion to her " error," whereupon Richard flew into a frenzy.

" Not a word! " he shrieked. " She is an angel if there ever was one! It is I — I — who was the guilty fiend! "

Despite the suffering occasioned by her illness, the last months of Elizabeth Sheridan's life were singularly happy. A new fire of love blazed between her and her husband. In 1791, so long after Tom's birth that she had forgotten the sensation of motherhood, they had a second child. A daughter whom they named Mary, after Mrs. Tickell. For a few weeks after the baby's birth Elizabeth was radiant. Her health seemed miraculously restored; seeing her so starry-eyed and beautiful it was difficult to think that she had ever been ill. But the change was short-lived. One day she was laughing, singing to the baby a difficult aria by Handel. The next day she could not leave her bed, or summon the strength to raise her voice above a whisper.

By May she had become much worse. She was pitifully thin; it was almost as though she had become a child again. Her eyes were bright with fever and with the insistence of a single question: was this the end — for herself, for Richard and her children? The doctors held out little hope. Perhaps at the Hot Wells Mrs. Sheridan might recover. But the Hot Wells,

Richard remembered, was where Mary Tickell had died.

The spring was burning in beauty when Richard brought Elizabeth to Bristol, to those waters which were her last chance of earthly improvement. Richard himself was beyond all hope. He poured into his diary all the formless thoughts that crowded his mind. His melancholy fears for the future, so black without Elizabeth. Praise for his wife — her beauty, her goodness. Not a word of reproach for her. Whatever she has done, Richard has forgiven her long ago. Only he is to blame. There is praise too for Mrs. Canning, who had left her home and children to fend for themselves while she accompanied the Sheridans to the Wells. Throughout the warm evenings when the noises of the town drifted through the opened casements with the exhalations of the surrounding gardens, Mrs. Canning sat with the dying woman, bringing to her the ineffable comfort of a dear and familiar presence.

To Richard each night was a time of torture, for he never knew when he might be summoned to Elizabeth's bedside for the last time. One night she begged them to seat her again at the piano. Pillows and rugs were brought; tenderly they raised her and bore her across the room. Candlelight fell softly across the pages of music, and Richard and Mrs. Canning waited breathlessly until her fingers found the keys. A fragment of melody in that little quiet room — then silence again. " Looking like a shadow of her own picture[5] she played some notes with tears dropping on her thin arms."[6] It was useless to pretend; still weeping she signed to them to snuff out the candles and carry her back to bed.

Her children's future troubled Elizabeth constantly: not Tom — he would be a man soon, and there was his father to watch over him and give him counsel — but Mary, her infant daughter! What was to become of her, motherless almost from the hour of her birth? Again Mrs. Canning's cool, capable hands stilled her sobbing. Elizabeth need have no fears. Mary Sheridan would grow up among the Canning children; her mother's dearest friend would be a mother to her.

The months dragged wearily toward the dust and heat of summer. June was almost over when the Linleys came, father and mother, and once again took up their stations at the deathbed of a beloved child. Thomas Linley and his wife were old and enfeebled. They had seen so many bright young flames blown out. Yet they themselves lived on, a pathetic broken man and a stony-faced woman. They were strong; even the ailments common to advancing age seemed to avoid them. Only the children they had begotten were doomed. Thomas and Samuel and Mary and baby William — the names were like a melancholy litany. Now Elizabeth, loveliest and dearest one of all.

She died at five o'clock of a June morning. Richard

[5] Reynolds' *St. Cecilia.*
[6] Sheridan's Diary.

Sheridan noted: " The loss of breath from a beloved
object, long suffering in pain and certain to die, is not
so great a privation as the last loss of her beautiful
remains, if they remain so. The victory of the Grave
is sharper than the sting of Death." She had often
expressed the desire to be buried beside Mary Tickell.
On the 13th of July a pageant passed through Wells
as they bore her to the vault of the Cathedral. Dr.
Harrington, her friend since childhood, composed in
her honor a fulsome Latin ode. Everywhere people
remembered how magnificently she had sung, how
peerless had been her beauty. The cadences of her
voice echoed on in Richard Sheridan's ears. Years
later when he heard Jane Linley [7] sing he could not
compliment her. Instead he exclaimed tragically, " If
only you had heard Mrs. Sheridan sing that particular
song! "

His grief was abnormal in its intensity. His friends
despaired for his reason — even for his life. Yet in a
few months he was dancing with Pamela, Mme. de
Genlis' lovely daughter, and entertaining her at Isle-
worth at a fête which sadly strained his depleted purse.
It was rumored later that the footmen who moved
among the guests handing punch and ices were really
bailiffs, who had come to collect and who remained to
serve. " They tell me that when he entertains his
friends, he can sit down to dinner with a dozen of his
own securities, have a score of tradesmen waiting in
the antechamber, and an officer behind every guest's

[7] Like her sisters Elizabeth and Mary, Jane also died at a very early age.

chair." So had Sir Benjamin Backbite described young Charles Surface in *The School for Scandal*.

Could he have forgotten so soon? Or was it because Pamela de Genlis, in her stiff ball-gown with the flowers at her breast and the diamonds twinkling in her ears, was so hauntingly like Elizabeth? People said he would soon marry Pamela de Genlis. And there was her mother smiling at the dancing couple; one could see that she approved. But time passed. It was three years since Elizabeth Sheridan's death, and the ravishing Pamela was now Lady Fitzgerald. Then suddenly came the incredible news. Richard Sheridan was married again! With the same romantic fervor which had characterized his first marriage Richard had eloped again. She was a young miss of nineteen named Hester Jane Ogle, and her father was Dean of Winchester.

The ties that bound him to Elizabeth were slipping fast. Tom, his great dark-eyed boy, was seldom with him. Tom had his own friends, his own place to make in the world. And Mary, Mrs. Canning's beloved fosterling, had died a year ago. Elizabeth was remembered beauty. She belonged to the raptures of first love, to the bright-winged dreams of youth. All that, sighed Richard, was gone. He was forty-three — a far more advanced age in the eighteenth century than it is considered today. There were lines in his face, and the heavy pouches of good-living under his eyes. Lately he had been feeling unwell. Gout of course — the inevitable. Gout followed a man into maturity as the sunset followed the dawn. He had other symptoms as well, vague but persistent. Headaches tortured him; he was restless and irritable. It was the loneliness, he thought. Loneliness and the frightening knowledge that the play was drawing to its close. And what had happened to the brilliant conclusion which the first act had promised?

CHAPTER FOURTEEN

A Vain Expectation

THE air was tense with intrigue. Lords and ladies moved warily and talked in whispers. Everyone was a conspirator; it was all rather like the old cape-and-sword tragedies at Covent Garden. French émigrés were being spirited away to England, where society listened eagerly as they recalled the days of the *Ancien Régime*. Fox and the Duchess of Devonshire concocted an intricate plot to save "poor Mrs. B." — Marie Antoinette. There was feverish correspondence, and couriers with money posted madly from London to Paris. But the mob cheered as the tumbril halted and the Queen walked upward to her death. . . .

With the collapse of the French throne in 1792 the English friends of the Revolution grew bolder. They harangued passers-by in the streets; they addressed each other in the approved French fashion. "Good morning, Citizen Smith!" "'Tis vastly pleasant meeting you again, Citizeness!" There was news of rioting in Birmingham. The outraged townsfolk, searching for revolutionary pamphlets to destroy, had broken into Priestley's study and burned scientific manuscripts of great importance. The country was enervated. There had been unmistakable signs lately that the King's madness was recurring. That meant the reopening of the Regency question; arguments and bad blood on both sides, and in all likelihood no settlement again. There was strife in Parliament over Russia. For Catherine II desired to annex Oczakow in Bessarabia, and while Fox supported the Empress' claims Pitt stubbornly opposed them. Now Spain was becoming obstreperous. War, thought the country, and all but the armorers found the prospect decidedly grim.

On November 5, 1793, the battle of Jemappes was fought. The French armies had marched on Brussels, thereby threatening the peace of Holland. War seemed at hand, albeit from another source, and the Duke of Brunswick published a manifesto denouncing France. Sheridan's feelings on war had not changed in almost two decades; they were still the same as when he had regarded the conflict between England and America as a major political catastrophe. He spoke in the House for peace, and again he and Edmund Burke locked horns.

Burke and Sheridan were more than political adversaries now. They hated each other as only men can hate who have once been friends. On the second reading of the bill which called for the creation of an asylum for aliens in England, Burke sprang to his feet in a fury. Dramatically he flung a dagger to the floor of the House to point out the source of the treason —

the corner where sat the bill's supporters. There was a silence, tense, electrical. Every member was struck mute by the sudden accusation. After a moment Sheridan stood up and looked from Burke to the dagger, and back again, with a quiet, contemptuous smile. Would not the honourable gentleman tell him, he asked softly, why the spoon and the fork were absent from so fine a display of theatrical cutlery?

Sheridan had already addressed to the House his motion on the " existence of seditious practises." [1] This was a well-timed and urgently needed speech, for the Habeas Corpus Act had been indefinitely suspended, and liberal thinkers everywhere were constantly being harassed by officers of the law bent on the literal exercise of the gag-laws. The glorious principles of free thought, free speech and assembly, for which so many Englishmen had shed their heroic blood, were being menaced now by fanatics whom a terror of the French Revolution so blinded that they failed to realize the significance of their own actions.

Sheridan held that a committee of inquiry was indispensable; such a committee to decide on the validity of all sedition cases. For either a real danger existed, or it did not — or was the Ministry simply trying to delude the nation and to sap its strength by sending it out on scores of sleeveless errands? Cries of " Treason! Down with the traitors! " were heard all over the country, yet investigation unearthed only

[1] March 4, 1793.

one mare's nest after another. In his best manner Sheridan set out to laugh these " conspiracies " out of existence. There was the plot the Lord Mayor of London had discovered at the King's Arms in Cornhill, where in the guise of a debating society people of dangerous tendencies met and, smiled Sheridan, " bought treason at sixpence a head, allowing each traitor five minutes for overturning the state! " There was the heroic service to his country of the Duke of Richmond who sounded alarums, summarily halted mail-coaches, and now had stationed himself " among the other curiosities, at the Tower." There was the matter of the insurrection at Edinburgh which had been fomented by distributing money among the soldiers of the garrison — which they had straightway squandered upon ale and porter! French spies were rumored to be in possession of plans for seizing the Tower; London was being menaced; a general hysteria prevailed which must do immeasurable harm in England's relations with France.

"Such has been your conduct toward France," Sheridan concluded one of his speeches in 1794, " that you have created the passions which you persecute. You mark a nation to be cut off from the world; you covenant for their extermination; you swear to hunt them in their utmost recesses, you load them with every species of execration. And now you come forth with whining declamations at the horror of their turning upon you with the fury which you inspired! "

He knew that Britain desired to witness the estab-

lishment of a " stable " government in France. But
in matters of government it was notoriously difficult
to please the citizens of the country concerned — how
impossible, then, to satisfy a foreign and none-too-
friendly power! "We commenced with reprobating
and reviling Lafayette, Rochefoucault, and the whole
party of the reforming Royalists. Brissot and the
Tenth-of-August Republicans overthrew and destroyed that party. We may boast of having assisted
Robespierre and Danton in the destruction of Brissot
and those Republicans. Robespierre and Danton
now possess the lead. Are you waiting until such
men as Hébert and Chaumette shall have destroyed
Robespierre and Danton? Would such a change give
you the stable . . . and trustworthy government you
desire, or do you see any class . . . which, in the revolution of enormities, gives you a fairer promise of your
object . . .? When can there arise the sort of government with whom you *would* condescend to treat? . . .
From only one possible source; from a general refor-
mation in the public mind . . . founded on a deep
sense of their calamities and a just abhorrence of their
past crimes. . . . Admirable prudence! Consummate policy! Whilst the certain seeds of internal dis-
cord . . . are sown among them . . . we will not
stoop to treat, because we cannot have *security* for the
future. But if . . . our perseverance . . . shall at
length eradicate all that is vicious in their internal system, strengthening the energies and solidity of their
Government, then our pride will abate, respectful ne-

gotiations will follow, and a happy peace be concluded
. . . for the terms of which we must be left in future
forever at their mercy."

He had often heard it said, he remarked once, that
" the French had no right to beat their enemies! " For
French prowess on the field of battle was increasing,
and the Englishman of " sound principles " felt his
fears increasing with it. To the end he always steadily
denied that the doctrine of the Rights of Man had
brought about the French Revolution, just as he
stoutly affirmed that Pitt and his terrorism of public
opinion had caused the panic in England.

In 1796 the cataclysmic figure of Bonaparte burst
upon the world. He was subtle, a master of statecraft,
and apparently invincible in arms. Across the narrow
waters of the Channel England cowered, awaiting an
attack for which she knew she was unprepared. For
the nation as a whole was not united in opposition to
the Corsican; to the Jacobins he was the liberator
who would assist them in throwing off the shackles
of the House of Hanover, who would help them stand
as free men in the bright sun of Liberty. In Ireland
the Jacobin faction was stronger than anywhere else
in the British Isles. It was there that Napoleon was
to strike the first blow for Freedom. In Paris, Wolfe
Tone and Hoche laid careful plans; but for an unusu-
ally heavy mist which made navigation impossible
the French fleet would have landed in Bantry Bay.

Once again, as in the case of the Spanish Armada, the Irish Sea rose in its might to repel Britain's attackers.

The closeness of that surprise move by the French shocked the country sober. Panic was for the moment forgotten. England set herself seriously to take stock of her defenses, her land and sea forces — and she learned some unpleasant truths.

The Navy, England's pride and the backbone of her power, was in very sorry straits. There was enough corruption and wasteful inefficiency at the Admiralty to float the mightiest man-o'-war. Sailors were poorly quartered and badly fed; they received the most fragmentary medical attention. Worst of all was the circumstance which permitted an officer to flog a seaman for the most trivial infraction of the rules. In many cases these " disciplinary measures " were merely vicious expressions of sadistic cruelty, and instilled in the sailors not a submissive respect for Authority in a laced cocked hat but a fierce desire for rebellion. The Lords of the Admiralty had frequently been besought to ameliorate the lot of the common sailor, but they had dismissed all reform measures as so much poppycock. It remained for the two mutinies of 1797 to show them how grave the situation might become.

Lord Howe having retired and settled in Bath, paradise of the ex-military-and-naval man, Lord Spencer was named his successor. His Lordship was a kindly eccentric whose claim to fame lies in his having given the world the garment called in his honor the " spencer." Of naval strategy and management he was most abysmally ignorant. In April of 1797 he sent orders to the fleet at Spithead to proceed immediately to sea; when Lord Bridgport, the officer in command, gave the signal to his flagship, the *Queen Charlotte*, his men ran up the shrouds and cheered — but they refused to weigh the anchor. Similar breaches of discipline were reported from the other vessels of the fleet. Amazed and terrified officers were forced to surrender their commands. The sailors had drawn up long petitions; a new day was appearing over the horizon. It was mutiny, and the Board of Admiralty moved with all its ponderous dignity to Portsmouth, there to deal with the situation.

But Portsmouth, too, had been infected with the dangerous new ideas of French origin. Representatives of the sailors refused to treat with the Admiralty; they planned to wait until the King and Parliament had granted them their demands. In a towering rage Admiral Gardner swore that he would hang every fifth man from the yardarm as an example, and almost immediately the red flag was raised on the *Royal George*. The fleet had sent its answer to the Admiral. Lord Spencer insisted on appearing personally before the sailors, for surely the presence of the First Lord must quell any mutiny, however fierce. But he was instantly voted down. There was only one man in whom the sailors reposed any trust at all — Lord Bridgport. At his request the offending red banner was struck, and the men consented to sail to St. Helens, although they did not entirely credit His Lordship's promise that their claims would be granted every just attention in their absence.

In the House the mutiny was the subject of long and acrimonious debating. But while Pitt and Fox quibbled over technicalities, Lord Spencer refused the petition of a delegation from the fleet, and the outraged sailors threatened to resort to the often-employed method of Authority, and hang a lieutenant from the yardarm. Swiftly the Admiral relented. Not to be outdone, the men also admitted that they might have been somewhat precipitate. But they sent all officers ashore, however, and were now in complete possession of the squadron.

To the House, debating in the early days of May the question of naval expenses, Sheridan deplored the mismanagement which had characterized the recent crisis. "Why had not the Minister brought his estimate of expenses down earlier? Had not the sailors received a promise from the Admiralty which the Government now had thought fit to neglect?"

And now Lord Howe roused himself from the lethargy of his retirement and visited all the ships lying at Spithead, Portsmouth and St. Helens. If anything at all could be done, Lord Howe was the man to do it. He did succeed in restoring a modicum of order. But there remained a group of sailors who refused to be bought with unsubstantial promises. Instead of surrendering the ships they controlled they set sail for Brest; on the way a new rebellion broke out, and Richard Parker, "Admiral" of this mutiny-within-a-mutiny, demanded that the ships put back at once for Spithead and the Nore. Parker was now in command of the fleet, and he proclaimed it a floating republic. And in answer to Lord Spencer's ineffectual mutterings from London effigies of Dundas and Pitt caught in the fresh sea breeze and swayed gently from the yardarm.

Since others had tried and failed, it was Sheridan's turn now to save the situation if he could. He ordered out the *Neptune* and other gun-boats, and stationed an armed battery on the Isle of Wight. Parker was posted throughout the Kingdom as a traitor and a price put on his head. Sheridan's sympathies might be with the sailors, but the dangers of mutiny were too great to be countenanced. In a few days the crisis had passed. The leaders were executed, and the country settled back to a calm life once more.

But across the Channel another rebellion persisted which demanded, averred Sheridan, "the absolute surrender of Party. If there was a rot in the walls of Old England, her decay could not be very far distant." [2] For the Directory was gathering strength in France, and Sheridan could not visualize its adherents as "republican Romans." In a speech whose patriotic fervor earned the praise of Pitt he urged his countrymen to unite against them, for only by a concerted opposition would they end their menace and their might.

[2] June 2, 1797.

Like Sheridan, Fox too was married in 1795. His bride was the beautiful Elizabeth Bridget Armistead who had been for ten years his acknowledged mistress. Mrs. Armistead's career of gallantry had begun almost twenty years before her association with Fox. She had been the mistress of the Duke of Dorset, of Lord George Germain, Secretary of State for the Colonies during the war with America; of Lord Cholmondely; and even of His Royal Highness the Prince of Wales. Now she and Fox settled down to a life of such complete domestic tranquillity and bliss as is seldom enjoyed even in the most fortunate of marriages. Mrs. Fox was beautiful, charming and gracious. Their home at St. Anne's Hill on the Thames was visited by all the great and prominent men of England. Fox and his wife knew in their life together a happiness as rare as it was perfect. A happiness which Sheridan's union with Hester Jane Ogle sadly and woefully lacked.

In the beginning " Hecca " had restored to a tired and worn-out man that youth which he had believed forever lost. Their honeymoon at Wanstead was a delightful game, he playing so eagerly at being young again, she aping a mature dignity which her giggles and her flying curls belied. " Your aged mother," Richard wrote to Tom, " sends you her blessing." And joyfully Tom sent his, for he was genuinely fond of Hecca and he saw her not as the usurper of his dead mother's place, but as a comrade for his father's lonely hours.

[213]

Yet it was an unwise marriage. Hecca was a creature of whims, of the "fashion." She was that Lady Teazle whom he had described so unerringly twenty years earlier — charming, pretty, hopelessly extravagant. She sang prettily and danced very well, but she lacked the depth and stability which Richard needed. "I am not handsome," she wrote to Richard's sister, Mrs. Le Fanu, in a remarkable piece of self-analysis dated October 24, 1816 — a few short months after her husband's death. "I am full of faults and very ignorant. I have a tolerant heart and not a little mind, and I adore merit in others, and that is all I can say for myself." Poor Hester Sheridan, so richly deserving of a kinder fate! She delighted to hunt celebrities, and was one of the plagues of Lord Byron's first social season. She reveled in the pleasures of the world, yet when troubles rained unrelentingly upon her young head, when illness and poverty confronted her, Hecca did not flinch. To the end her devotion to Sheridan remained constant. If she did not bring him happiness Hester Jane certainly did give him an overflowing measure of tenderness and loving care.

Her gaiety had charmed Richard from the first. It was a quality which Hecca never lost and it was always able to refresh her husband. He was never as considerate of her as he had been of Elizabeth, and certainly he never pretended to be completely faithful to her. But he needed her desperately — much more than he had needed Elizabeth, or anyone else. Constantly he would beseech her not to fail him. She was

his prop, his mainstay in an insecure and unpredictable world. And until that moment when she closed his
eyes forever Hecca Sheridan remained at Richard's
side.

On January 14, 1796, their son Charles Brinsley
Sheridan was born. Grey and Fox were his godfathers,
and Dr. Parr officiated at his baptism — " christened
at the Font of the Opposition " the newspapers jest-
ingly reported. Tom Sheridan adored his baby
brother. He was a pretty child, large-eyed and somewhat elfin of feature, like his mother, and he wrote
verses which were commendable even for a poet's son.
Richard regarded Charles as a toy, a plaything to
charm away his fits of despondency. He called him
his " darling Robin," and he would keep Hecca
amused for hours on end painting for her the glory of
their boy's future and the brilliance of his success.

Despite the disparity in their ages and tempera-
ments, the Sheridans might still have lived a normal
life, — if Hester had been able to control her temper,
and if Richard had not spent weeks away from home,
drinking and gambling with his friends.

He was drinking more heavily than usual and the
effects were becoming visible. His friends who knew
the signs shook their heads and sighed. In 1804 died
Joseph Richardson, one of the authors of *The Rolliad*.
Sheridan arrived at his funeral too late to hear the ser-
mon, but so persuasive was his smile and so winning
his apology that the flattered minister lost no time in
repeating the whole thing for his benefit. Shortly

[215]

afterward Lady Bessborough wrote to Lord Holland: "Poor Richardson is dead. Sheridan will do the same, for he is never sober for a moment. . . . He has quarreled with Mrs. Sheridan. A sort of separation took place, but I believe it is partly made up again, — at least I believe they live in the same house again, but are not very good friends. I am sorry for it, for she was the only chance there was of his stopping drinking." Apparently Hecca's youth and her gay tenderness had not been able successfully to combat the forces of the whirlpool which were drawing Richard down.

There were so many reasons why he should seek a temporary respite in drinking. His health, which had not improved. His Parliamentary career — outwardly satisfactory and creditable enough, but proving upon close scrutiny merely a hollow semblance. His debts, which he knew were increasing every day, although it is said that Sheridan never in his life was certain how much he owed and to whom he owed it. He resembled Charles Surface of whom he had written: "Why, if the old Jewry was a ward, Charles would be an alderman! No man's more popular there, 'fore Gad! I hear he pays as many annuities as the Irish tontine, and that, whenever he is sick, they have prayers for the recovery of his health in all the synagogues!"[3] Sometimes when the exhilaration induced by the brandy had faded he imagined all London to be his creditor, — one vast, grinning,

[3] *School for Scandal*, Act I, Scene i.

[216]

composite figure waiting until he was no longer a member of Parliament and could be thrown into the Fleet, like any other man who failed to pay on time.

On the occasion of his marriage he had made a settlement upon his wife in which much of his capital was involved. And fancying himself in the rôle of a landed gentleman, he set out to acquire country estates through various agents and brokers to whom he delegated extraordinary powers. In 1796, learning that Admiral Geary's estate of Polesden in Surrey was being put up for sale, he authorized Grey and Whitbread to purchase it for him. He tore down the house and had it rebuilt according to his own plans; he bought adjoining acres which he hoped to rent as farms to sturdy and industrious yeomen. But the part which he had elected to play could prove incalculably expensive. Walter Scott bankrupted himself in the rôle of the Laird at Abbotsford. Sheridan was soon to discover that he had lost a fortune at Polesden and must continue to lose more before he could realize anything on his investment. After his death the estate, heavily mortgaged and bearing unmistakable evidences of slipshod management, passed to his son Charles, since Tom did not long survive his father. Charles retained it until his own death in 1843.

He still possessed Drury Lane. Four years before his marriage to Hester Jane Ogle, Sheridan had decided that the old theater was no longer safe; certainly it was not the bright and fashionable structure which

the elegant tastes of the day demanded. Drury Lane
must be rebuilt. At first he planned to surround the
theater with shops which would serve at once to increase the value of his property and to swell his annual
revenues. This was never carried out. The new
theater would open its doors in 1794. Meanwhile the
acting company performed at the Pantheon or at the
King's Opera House in the Haymarket. Sheridan's
days and nights were spent in complicated financial
transactions which would have daunted a Secretary
of the Exchequer. The maze of mortgages in which
he moved grew more and more confused, but still he
forged ahead. Was it possible that he did not fully
comprehend to what a vast undertaking he had committed himself? Or was he still imbued with that
courage which comes of success — a success which
lay twenty years in the past and which he was never
to repeat? The architects and bankers went on fig-
uring; yet the estimates for the new theater fell below
the costs of construction by almost seventy-five thousand pounds, and from this staggering deficit Sheridan could never free himself as long as he lived. As
soon as the theater opened, and again two years later,
he was compelled to assign his theatrical properties
to a board of trustees, chief of whom was Adam, the
Prince's crony. But his affairs still continued to
decline.

He was the victim of a literary hoax which was to
prove quite costly. A certain William Ireland, a boy
of nineteen, fathered a fraud which was far cleverer

than any perpetrated by Chatterton. Ireland appeared one day with a manuscript under his arm. It was, he announced calmly, an undiscovered tragedy by Shakespeare. His imperturbable plausibility convinced not only Sheridan, who immediately undertook to produce the play, and " Glorious " John Kemble, who was to play the leading rôle; he deluded Shakespearean scholars like Malone and Richard Porson. The drama was entitled *Vortigern and Rowena,* and even before its production at Drury Lane it was the sensation of London. Boswell kissed its pages and asserted reverently that now he could die happy, since another of the Master's immortal works had been revealed to him before his end.

On April 2, 1796, the curtains parted at Drury Lane and Mrs. Jordan and John Kemble appeared to wild applaudings. But before an hour had passed the audience grew restive. Someone laughed, someone else in the gallery replied by an unmistakable hiss, and suddenly from all over the theater came shouts and derisive hootings. Ireland might have fooled the experts, but a London audience could not be taken in by his forgery. The next night *Vortigern and Rowena* with all its magnificent scenery and elaborate costumes was recalled. Sheridan found himself searching feverishly for a play which would recoup the losses he had sustained on Ireland's tragedy and would still the laughter all London was enjoying at his expense.

He found it two years later, when he cast Mrs. Siddons as Mrs. Haller in Benjamin Thompson's translation of Kotzebue's *Menschenhass und Reue*, which he produced as *The Stranger*. Sarah Siddons, tall, regal, with the flashing dark eyes and the haunting deep voice, was overnight the toast of London. There was something awesome in her beauty which audiences found fascinating and at the same time disturbing. " One would as soon make love to the Archbishop of Canterbury as to Mrs. Siddons," some wag remarked. But until her death she remained the undisputed queen of the English stage.

Mrs. Siddons and Kotzebue were an unbeatable combination, and Sheridan tried them again. Miss Phillips rewrote *The Spaniards in Peru,* or *The Death of Rolla,* and Sheridan offered it as *Pizarro: A Tragedy,* with Kemble, Mrs. Siddons and Mrs. Jordan cast respectively as Pizarro, Elvira and Cora. The play abounded in long, fulsome speeches of which patriotism was the keynote — ideal for a season when everybody talked of Nelson's victories and England's newly asserted dominion of the seas. The " sentiment " which he had scorned in his comedies, the bombast and bathos which he had ridiculed in *The Critic,* riot without check through *Pizarro.* It was almost as though Sheridan the author saw and criticized dramatic defects to which Sheridan the producer remained totally blind. The very type of historical drama which he had killed with *The Critic* was revived. This time its hold was stronger than before, for *Pizarro* remained popular with playgoers for generations, and it fathered a whole tribe of similar tragedies. Artifice and artificiality were back again in favor.

The thousand pounds which Sheridan realized on *Pizarro* were soon spent; success was once more eluding him. In 1800 he approached Kemble and offered to sell out to him; but nothing came of the long and tedious negotiations, and when Kemble finally embarked upon his career as an actor-manager it was in Covent Garden that he lost his money and not in Drury Lane. Two years later a suit in Chancery was filed against Sheridan. He appeared in his own behalf and pleaded his case with his customary suave eloquence. In the same year he pleaded and won the case of the actors against the bankers who claimed a prior lien on the Drury Lane salaries. Sheridan waited for months to hear from his solicitors; at last he wrote, roundly cursing the delay, and was told that his request had been granted the year before. Impossible! Yet a search revealed their letter, unopened, at the bottom of a pile of other letters, the seals of which were still unbroken.

Sheridan's struggles with his theater dragged on until at last he was forced to admit himself defeated. For thirty years he had guided the destinies of Drury Lane. Now he was growing old, and he seemed no longer able to gauge the taste of the theater-going public. If Drury Lane was to survive at all it must do so under another's ægis. In 1806 Richard Sheridan surrendered the directorship of his theater to his son Tom.

The three years from 1795 to 1798, during which Sheridan had labored at his Herculean task of making Drury Lane pay, had been serene ones for Fox. Having failed to reach an understanding with Pitt, his political stature was, at the moment, shrunk to microscopic size. He retired to the green slopes of the Thames and discovered how pleasant was the idyllic existence of the country squire. Fox went hunting, he wrote methodically each day in his diary; accompanied by Mrs. Fox he visited the homes of his friends.

In 1798 Sheridan appealed to him to enter the political maelstrom once again. It had been one of the most tragic years in all the dark history of Ireland. The conspiracy which the heroic Edward Fitzgerald had headed had been discovered; its leader himself had been killed. Now the forces of repression were in control. Lord Clare had been sent to Ireland to restore order and quiet, and Sheridan found his conduct reprehensible. On June 18th he voiced his protests on the Irish situation, and so scathing were his indictments of His Lordship that Sir John Macpherson remarked, " You have *begum-ed* the Chancellor-Governor of Ireland. I have heard your speech. If it is printed . . . he must end in impeachment. I conjure you to print it for the sake of a million people."

" To keep Ireland against the will of the people," Sheridan had stated, " is a vain expectation."

Lord Clare pursued his ruthless course and exposed an organization called the United Irishmen, one of the many formed to oppose him. He ordered the arrest of Arthur O'Connor, his brother Roger, and a priest named O'Coigley, and had them tried for treason. O'Coigley was hanged and afterwards beheaded; he went to his death like a hero and a martyr, and won for the cause of freedom a legion of new recruits. When he heard James Mackintosh refer unflatteringly to the dead priest, Dr. Parr, Sheridan's friend since his school-days at Harrow, reproved the speaker in the following classical sentence: " Yes, Jamie, he was a bad man, but he might have been a worse. He was an Irishman, but he might have been a Scotsman; he was a priest, but he might have been a lawyer; he was a Republican, but he might have been an apostate."

CHAPTER FIFTEEN

Treasurer of the Navy

THE year is 1803. Napoleon continues to terrorize Europe, and mothers frighten naughty children by whispering that the Corsican Ogre will take them away. All London is laughing delightedly over a riddle which some coffee-house wit has propounded: " Why is the Duke of Portland like an old woman? " " Because he's past bearing! " Men are saying that once again His Majesty is mad, and at Brooks' they have begun to place bets on the Prince's chances of retaining his Regency longer than a few days. Grenville has hurried to Stowe to ascertain exactly what is the King's condition, but the reports he brings back tell nothing. Is George shamming? Will Pitt and Addington convince Parliament a second time that His Majesty is " as sane as ever "? Or will the victory go to Fox?

Sheridan stood now at the pinnacle of his friendship with the Prince. That he was pleased and flattered by His Royal Highness' attentions was only natural; he refused, however, to submit to him entirely. Sheridan was loath to be drawn again into the suffocating tangle of the Prince's domestic affairs. Princess Caroline might be the thoroughly unspeakable creature which her husband maintained she was — and actually history has done an ineffectual job of whitewashing her character — yet Richard shrank from investigating her affairs in order that he might supply the Prince with grounds for a divorce action. He prided himself that never had he asked of the Prince a favor for himself. Now when he came before " Prinny " to plead for a plum it was for Tom, his son, that brilliant young scapegrace.

Tom Sheridan had pursued up to now the delightful — if costly — pleasures of the Great World. He had already cost his father fifteen hundred pounds when he had been named in a fashionable divorce suit, and a career of gambling and gallantry was apparently the extent of his ambition. Tom was not anxious to enter politics. It was too troublesome to " stand " for some borough, and the prospect of electioneering was altogether too appalling. If his father could use influence, now, and get him a post somewhere . . .? Meanwhile there were those debts of his. What, Tom wondered, did his father propose to do about them?

His father asked for and obtained a sum of money from the Prince — eight thousand pounds. It cleared up most of the young man's debts; it was also the springboard from which Tom plunged into the world and discovered that there was a place for him after all. Within a few months he had eloped with Miss Caroline Callander, a Scotch heiress. In 1804 he was

GEORGE FREDERICK, Prince of Wales

From the painting by Lawrence

appointed an aide-de-camp to Lord Moira in Edinburgh, and the following year he had risen to the position of Muster-Master General of Ireland. Tom became a hard-working public servant. When he died he left a good name and a grieving widow. As for his children, they too rose in the world, as their father and grandfather had so earnestly hoped they would.[1]

The problems of the Prince could not be settled as easily as Tom Sheridan's. He had pledged himself to assist the Catholics, yet he was afraid to reopen the question of Catholic Emancipation. He had learned from his tentative overtures in that direction in 1789 that his father would brand any compromises with the Catholics as treason both to his conscience and his coronation oath. His friendship with Fox had cooled; Mrs. Fitzherbert still hated Fox, and Fox's behavior during the Regency crisis had made him *persona non grata* with the restored King. Since the Prince was playing the rôle of the dutiful son he was compelled to let Fox go.

The King, to his son's immense relief, shared his fondness for Richard Sheridan. To the fuddled old man Sheridan was a public benefactor, a national hero; for had he not himself protected the royal person from an assassin's bullet? His Majesty could not remember clearly all the details, but they remained vivid in Sheridan's mind until the day of his death. It had happened at Drury Lane shortly after the be-

---

[1] One of Tom Sheridan's daughters was the beautiful and accomplished Mrs. Norton, and the other was Lord Dufferin's mother.

ginning of the new century. A madman named Hatfield drew a pistol and fired upon the madman in the
royal box. The ensuing panic was terrific, but Sheridan soon had everything calm. He was everywhere
at once, issuing orders and executing them. He
soothed the squealing, hysterical Princesses; he ap-
prehended the culprit. He made the occasion even
more memorable by composing on the spot a new
stanza to be added to the National Anthem, which the
orchestra played while quiet settled itself over the theater and the actors prepared to continue the play.

Pitt was no longer Prime Minister. He had resigned — or was it abdicated? — in March, 1801.
But his spirit controlled succeeding ministries, just as
his hand was discernible in every important piece of
statecraft his country undertook. The truce of
Amiens [2] was a case in point. Sheridan was dis-
pleased with it, dubbing it " a perilous and hollow
peace." He continued: " We have gotten Ceylon and
Trinidad. Ceylon should be named *Security* and
Trinidad *Indemnity*. Is this armed repose . . . the
fruit of our glorious war? " His eyes chanced to fall
on Pitt, occupying an elevated seat three or four
benches above that of the Treasury. With that little
fleeting smile which his hearers had come to recognize
Sheridan said, " I remember a fable of Aristophanes;
it is translated from the Greek into decent English —
I mention this for the country gentlemen. It is of a

[2] May 14, 1802.

man who sat so long upon a seat . . . that he grew to it. When Hercules pulled him off he left the sitting part of the man behind."

But he could still recognize Pitt's greatness and the validity of the motives which had inspired him — even if to Sheridan those motives might seem completely misguided. " Of the ex-Minister I would say that no man admires his splendid talents more than I do. . . . He has no low, little, mean, petty vices. He has too much good taste and talent to set his mind upon ribands, stars, and other appendages and idols of rank. He is of a nature not at all suited to be the creature or tool of any Court. . . . But I must tell him how grossly he has misapplied his great talents in the politics of this country; I must tell him how he has augmented our national debt, and of the lives he has lost in this war. I must tell him that he has done more *against* the privileges of the people, increased more the powers of the Crown, and injured more the Constitution of this country than any minister I can mention."

In order to hear her husband's speech on the Army Estimates, December 2, 1802, Hester Sheridan disguised herself as a man. She was still at heart a child who loved to play games; the thought of dressing up and slipping unrecognized into the House of Commons thrilled her beyond description. She never regretted that she had listened that night, for rarely had Richard surpassed himself in invective and in statesmanlike spirit. His drinking might have reddened his eyes and coarsened his features, but it had certainly not affected the preciseness of his thinking.

He was attempting to convey to his hearers some realization of the growing might of France which menaced their security. " Look," he thundered, " at the map of Europe! We see nothing but France! It is in our power to measure her territory, to reckon her population, but it is scarcely within the grasp of any man's mind to measure the ambition of Bonaparte. Russia, if not in his power, is at least in his influence. Prussia is at his beck; Italy is his vassal; Holland is in his grasp; Spain at his nod; Turkey is in his toils; Portugal at his feet." He had heard men crying that Pitt and Pitt alone could save the nation, and he answered them now. " No single man can save this country. If a nation depends upon one man only, it cannot, and, I will add, does not deserve to be saved. It can only be done by the Parliament and by the People! "

Once again he returned to Bonaparte. " He says he is an instrument in the hands of Providence — an envoy of God . . . to restore happiness to Switzerland, and to elevate Italy to splendour. . . . Sir, I think he is an instrument in the hands of Providence to make the English love their Constitution the better, to cling to it with more fondness, to hang round it with truer tenderness. Every man feels, when he returns from France, that he is coming from a dungeon to enjoy the light and life of British independence." If there is aggression to be made his convic-

tion is that England " meet it with a spirit worthy of
these Islands; that we ought to meet it with a convic-
tion of the truth of this assertion, that the country
which has achieved such greatness has no retreat in
littleness; that if we could be content to abandon
everything, we should find no safety in poverty, no
security in abject submission; finally, Sir, that we
ought to meet it with a fierce determination to perish
in the same grave with the honour and independence
of the country." The great and all-embracing truth
of what he said that day seems particularly vital in
the light of present history. Strange that its message
should have escaped Fox, who was as a rule so discerning. For he wrote to his nephew, the future Lord
Holland: " Sheridan made a foolish speech, if a speech
full of wit can with propriety be called foolish, upon
the Army Estimates, of which all who wish him ill are
as fond as I, who wish him well, am vexed at it."

In May, 1804, Addington went out, and Pitt returned to rule England for the last time. He was only
forty-five years old but he might have been a man of
seventy. Never too robust, his health was now completely broken; but far more tragic was the collapse
of his indomitable spirit. As Napoleon grew stronger
Pitt became more and more feeble. The double tri-
umphs of Ulm and Austerlitz were his death-blows.
He died in January, 1806, and again Sheridan spoke
sincerely and honestly in his praise: " There were
many who flattered him more than I, and some who

feared him more, but there was no man who had a higher respect for his transcendent talents, his matchless eloquence, and the greatness of his mind. I may have considered that there was too much of loftiness in his mind which could not bend to advice, or scarcely bear coöperation; I might have considered that as a statesman his measures were not adequate to the situation of the country in the present times; but I always thought his purpose and his hope were for the greatness and the security of the Empire."

After Pitt's death Fox brought in a ministry the apparently unlimited accomplishments of whose members earned it the name of " All the Talents." Fox filled the post of Foreign Secretary; Grenville was Secretary of the Treasury; Wyndham, who had supported both Pitt and Fox, was Secretary of War; and Petty, Lord Landsdowne's heir, controlled the Exchequer. Addington, now Lord Sidmouth, was Lord Privy Seal; Lord Ellenborough was Lord Chief Justice; and Lord Spencer, having exhausted the possibilities of the Admiralty and surrendered his post to Grey, had consented to serve as Home Secretary. Erskine was Lord Chancellor; Lord Moira was Master of Ordnance; and Sheridan was awarded the Treasuryship of the Navy — which he was to have received once before, in 1789.

Sheridan's new position called immediately for an increase in his already enormous expenditures. He refurnished his house in George Street and added to the staff of servants; he purchased two elaborate new four-wheel carriages; and in honor of the christening of his grandchild, Tom's first baby, he gave a magnificent reception to the Prince and the Party. Everything was as lavish as at one of his Royal Highness' own functions. The house had been decorated with tall palms and orange trees; Rovedino and the popular Irish tenor Kelly had been engaged to sing. Everyone made merry and drank the health of Tom and Lord Moira, who were both presently to depart for the scene of their duties.

One year earlier the Prince had bestowed upon Sheridan the receivership of the Duchy of Cornwall, a sinecure which in good years sometimes brought in as much as nine hundred pounds. Sheridan was deeply touched by this further evidence of His Highness' kindness and consideration. So touched was he that he did not at once realize that the benefits to be derived from the receivership must be deferred until the death of Lord Lake, the present Receiver. Hester Jane, who had grown with the years a trifle shrewish, berated the Prince and his gift. She said that one was without merit while the other lacked either honor or faith. Her husband was less vindictive. Lord Lake might survive *him*, of course, and then the receivership of the Duchy would have done him no good at all. But the Prince must be shielded from any suggestion of insincerity or faithlessness. "He was not to be suspected," he told Hecca sternly, "since he was acting as honourably as a man can do."

Fox was in the saddle now. But the man who had so

persistently opposed Pitt did not long survive him. Afflicted for years with a dropsy for which he had twice endured the excruciating tortures of " tapping," Fox left his house in Stable Yard, St. James' Square, on August 27, 1806, for Chiswick, which the Duke of Devonshire had lent to him. Slowly and in great anguish he made the journey from London to St. Anne's Hill, for he had resolved that he must see that happy place before he died. His passing left both Whigs and Tories leaderless. Without any careful or competent guidance both parties were now afloat upon an ocean of problems — some old, others new, but all equally involved and perplexing.

First Pitt, then Fox. Now Georgianna of Devonshire, Fox's lovely Duchess and the Whigs' tutelary goddess, closed her eyes. She had possessed great beauty and great wealth, and a name which was one of the most distinguished in the country. Yet her life had been lonely and she had been pursued until the end by a deep and tragic unhappiness.

They were vanishing fast, the familiars of his youth. Often the Prince became frightened as he remembered how little remained of those magnificent old days. Everything was changing. And His Royal Highness felt the tears starting to his eyes. His friends were gone. The quiet and serene world of his youth was vanished also — blown away in the smoke from that fellow Bonaparte's cannons. Worst of all, his beauty had disappeared. He was a fat man now — a very fat man indeed. The curls which had clustered low on his brow were thinning fast, and when he walked he breathed with difficulty. He had left his wife, wretched creature, and was once more reunited with " his true, his only Maria." In her company he tried to shake off those despondent moods which plagued him. He built the Pavilion at Brighton, and experienced the artist's peculiar satisfaction in knowing that he had created the largest and most perfect palace of pleasure which ever existed. There he sat, the Master of the Revels described with such Pepysian detail in the *Creevey Papers*. He applauded the dancers with his enormous beringed hands and squinted at them through his little porcine eyes. The heat and the wine made his bloated face monstrous; his stays tortured him. The music played on and the dancers spun more wildly, and presently a wan, sickly light crept past the guttering candles. Surprised, the guests saw that it was morning. His Royal Highness rose. Everything stopped as he stumbled from the room and flung himself, a grotesque and weeping hulk, upon his bed.

The politics of the eighteenth century had been buried with Fox and Pitt. There were new men around him now. Younger voices counseled him, and the Prince was not sure that he trusted a single one of them. They were all unprincipled place-seekers whose devotion to His Royal Highness was not unmixed with a very real desire to better themselves. For the Prince, perhaps because he was so incapable of it himself, demanded an intense and unswerving devotion in the men he chose to serve him.

[235]

One by one the ranks of the giants were thinning. Sir Walter Scott mourned them in his *Requiem,* friend and political adversary alike:

> But search the land of living men,
> Where wilt thou find their like again?

Fox's death left vacant his seat in the House. The following year Sheridan consented to replace him as Member from Westminster, and his constituents at Stafford never forgave his desertion.

The old King disapproved heartily of " All the Talents." He could not decide whether he disliked Grey or Grenville more thoroughly. But his sick brain feared and distrusted them both. At any moment the fiery vehemence of one or the icy inhuman calculations of the other might accomplish what George III so dreaded. The Catholic question might come to a head. Fox had sworn to the Prince that as long as the old King lived he would not agitate him by raising the horrendous issue of Catholic Emancipation. His Majesty, although he had never approved of Fox as a suitable companion for the Prince, knew that he was a man who respected a promise. But Fox was dead. The destinies of England were in the hands of a group of men who gave not a thought to an old man's feelings. They would bring up the matter of Catholic Emancipation just to plague him. .

In March " All the Talents " collapsed. The Cabinet post which he had so briefly filled was once again wrested from Sheridan's grasp. His remark on the occasion of the ministry's dissolution has become historic. He had often heard, asserted Sheridan, of men knocking out their brains against a wall; but never had he heard of men building a wall for that particular and express purpose. The story went the rounds and a wit replied to it in doggerel:

> "I've heard very often," shrewd Sheridan said,
> "Of a man who against a stone wall ran his head.
> But my friends had no wall, so with wonderful pains,
> They built one on purpose to beat out their brains!"

> No, no, Master Sherry! Though pleasant thy wit,
> For once it has failed the true matter to hit;
> For men who thus wantonly build up a wall,
> Have convinced the whole world they have no brains at all!

His Majesty had guessed correctly. The Catholic question was raised, and Sheridan spoke on a matter upon which his feelings had always been pronounced. He advocated reforms in Ireland, but reforms which must be all-inclusive and swept clean. "The place to set out in Ireland for the relief of the people is the cottage." [3]

The end of "All the Talents" chilled Sheridan's heart with a premonitory warning of the disaster which would eventually overtake him. Grenville had been for years his avowed enemy. Now he exerted all his

[3] August 13, 1807.

influence to keep Sheridan from carrying the elections at Westminster. The campaign was vicious. Sheridan worked tirelessly, but he knew almost from the outset that he had little hope of prevailing against the combined strength of Grenville, Horne Tooke and Cobbet. When the votes were counted Grenville's henchman Paull, the rabble-rousing tailor, had been returned. For the first time in twenty-six years Sheridan was without a seat in Parliament. Terrified, he took counsel with his friends. Was this cheap defeat to be the end of a career which had begun in such a burst of glory? But Fate had not finished playing her game with Richard Sheridan. His friends maneuvered skilfully, and Sheridan discovered to his surprise that he had been the successful candidate in Ilchester — a borough which had, ironically, been created by Grenville himself. He had been spared for a little while the ignominious oblivion of debtors' prison.

The Duke of Portland, more than ever past bearing, came back on March 25, 1807 to preside over the tattered remnants of a ministry. His Chancellor of the Exchequer was that Spencer Perceval, the mathematical barrister who established banknotes as legal tender. At last a man who understood finance and was not ashamed of his knowledge was put in charge of the nation's purse-strings. Perceval soon had the reputation throughout England of being a cross between a magician and Lord Bountiful, but his popularity with even the most ignorant peasant was enormous, and when His Grace died in 1809 Perceval moved up into his place.

The prominence now being accorded the Irish question made Sheridan anxious to secure for himself an Irish seat. He had never been wholeheartedly welcomed by Ilchester, and Stafford seemed lost to him forever. It seemed for a while as though he might be elected in Wexford, where the Independents had given him the nomination. But Wexford was far away; the Irish Sea separated candidate and constituency. Mr. Colclough, his running-mate, secured votes for himself and none for Sheridan. His methods were finally questioned by their opponent, Alcock. In the presence of eleven men who had been selected to decide the issue and who lifted not a finger to help the doomed man, Alcock killed Colclough — and at the same time won the election.

Sheridan was forced to continue as the Member from Ilchester. But although he might have failed in his attempt to represent an Irish borough, he could still speak out in behalf of the country of his birth. " The fact is that the tyranny practised upon the Irish has been throughout unremitting. There has been no change but in the manner of inflicting it. . . . You ask Ireland for bravery and take away the motives for it; for loyalty and deprive them of the benefits of a Constitution. By the hapless Bill proposed but defeated, at least a Catholic officer might have been enabled to make a career and need no longer rise in his own degradation. Charles I had asked Selden what was the best way to put down rebellion; to which Selden answered, ' Remove the cause.' Remove the cause of disaffection in Ireland, and disaffection will end! " [4]

[4] August 13, 1807.

CHAPTER SIXTEEN

Neither Place nor Purse

NO ONE believed any longer in the King's recovery. It was an established fact that he was mad,
and people had tired long ago of discussing each new
manifestation of his ailment and of hurrying out to
Stowe or Windsor to catch a glimpse of the illustrious
patient. The Royal Family was providing little
either novel or entertaining in the way of gossip. The
Prince, his brother the Duke of York, and their uncles
the Dukes of Clarence and of Cumberland — the latter certainly the most reviled gentleman in the realm
— were continually at each other's throats. Lately
these quarrels had been receiving some public attention. " The conduct of these illustrious personages
is a most melancholy and alarming feature in the
difficulties which every hour increase upon us; and
it is not without great forbearance one can impute it
to any other ground but an affection of the same nature as that under which the King labours." [1] The
Prince and his wife continued to live apart. She
maintained a separate residence at Kensington Pal-

[1] From a contemporary political writing.

ace; their daughter Princess Charlotte, who could not get along with either one of her parents, lived at Warwick House. In an age when marital upsets were diligently shielded from scrutiny the entire nation was privy to the troubles of the royal pair. Princess Caroline had her staunch supporters, her husband had his.

The Peninsular War was raging. The nation spoke of Horatio Nelson and of a young officer who would later be the Duke of Wellington. Mr. Sheridan, the Member from Ilchester, was heard frequently on the subject of the Spanish campaign. He had a good deal of vituperative comment to make on those ministers who, by their stubborn refusal to increase the army's appropriations, would end by starving the troops and rendering them too feeble to fight. Sheridan was drinking more than ever. Sometimes when he spoke his voice thickened and a few sentences blurred unintelligibly; there was a fixity, a glaze to his eyes which destroyed forever that look of bright alertness, his chiefest charm. Drink was to Sheridan more than a refuge from the world. It *was* his world — the only place left him now that so many doors had slammed abruptly in his face.

He was excluded from Drury Lane. His theater no longer looked to him to guide its destiny. The men who had since Fox's death been the Whig leaders — Grey and Grenville and their allies — had made no secret of their dislike of Sheridan. Every day it was becoming more and more obvious that his career in

MRS. FITZHERBERT

From the painting by Russell

politics was ended; the meteor which had flared upward with such consuming brightness was dropping
now, faster, faster, until it must expire in the darkness
below. The portals of Carlton House stood wide no
longer. "Prinny" had found new friends. Never
known for his constancy, he was become as capricious
and full of whims as a Court beauty. He quarreled
with his mother, he berated his wife, he bullied his
daughter. Recently he had importuned Lady Bessborough to become his mistress, but the grotesqueness
of the fat man's wooing had made the lady laugh. She
had refused him, and her reply had not improved his
temper. Having served His Royal Highness faithfully
and honorably most of his life, Sheridan was now to
be tossed aside; the years when he had worn the
Prince's livery had netted him neither place nor
purse.

Sheridan sat in the House waiting to speak on Mr.
Ponsonby's motion concerning the war in the Penin-
sula. It was February 24, 1809 — and outside the
night was starless and very cold. Sheridan slumped
in his chair. He was drowsy, and troubled by that
vague yet persistent discomfort which lately never
seemed to leave him. Suddenly the darkness which
had blotted out all the windows vanished. There was
no longer night outside, but a hideous and hectic trav-
esty. Somewhere a fire was burning, Sheridan noted,
and closed his heavy eyes again.

When he opened them a moment later it was to learn
that his world had been entirely consumed. What re-

mained was a charred and twisted ruin — and a strong-box crammed with mortgages. For Drury Lane, like his father's theater in Dublin, had burned to the ground. . . .

Mr. Ponsonby did not make his motion. Shocked at the cataclysm which had overtaken a fellow member, the Speaker proposed an adjournment. But Sheridan merely rose and shook his head. Whatever might be the extent of the calamity which had befallen him he saw no reason why it should interrupt the proceedings of the House on a great national question. The flush in his face had deepened; the fixed look in his eyes grown more marked. Otherwise he appeared so unmoved that the men watching him were far more shocked than by the wildest hysterics. For that sculptured calm of Sheridan's was almost the calm of death.

He picked up his hat and walked with a deliberate step through the familiar streets which led to Drury Lane. Ahead of him, growing unbearably bright as he approached it, blazed the fire. Now he could smell the smoke. It caught in his lungs and sent tears starting from his eyes, but fiercely he wiped them away. Let no man say that he had seen Richard Sheridan standing in the street, blubbering like a baby!

Across from where Drury Lane had stood there was a cheap little tavern. Sheridan had never patronized it before, but tonight he entered its foul-smelling taproom and calling for a bottle of wine, sat himself at a table near the window. From here, although the glass was grimed and filthy, he could perceive a spreading redness outside and he knew that the fire still raged. He was sitting there, drinking and peering steadily through the window, when some of his friends found him and insisted that he leave with them.

But Sheridan would not move from his chair. He gave them a twisted and bitter smile. "Surely," he said, "a man may enjoy a glass of wine at his own fireside?"

Drury Lane had been insured for a trifling amount, which would not begin to recompense him for its loss. In the fire many personal souvenirs of an inestimable intrinsic value had disappeared; among them was "St. Cecilia's harpsichord" — the instrument at which Elizabeth Sheridan had been seated when old Sir Joshua Reynolds painted the famous portrait.

The last spark had hardly died away, however, before Sheridan's plans were afoot to rebuild Drury Lane yet again. He also considered a proposed merger with Covent Garden, whereby the two theaters as one powerful combination might control the dramatic firmament. Now that London was spreading out into so many unforeseen directions Drury Lane was somewhat inaccessible, and might become even more inconvenient since the world of fashion dined in the evening instead of between three and five in the afternoon, as formerly. Covent Garden possessed a "dormant" as well as an actual patent. Sheridan, anxious to secure both, reasoned that he might in this way keep two potential rivals from devouring each other. He approached Samuel Whitbread, his friend and for many years the agent in charge of his affairs.

Whitbread was prominent in Whig circles. He had inherited Thrale's brewery, and was therefore a man of unquestioned — some said of unlimited — means. In 1805 he had incited and led an attack on Pitt's friend Dundas [2] which had resulted in the latter's impeachment. There had followed what for Richard Sheridan must have seemed like a renascence of those stirring days of Warren Hastings' trial, for he had been put in charge of the impeachment proceedings against Dundas. Unfortunately they had accomplished nothing. Dundas had speedily been acquitted. That decision, which until the end of his life Whitbread regarded as the public vindication of a scoundrel, was a blow from which he never fully recovered. He sought about him frantically for a cause to espouse and found that of Her Royal Highness Princess Caroline and her daughter, Princess Charlotte. He undertook to justify them to the British nation and at the same time to right their grievous wrongs. But when, in 1815, he took his own life he had succeeded in doing neither.

Sheridan besought Whitbread to form a committee which was to rebuild and refinance Drury Lane. A committee upon which Lord Byron sat. Elaborate plans for the erection of a fireproof structure were begun; as he had in 1793 Richard now watched con-

[2] Lord Melville.

struction costs rocket dizzily away from any proximity to the estimated figures. All the existing mortgages were renewed and new ones arranged. Meanwhile the work progressed at a feverish pace. Two years after the holocaust the cornerstone was laid; the theater itself opened its doors to the public a year later, in October, 1812. It was the very ultimate in architectural and artistic achievement. Travelers who stepped through its portals agreed with the proud Londoners that nowhere was there such another.

One of the first productions to grace the stage of the new playhouse was a dramatizaton of Frances Sheridan's *Nourjahad,* which had appeared as a novel when her son was a little homesick boy at Harrow. Everyone in England who could sharpen a goose-quill wrote a Prologue for *Nourjahad.* Sheridan's desk was snowed under with manuscripts, and each post brought in a fresh armful. He read them through and discovered that they had all been composed, as it were, on the same pattern. Each one contained allusions to the Phœnix arising from its ashes — and damned little else! Even Whitbread sent his own verses, which like the rest referred to that miraculous and legendary bird. And of them Sheridan remarked to Lord Byron that they had been indited by a " rhapsodizing poulterer."

It was Byron who, scorning at first to vie with other poets of less distinguished birth in a public scramble involving a mere prologue, descended at length into the arena. And won.

[247]

As soars this fane to emulate the last,
Oh! might we draw our omens from the past,
Some hour propitious to our players may boast
Names such as hallow still the dome we lost.

. . .

Dear are the days that made our annals bright,
Ere Garrick fled, or Brinsley ceased to write! [3]

Sheridan was to receive £24,000, out of which he
would reimburse the Linleys and all other claimants.
His son Tom was allotted an additional £12,000 for
his share of the old patent. Between them father and
son possessed a sum which appeared at first glance as
staggering as the national debt. But it vanished —
Sheridan could never say why or how. He told Hecca
ruefully that he should have greased all his pockets.
Then perhaps a few of the banknotes might have remained with him.

Of all the horror and despair connected with those
confused days after the fire one pleasant memory remained. Lord Grenville had been appointed Chancellor of Oxford, and though he had opposed Sheridan
politically for years he felt that both as a dramatist
and a public figure Richard should be awarded an
honorary degree. Sheridan was flattered and deeply
humbled. He came to Oxford, to the silent gray buildings and the satin-smooth green lawns, and recalled
how he had been here in a previous existence. His
mind walked back among the tombstones of the years
to the bright July of 1774. He and the world had been
so young, and Lord North had worn such splendid

[3] Published in the *Morning Chronicle*, October 12, 1812.

robes as now hung from Grenville's shoulders. And Elizabeth had sung. He could not recollect clearly her song; even the face of the singer seemed blurred across thirty-six years. But he heard her voice distinctly — high and clear, and so miraculously sweet.

Just before the ceremony came the revelation of a last-minute change in plans. "Three churlish *non-placets* of Corpus" had dissented, and the name of Richard Brinsley Sheridan was withdrawn from the list of candidates for the degree *honoris causa*. He was disappointed, of course; more so than he would have admitted. But with his usual charming smile he deprecated the whole occurrence and took his seat among the spectators. The ceremony began. And soon he heard echoing from everyone around him loud cries of "Sheridan! Sheridan among the Doctors!" The Voice of the People had spoken; it was a command which none could disobey. Sheridan's smile deepened as he rose and made his way, unrobed, to the platform.

In 1810 Princess Amelia breathed her last. She had been His Majesty's favorite child; upon her he had lavished all the tenderness and devotion which the rest of his family rejected. For weeks after her funeral the King appeared distrait. He muttered, he played the harpsichord, he sat weeping in darkened rooms. He was mad again, said the little whispers which floated from the palace. His ministers shook their heads; his people mourned. Twenty years earlier, at the time of his first seizure, George III had been aware of his condition. It is said that once he turned his face to the wall and whispered so mournfully that those who heard him could not restrain their tears, " God help me, for I am going to be. mad." And from that madness there had been a temporary respite. But this time there was no hope at all. He kept to his apartments at Windsor while his thoughts strayed among those shades who had once been his friends. He granted audiences to Pitt, he conversed amiably with Lord North. A decade was to pass, with the old man still living on among his ghosts. His most dreaded enemy, Bonaparte, would be a prisoner upon a rock in the ocean and the Congress of Vienna five years past before that dark winter's dawn in 1820 when the cannon would roll and the nation know that the old King's misery was ended.

The King's madness meant another repetition of the old Regency question. This time it appeared more than likely that the Prince would at last realize his fondest wish. The walls of the House heard reiterated the old arguments for and against; now, however, fewer dissenting voices were raised. Sheridan also took part, replying to that frequently advanced theory that a Regent was not immediately urgent, but that Parliament might arrogate to itself some of the King's peculiar powers. The Whigs were in fact playing that game of deferment and delay which Pitt had tried twenty-three years earlier. And though the actors were changed, the reasons were still the same; they feared — as Pitt had feared — that when the Prince came into his own he would bring in his friends to supplant them.

"We seem to act," he declared, "under the impression that what [power] the monarchy has lost has been divided amongst ourselves; whereas the Royal power is so fundamentally interwoven with every other interest in the State that by even its temporary interruption the life and power of Parliament is paralysed."[4] There ensued a great deal of agitation as to which one among the ministers should frame the Prince's reply to Parliament on the Regency Bill. Such a delicate matter required tactful handling and the most consummate finesse; it was furthermore an open secret that the men whose fingers shaped that answering address would mold the Prince's future policies.

Grenville and Grey decided that the task belonged to them. They had conferred together constantly, and their talk had not been wholly confined to the Prince and his speech. Having graciously received the Royal permission to draw up that speech they were still not satisfied. Both were aware that things had a habit of repeating themselves with the Prince. Himself inconstant and unstable, events moved about him with a wonderfully fixed regularity. Thus, as in 1789, Sheridan and Lord Moira and his other friends were all writing addresses for him. And at the last minute "Prinny" would hand them all to Sheridan and tell

[4] January 2, 1811.

[251]

him to select the least objectionable of the lot. Sheridan's friendship for the heir, which had once appeared to be waning but which flourished again mightier than ever, his constant presence at Carlton House — these constituted a menace. They determined at all costs to rid themselves of Sheridan. He must be sent forth without delay from the councils of his Party. Then and then only could they anticipate those days of feasting and general rejoicing in which Sheridan would not share.

Some hint of their plans must have filtered through to Richard. He knew how deep was their dislike of him. For himself, he distrusted and despised both with a fine impartiality. They had determined to sever him from the royal master he had served so unselfishly? Sheridan's smile was defiant. No one yet could boast that he had worsted Richard Brinsley Sheridan — at anything. He kept his own counsel, and the ministers planned what His Royal Highness should say to Parliament. They deluged the impatient Prince with tentative drafts and fragmentary paragraphs; they sent couriers hurrying around to Carlton House with revisions and emendations.

Sheridan's reply was eventually adopted and presented before the House soon after the New Year. The paper prepared by Grenville and Grey was returned to them for " correction," and was followed by a few suggestions which Sheridan had written. The two ministers swore that the sentiments in the document were not their own and loudly disclaimed all responsibility for them; when Sheridan attempted to answer them the feeling of hostility among the three men mounted. Grenville wrote the Prince a letter whose every paragraph dripped venom and bitterness toward Sheridan. Richard's reply was a long and circumstantial retelling of the whole incident, and the picture it paints of the two schemers is far from flattering:

> I have only shortly to express my own personal satisfaction — I will use no other word — that I should have been considered by any persons . . . as one so little attached to His Royal Highness . . . as to be held out to *him* whose fairly earned esteem I regard as the first honour and sole reward of my political life . . . in the character of an interested contriver of a double government . . . and an apostate from my former principles. To Lord Grenville I have the honour to be but very little personally known. . . . From Lord Grey, intimately acquainted as he was with every circumstance of my conduct . . . in the years 1788–89, I confess I should have expected a tardy and reluctant interpretation of any circumstance to my disadvantage. As to the nature of my endeavours at that time, I have the written testimonies of Mr. Fox and the Duke of Portland.

Sheridan expressed himself as willing to forego any high office for which he had been considered in favor of Grey. He advised his son Tom to think, as he himself had always thought, of the Party before any personal gratification. Yet Grenville and Grey refused to be pacified. They would make their peace with the Prince on one consideration only — that Sheridan's head fall in the process.

The Privy Council met on January 25th at Carlton House, and His Royal Highness took office, reaffirming his political principles by standing conspicuously close to a bust of Fox during the ceremony. But it was soon obvious that the Prince's allegiance to Fox was purely one of sentiment. Despite Sheridan's frantic efforts he capitulated to Queen Charlotte and his uncle the Duke of Cumberland, and informed Grey and Grenville that they need not trouble themselves about a ministry. Perceval was to retain his old place — some said this was a gesture of respect to the poor mad King. The great days of enlightenment which the Prince's assumption of office were to inaugurate were just as remote as they had always been. " Prinny " was growing heartily sick of ministers and cabinets, and of well-meaning friends who worried him about unimportant trifles. He was far more interested in the pleasant side of being a king, and during the summer of 1811 he antagonized the critics of his short reign by the sumptuous banquet which he gave at Carlton House. It was unlike anything of which the old King had ever dreamed. Down the table's length water flowed, coming from a continually-playing fountain. At the head of the table sat the Prince. His guests were served by footmen wearing medieval armor; behind his chair was a " Royal Crown and His Majesty's cypher, G. R., splendidly illumined." [5]

There were many other reasons to despair of the

[5] From a contemporary account.

Prince's behavior. Conditions among the starving weavers in Glasgow and in the north of England were unspeakable; nowhere was there an overabundance of either food or money. Reports of riots were common, and Londoners read almost every day how regiments had been dispatched here and there to quell the mobs. Through it all the Prince moved, intent on nothing but his own amusement, and the Opposition at length came to realize how little trust they might repose in the Regent. They made terms therefore with that indiscreet but much-harassed woman, his wife the Princess Caroline.

Although the rich man on his great estate or in his magnificent London house might be gazed upon with envy by his less fortunate brother, he was just as dissatisfied with his lot as the meanest beggar — and he felt equally insecure. For Napoleon was still a major menace. He had been held back so far, to be sure, but no one could predict when he might succeed in reaching out to encompass England. At home the first factories were fouling the northern landscapes; the diseases, filth, starvation and wasteful cruelty they brought with them passed blightingly across the lives of the once-contented workers. Strange thoughts moved in the air. Words like " Reform " and " Universal Male Suffrage " and " Catholic Emancipation " upset the digestions of the Opposition's leaders and ruined many a day's shooting.

London, whose population numbered more than one

million, was still surrounded by pretty green gardens and fields through which wide canals wound sleepily. Pimlico, Bayswater, and Hammersmith were entirely rustic, places to which one drove in shining carriages behind smartly stepping horses, and lunched in the stillness under the trees. There were many wealthy people in London — merchants, mostly, and returned " Colonials " — who had built their mansions in Berkeley Square, Portland Place and Hanover Square. The windows of the Bond Street shops attracted thousands of eyes daily, for everybody walked down Bond Street — if only to be seen by everybody else. Gentlemen on their way to White's or Brooks' or Watier's. Ladies with gossamer scarves clouding their shoulders and reticules swinging from their wrists, in quest of a new bonnet, the latest in French gloves — or a gallant.

The day of the great dandy was in its radiant noon. His Royal Highness might be the First Gentleman of Europe, but there was in England one man whose slightest word carried more weight than the Prince's. That man was George Bryan Brummel. His praise of a cravat set the fashion, and to the dictates of Fashion even Royalty must bow. Brummel was the Prince of Dandies, and he had a legion of disciples. In the late hours of the afternoon and on through twilight they walked abroad in Hyde Park — " reserved," notes a contemporary observer, " for persons of rank and fashion." The sunlight glanced blindingly away from the sides of their tall varnished boots ; their collars were stiff, their coats long and full-skirted. Thus one might see the Duke of York and Lord Alvanley, whom Byron regarded as a " delightful companion, brilliant, witty and playful "; Lord Sefton and " Poodle " Byng. Sometimes Mr. Brummel joined them in their stroll, and then they seemed all at once exaggerated caricatures of his own effortless and supernal elegance. Sometimes the Prince drove by, nodding and smiling as he recognized in the crowd a favored friend. It was a remarkable scene. Surely, thought the Englishman — and with justification — nowhere else in all the world was there anything like the Prince Regent's England.

CHAPTER SEVENTEEN

The Last Speech

THE new century was scarcely ten years old when a startling personality appeared in its skies. He was truly the darling of the gods. He possessed a pale and perfect beauty, great wealth, an ancient and noble lineage, and one of the most authentic and unusual talents ever to emerge in England. He had not been in London many weeks before the town rang with his name. " Byron! " fluttered the ladies at dinners and at dances, where he had made known his disapproval of the intimacies of the waltz. His Lordship's *The Waltz: An Apostrophic Hymn* was not published until February, 1813, but long before Londoners were privileged to read his stanzas they knew that Byron considered the dance a shameless and immoral innovation. The handsome poet fulminated — and everyone went on waltzing. Cannon might roar and brave young men in gleaming uniforms might ride away to die, but orchestras everywhere played on above the fury of battle their lilting melodies in three-quarter time. Milliners waltzed, and brokers' clerks; governesses, ladies and gentlemen; even diplomats suc-

[259]

cumbed to this wild and contagious pleasure. On and on they whirled — until in 1814 Prince de Ligne remarked, "The Congress of Vienna does not walk, but it dances."

Fathers and husbands and brothers of the waltzing ladies, meeting the poet in drawing-rooms or passing him in Hyde Park, muttered "Byron!" and scowled until he moved away.

The critics, too, exclaimed "Byron!," but their tone was full of admiration, for they had just read the first published cantos of *Childe Harold's Pilgrimage,* and neither the author's money nor his morals concerned them as much as his amazing facility of rhyme and felicity of phrase.

Sheridan had made Byron's acquaintance at the time when a prologue was being sought for his mother's *Nourjahad.* Thirty years stretched between them. When he looked at Byron Sheridan saw himself as he had been in that wonderful year 1775 — young, handsome, successful, with the world at his feet. Byron sensed in Sheridan a fellow-Arcadian — consumed by the same desires, tortured by the same fears. He had already apostrophized him in *English Bards and Scotch Reviewers:*

> Oh! Sheridan! if aught can move thy pen,
> Let Comedy assume her throne again;
> Abjure the mummery of German schools;
> Leave new *Pizarros* to translating fools;
> Give, as thy last memorial to the age,
> One classic drama, and reform the stage.

Constantly they encountered one another. At one of the Regent's parties; at Melbourne House, that divided and distracted ménage, where downstairs Lady Melbourne, who had been one of "Prinny's" loves, smiled graciously upon her guests, and upstairs her daughter-in-law Lady Caroline Lamb sobbed over a love-letter from Byron. To one of the Prince's banquets Byron came, flushed and excited because he had just spoken for the first time in the House of Lords. He found His Royal Highness drunk, quarreling with those who attempted to soothe him, raining raucous maledictions upon the heads of Grey and Grenville. It was a sight to unman the strongest, and the Regent's daughter, who was present, burst into a flood of frightened tears. Sheridan led her away to a quiet antechamber, and Byron, upon whom the scene had made a profound impression, wrote some verses.

> Weep daughter of a royal line,
> A Sire's disgrace, a realm's decay;
> Ah! happy if each tear of thine
> Could wash a Father's guilt away!
>
> Weep — for thy tears are Virtue's tears —
> Auspicious to these suffering Isles;
> And be each drop in future years
> Repaid thee by thy People's smiles.[1]

On May 11, 1812, the prodigious Perceval was killed by a maniac. His death left vacant an important position, one which the Regent was certain to fill by the

[1] Published in the *Morning Chronicle*, March 7, 1812.

[261]

appointment of a " new " man. For His Royal Highness had fallen completely under the sway of Lady Hertford; it was understood that he would find places for her friends and pull down the juiciest plums for her protégés. Lady Hertford had sponsored Lord Yarmouth, who made no concealment of his disapproval of Lord Moira and the other surviving Foxites. Sheridan realized that he, too, stood outside the charmed circle of Yarmouth's favor, but the years had not yet taught him how to turn his coat according to the prevailing political mode. He still believed as he had always believed on three fundamental issues: the absolute freedom of the Press; the continuation of the Peninsular War until a just and lasting victory had been achieved by England; the Catholic Emancipation.

This last troubled the Regent's slumbers. The days of his youth, when he had spoken out so uncompromisingly in favor of Catholic Emancipation, lived on to haunt him in the person of Sheridan, who flatly refused to vote against such a Bill. Every year the Prince grew to resemble his father more, and when the merest mention of the Catholic question caused him to fall into a fit of hysterical weeping, it was only logical that doubts as to his sanity should be raised. Those domestic intrigues which had colored so much of the Prince's life had erected in the Court four rigidly marked camps: Princess Caroline vs. Princess Charlotte vs. the old Queen, George III's unhappy wife, vs. the Prince Regent himself. His Royal Highness was accustomed to his own way. For even those who might deny the man could not very well refuse the Prince. But Sheridan remained firm alike to blandishments and to threats, although he regretted having incurred " the appearance of ungrateful neglect and disrespect towards the Person to whom I am most obliged on earth."

Sheridan cannot wholly be blamed for failing to see that by opposing the Prince he was hastening his own political doom. His health was worse. He thought more frequently now about rest and relief from pain than about trying to achieve that greatness which, despite all his efforts, he still could not claim. He attended parties and drank as much as ever. Byron has recorded many of their heroic evenings in 1812. " It occasionally fell to my lot to convoy him home — no sinecure, for he was so tipsy that I was obliged to put on his cock'd hat for him; to be sure it tumbled off again, and I was not myself so sober as to be able to pick it up."

He had a persistent choking cough. He was giddy at times ; he worried poor Hecca continually about the mysterious nature of his malady, from which he knew he would not recover. He thought a lot about death, and speculated how one attained that calm and detached resignation with which the sane man approached eternity. But his philosophical contemplations were soon shattered. Once again there was tragedy among the Sheridans.

It struck this time at Tom, Elizabeth's son. He had

inherited from his mother not only her features but a predisposition to that illness which had brought about her death. Tom was a young man, actually only a few years past thirty, but the doctors had told him gravely that he must leave England and go to a milder climate if he wished to live. They suggested Madeira. To Tom Sheridan they might just as well have suggested the moon. He had no money, having always lived well and indulged himself after the fashion of the true gentleman. His departure from England would mean the abrupt conclusion of his political life, and even if he should survive physically it would be without any hope of sharing in the bounties of his Party.

He appealed to his father. Listening, Richard wept tears of loving pity for his son and of impotent rage at his own inability to aid him. He was penniless. Then at last he thought of Samuel Whitbread and his heart grew easier, as though his purse were already heavy with guineas to give to Tom. Whitbread had never failed him; it was inconceivable that Whitbread could hear of Tom's plight and remain unmoved.

But Samuel Whitbread was himself fast nearing the tragic hour when his mind would crack, when his own hand would lodge a bullet in his breast. He informed Sheridan coldly that he would not yield up a single farthing of that sum which could be realized on Sheridan's share in Drury Lane until he was certain no prior lien of any kind existed on that share. Father and son pleaded, alternately begging and cursing, but Whitbread stood his ground. He could do nothing, he told them. They must possess themselves in patience, and wait. Wait they did, with each day a century, and Tom saying ruefully sometimes that the money, when it came, could be used to purchase six feet of ground for him in England, since he doubted he would ever see Madeira now. At last Whitbread was satisfied; the Sheridans might have their money. And he presented it to them, thousands of pounds not in cash, but in " shares " of the Drury Lane Theatre. . . .

Whitbread's refusal to advance him money may have hastened Tom Sheridan's death. No one can say definitely. But there can be no shred of doubt that by denying Sheridan sufficient funds to carry an election he accomplished his permanent defeat. Sheridan was now without any post at all, either theatrical or political. The wheel had turned full circle; he was back once more at the same place where he had stood in 1773, when he had first journeyed up to London. His friend Lord Moira, to whom he had appealed, was unable to form a ministry — and consequently unable to assist Sheridan. No one could aid him, it seemed; and he had long been powerless to help himself.

There began for Richard Sheridan a time of perpetual worry. Presently his creditors would grow bolder, and since he could no longer claim the old Parliamentary immunity he knew only too well what was the fate which mocked him. Two things in his life had received from him an unfaltering devotion — the Prince Regent and the Party — and from both he had in turn received nothing. Neither recompense nor favor, he thought grimly, nor a safe place to lay his tired grizzled head.

"A devil haunts thee in the likeness of a fat old man." A stubborn fat man, one who made short shrift of the Whigs and their "advanced" counsels. The Regent had found his voice, and its roar was unmistakable. There ensued an upheaval. When calm had been restored the Whigs were out, where they remained until the great days of Reform, in 1832. The country belonged now to Lord Liverpool and the Tories.

> Where are the Grenvilles? turned as usual; where
> My friends the Whigs? exactly where they were.[2]

It was a blow to Moira. He had been outplayed by Florizel, by the gross and unfeeling "Fat Boy." He marched past the flunkies and through the corridors of Carlton House, and confronted the Regent, who appeared somewhat apprehensive over his visit. He was come, announced Moira, to make his last bow to His Royal Highness before quitting the country.

Now the Prince was indeed disturbed. Moira had been invaluable in the old days about which he preferred not to think too often. Why not again? He leaned forward and whimpered that he wished his old friend would remain.

"You must never desert me, Moira," whined the Fat Boy.

[2] Lord Byron in *Don Juan*.

But Moira knew that his departure was not desertion. He loved the Prince; he asked nothing better
than to die in his service. Yet now he must go.

"When the friends and counsels you have chosen
shall have brought your throne to totter beneath you,"
he exclaimed, "you will then see one by your side to
sink, if it should so please God, under its ruins with
you."

The Regent could not move him. He sighed and
even wept a little, for he knew he would never look
upon Moira's like again. Then he conferred upon his
erstwhile minister the order of St. George, and Lord
Moira departed with his ribbon and his inflexible principles to govern Bengal.

The black waters of infamy and oblivion were closing over Sheridan's head. He heard himself condemned on every side, reviled as a turncoat, as the
basest political hireling. He had betrayed Yarmouth
— even the Regent himself. In all the vast treasuries
of the English language no one appeared able to find
for Sheridan a single kind and condoning word.
Sheridan resolved to answer his accusers and clear his
name. He who had neither riches nor rank to leave
behind him desired passionately to bequeath to Tom
and Charles Brinsley Sheridan the legacy of an un-
sullied name.

> Hard is his fate on whom the public gaze
> Is fixed forever to detract or praise;
> Repose denies her requiem to his name,

And Folly loves the martyrdom of Fame.
The secret enemy whose sleepless eye
Stands sentinel — accuser — judge — and spy.[3]

On three separate occasions he attempted to address
the House in his own defense. The first was on June
15, 1812. When he found himself unable to continue
because of a sudden weakness he postponed his speech
and resumed it two days later. But his illness and his
anguish, to which must be added the very real panic
at the state to which he was now reduced, combined
to take from him all his powers. No longer could he
hypnotize his hearers, "charming," as they had once
said of him, "the very birds off the trees." No longer
did they rise and cheer each flashing, crystalline
phrase, as in the grand days of the Hastings trial.
Fountains of oratory had gushed from him for unin-
terrupted hours, without the slightest diminution of
vigor or the slightest sign of fatigue. Now he faced his
audience halting, unable to proceed. Once his jaws
locked stubbornly, and while the House jibed and
mocked him he stood mute, trembling with shame and
rage. He moved to have published all those documents which had passed between him and the Prince,
but the motion was set aside. The entire nation as
well as his peers appeared determined to condemn him
without even the semblance of a trial.

A few of his former colleagues recognized how grave
was his condition. They advised Sheridan to spare
himself, suggesting that he ask for an adjournment

[3] Byron's *Monody on the Death of the Rt. Hon. R. B. Sheridan.*

[268]

until his health was improved. But Sheridan laughed them down and disparaged his illness. In his heart he pleaded for no false sympathy; if they would only hear him through in honesty and fairness he knew he would manage to survive until the trial was over.

"I have differed from him [the Prince]," he told his audience, "at times in opinion, and I have differed from the Party with which I am connected because I loved what I conceived to be the welfare of my country better than the approbation of either." Ringing words! In another day those who listened would have thrilled to their clarion. Now they sat before him, still, expressionless. But he knew what they were thinking; the silence crackled with it. There was a sentence from Cicero spinning around in his tired brain. "*Cum tacent, clamant.*" When they are silent they cry aloud. He shut his eyes a moment, but it was no use. Behind his eyelids he could still see those frozen faces. He forced himself to go on.

"The income I derived from the bounty of the Prince I will explain." His voice broke several times while he poured forth the pitiful tale of his receivership of the Duchy of Cornwall; of Lord Elliott's death, and how until Lord Lake's death four years later Sheridan had not drawn a shilling from the "sinecure" he had been awarded. So harrowed was he by the recital of those ancient wrongs that he could not speak, and was forced to consent to a two-day's adjournment.

On June 19th he resumed his speech. The temper of the audience was unchanged. Not a single sympathetic glance reached across to lend him courage. This time he told them about the problem of Catholic Emancipation, which from the first he had believed essential to the safety and prosperity of the realm. " I will never give my vote to any administration that opposes Catholic Emancipation. Nor will I even receive a furlough on that question, though a ministry were carrying every other that I wished. . . . If they were to be the last words I should ever utter in this House, I should say, ' Be just to Ireland as you value your own honour, be just to Ireland as you value your own peace.' " But it no longer mattered what Sheridan said or thought. He was a failure — his great days were in the past, and not a few of his hearers had been infants in their cradles when *The School for Scandal* was produced, or when the trial of Warren Hastings was news. They were listening now not to a distinguished playwright, a peerless orator, but to a feeble and querulous old man who had been accused of shamelessly deserting from his Party.[4]

On June 21st, when he appeared before the House for the last time, he touched on the French negotiations for peace. " Submission to France! " he thundered, and his listeners shivered. That voice, that menacing outthrust finger, that stern, unbending look — it was the old Sheridan restored to them, and they welcomed his return with frantic applause. Na-

[4] Byron indignantly refuted that charge in a letter to Tom Moore which he wrote from Venice July 1, 1818. The Whigs, he declared, had abandoned Sheridan, using him as long as they might derive benefit from his efforts, then tossing him aside.

poleon's ultimate defeat was still a year or so away;
he sought now not only peace with England but also
her assistance in the form of troops and money, and
it was Sheridan's avowed purpose to reveal his in-
famous schemings. "Not an Englishman lives who
would not perish rather than consent to it. To com-
mence a dishonourable negotiation is little less reprehensible than to conclude a dishonourable peace. . . .
Napoleon's sole object was to destroy our maritime
superiority. . . . Even Great Britain for her rights
and honours might spend her treasure . . . and yet
at last might fall. Yet after the general subjugation
and ruin of Europe, should there exist a historian to
record the awful events that produced the universal
calamity, let that historian, after describing the greatness and the glory of Britain, have to say, 'She fell
and with her fell all the best securities for the chari-
ties of human life, for the power and honour, the fame,
the glory, and the liberties of the whole civilized
world.' "

CHAPTER EIGHTEEN

Curtain

SHERIDAN was out of Parliament. He had nothing but his debts and his poor health, and he re-marked wryly that sooner or later one or the other must make an end of him. Before his departure for Bengal Lord Moira had taken the Regent to task for his conduct toward Sheridan. The Duke of Norfolk was prepared to sell a seat in Parliament for four thousand pounds. His Grace would contribute one thousand pounds, if Mr. Sheridan could manage the rest. The Prince promised Moira to make up the deficit. But this would have established Sheridan as the Duke's political henchman, and he refused to wear any man's livery. Shortly afterward he learned that the seat of Wooton Bassett was available for three thousand pounds, and Sheridan declared with a flash of his old pride that if His Royal Highness would " lend " him the money without any claims upon him, he would offer himself as a candidate. When he discovered this, Samuel Whitbread promised to pay Sheridan the two thousand pounds he owed him on the somewhat pe-culiar condition that Sheridan consent to remain out of Parliament. Because his spirit was so completely broken, because he was certain he could never summon the strength needed to come before a hostile House, Sheridan agreed.

The Regent said that Whitbread's money was paid to Sheridan to leave his service. He made the additional allegation that Sheridan had obtained three thousand pounds from him — without offering anything in return. Sheridan now found himself the storm-center of another scandal — not quite twelve months after his speeches before the House of Commons had resulted in the dubious satisfaction of having the charges " withdrawn " without a verdict which would definitely clear him of their stigma. The three thousand pounds promised him by the Regent had been paid, not to Sheridan himself, but to Cocker and Fonblanque, his solicitors, who had been instructed to part with it only to the man who controlled Wooton Bassett. But the Prince swore roundly that Sheridan and Cocker between them had cooked up a little scheme of their own. Cocker was to take the money to settle one of Sheridan's debts to him; whereupon Sheridan would explain the circumstance by stating that Cocker had embezzled the money. Like so many of the tempests which had raged about him, this one blew itself out before long, but Sheridan was becoming too weary for such buffetings. When the House met for its first session in 1813, however, the member from Wooton Bassett was not Mr. Sheridan.

He was still trying to find his way back into Parliament, for he had begun to regret the promise he had given Samuel Whitbread. To this end he feverishly kept up all his contacts with the Great World. He continued his correspondence with Lord and Lady Holland, he called on Lady Westmoreland, he dined with Lady Cork. As at the outset of his career he searched each roomful of people for someone willing to take up the cudgels for him — and able to stand the expense. "What a wreck is that man," Byron noted in 1813, "and all from bad pilotage; for no one had ever better gales, though now and then a little too squally." As that sentence stands it might serve for Byron's own epitaph.

Hester Jane Sheridan, who had been the very breath of buoyant gaiety, now began to droop. She too was ill. She smiled and shook her head when Sheridan questioned her about her health; when he pleaded with her to consult a physician Hester Jane promised that she would. Whether or not she did he never knew, for she always said that she was feeling better, and dear Richard was not to trouble about her but to take care of himself. So they clung to each other for comfort, two sick and frightened people, and the darkness closed about them.

Money was scarce. There were days when they dined on very little; when there was no fire in the grate and only one short candle to pierce the shadows with its feeble flame. They had removed to lodgings, but they found in their surroundings only squalor and not security. The bailiff's men were gaining on them fast.

For all its outspread vastness London was not large enough to hide the Sheridans from the sheriff and his officers.

Someone told the Prince of Sheridan's plight, but His Royal Highness only sneered and called him a " damned neutral." Afterwards he expatiated on what he had heard and even added a few details. " He now took to live in a very low way, and all he looked for in the company he kept was brandy and water." Yet this was scarcely the truth, for the " company he kept " in those closing months of 1813 was the finest in the land. Sheridan's purse might have been so empty that as he said himself he'd be forced to apologize to any footpad who snatched it from him. But his wit was as keen and trenchant as ever, his conversation as diverting. When he sat at the tables of the great he sang for his supper.

Those brilliant gatherings which Samuel Rogers assembled listened enraptured to Sheridan. He talked effortlessly for hours, and never for a single instant did his prodigious powers seem to flag. Lord Byron sat beside him during many of these evenings, spellbound with the rest. " I have seen him," he recalled years later, " cut up Whitbread, quiz Mme. de Staël, and annihilate Colman."

The Frenchwoman, whom Byron thought " too, too clever " — but then he had never been attracted to women of intellectual attainments — was the rage of London that season. Everyone fêted her. Her most inane remark was repeated and examined for concealed philosophical profundities. But her fame failed to impress Sheridan, for since she had been exiled by Napoleon she had changed her political complexion — and Sheridan still abhorred apostasy. "*He* talked," continued Byron, "and *we* listened without one yawn from six until one in the morning."

But when he walked home in the cold and pitiless light of early morning the exhilaration of Rogers' party left him. His head throbbed, and there was that pain again, prodding him with an insistent finger. Wretchedness was abroad early in the mean streets down which he passed, for the Sheridans' neighbors were all very humble folk who could not afford to lie long abed. Hecca too was awake; perhaps, thought Richard, she had not gone to sleep all night. She sat with a shawl pinned across her shoulders, for although it was August and the weather quite oppressive Hecca never seemed able to get warm. She had started when the door closed behind him, and a spasm of pain crossed Sheridan's face. Poor soul! Dreaming of the bailiffs again! He tried to speak to her, but he was of a sudden speechless. The man who had talked for seven hours to Rogers' guests had not a syllable for his wife. But Hecca understood. With little dragging steps she brought him his threadbare dressing-gown and a bowl of warm and fortifying punch. "Dear Richard!" she said softly, and her pale lips brushed against his cheek.

They were alone in two bare dark rooms. Charles was away at a school "for gentlemen," happily ignorant of the poverty of his parents. Tom had departed from England forever. He had the post of Colonial Treasurer at the Cape of Good Hope, and that was a splendid thing truly, since he need not ask his father for money, and the mere fact that he had some work to do would keep him from brooding about his health. Richard and Hecca talked of him often, though they never mentioned the illness which had sent him away from England. Desperately they strove to maintain the fiction that Tom was at the Cape to further his career.

At last the bailiff and his minions caught up with Richard Sheridan. He had eluded them always; even when they found him his nimble tongue had kept him out of prison. But now he was old and his words came slowly. And there was a new generation of bailiffs in the land to whom his name meant nothing. In August, 1813, he was arrested and thrown into a Cursitor Street spunging-house for a debt of six hundred pounds which he had expected to pay out of funds due him from Drury Lane. Distractedly he wrote to Whitbread: " Putting all false professions of friendship and feeling out of the question, you have no *right* to keep me here! For it is in truth *your* act. If you had not forcibly withheld from me the twelve thousand pounds . . . I should at least have been out of reach of this miserable insult — for that and that only lost me my seat in Parliament." For three days he waited, torn between fury at Whitbread and fear lest he pay no attention to his letter. Then on the morning of the fourth day Samuel Whitbread arrived, calm and unruffled. He handed over six hundred pounds and obtained Sheridan's release.

They say that Sheridan wept as he walked home beside Whitbread through the bright windy sunshine. Freedom was his once more — but for how long, and for what? He regarded those three days of horror from which he had just emerged as a prelude to all the similar days to come. For this reason his tears fell unchecked. It was a terrible blow to his pride that he, Richard Brinsley Sheridan who had once been Fortune's darling, must end his days in a filthy prison. He wept too for Whitbread, the man at his side, who had betrayed him, and upon whom he nevertheless still depended.

Before the year was out he had one small taste of the old happy times. Lord Essex took him to Drury Lane. He sat again in a stage-box and watched while Edmund Kean — he was the favorite of the pit these days — thrilled the house. When the curtains closed after the first act he slipped unnoticed from the box and his feet found their way backstage to the greenroom. There was a crowd assembled; he heard Byron's laughter. Suddenly he felt frightened of the actors and the people who joked and talked with them. He stood in the doorway, timidly. Then someone recognized him. There were shouts of " Sheridan! Sheridan! " Hands reached out to pull at his coatsleeves. He was dragged over toward the fire and a glass of brandy thrust upon him. The warmth of his old friends' welcome moved him so deeply that he could only stand there muttering "Thank you!" over and over in a shaking voice. But he raised his glass and emptied it to the toast one of them proposed. "Good health, and a speedy return to Drury Lane!"

They fired cannon on the first day of January, 1814. Those muffled shots shattering the dawn were to be the *motifs* which characterized the New Year. For during 1814 many guns would be fired and many heads would fall. Sir John Moore died at Corunna, and the nation mourned in united sympathy the passing of a great and noble heart. Across the stormy Irish Sea guns roared; the Corn Rioters terrorized Dublin and other cities, and country houses were razed to the ground. A spate of bitter words rushed through the House over Home Rule. Europe, which had been quiescent of late, rocked once again with a new disaster. The news from abroad was incredible, presaging the renewal of war and the continuation of panic and hard times. Napoleon had escaped from Elba! [1] Hardly had those dreadful words been received in London when new intelligences kept arriving as fast as the swiftest messengers could bring them. He was at Marseilles. . . . He was marching northward, northward, gaining on Paris. . . . Behind him marched an army, recruited no one knew whence. Ten thousand . . . half a million? Who could say

[1] February 27th.

whether the ghosts of all his dead legions had not risen to follow once again the Corsican's blood-soaked standard?

"So all is over in France!" wrote Sheridan. "And Napoleon is again Emperor! Good God, what an event!"

A kind of lurid and frightful red broods over those ultimate hours of Napoleon's return. The world had believed itself safely rid of him; he had been banished like one of the deposed Titans and flung into the outer darkness. Two months passed; a third. Yet still cannons shook across Europe, and the fields that should have been bright with tall and supple grain were trampled by the charging cavalry. All the world united in pursuit of the squat figure in the green coat, until behind the whitewashed farm buildings at La Haye Sainte the chase ended. Before the year was over the threat of Napoleon had been blotted out forever.

Richard Sheridan and his wife had grown to loathe London. The metropolis was filled with strangers, to most of whom the name Sheridan was a synonym for a bad debt. They packed their meager belongings and set out in quest of health. They journeyed from Windsor to Bristol and to the Isle of Wight, an ailing woman and a broken aging man, exhausted by days in a post-chaise and sleepless nights spent in strange beds. Wherever the coach stopped they sought the advice of physicians, for neither Hecca nor Richard attempted now to conceal their illness from each other. He was racked by interminable fits of coughing; his appetite failed; he paced up and down the inhospitable inn bedrooms and longed pitifully for a quiet place in which to close his eyes. The play was almost over. Their money too was practically gone. One morning they boarded the London coach, and clinging tightly to each other's hands they watched the familiar towns and villages pass outside their window until the postillions' whips crackled for the last time, and the coach rumbled through the archways of the city.

In his absence his creditors had grown more persistent. Sheridan pawned the few things which remained to him — the books presented on happier occasions by his friends, a suit of clothes, and the silver cup which he had once received from his constituents at Stafford. Some pictures painted by Gainsborough were sold for a few hundred pounds; finally he was compelled to part with the portrait of Elizabeth Sheridan as St. Cecilia. It was like losing Elizabeth a second time. He cried whenever he looked at the empty place upon the wall which still retained the faintly discernible outline of the picture's frame. There was nothing left except the clothes he and Hecca stood in and the bed in which they lay beside each other when darkness fell.

Hecca wrote to Peake, the treasurer of Drury Lane and for many years a close friend of her husband's, begging him to favor them with ten pounds. She wrote again. Could he spare a few pounds for a creditor

DRURY LANE THEATER, 1809

From an old engraving

more importunate than the rest? " Even two would be acceptable."

The Regent heard that Richard Sheridan was dying in poverty in a foul and filthy house in Savile Row, and His Royal Highness had an instant's recollection of other days, when Sheridan had been rich and they had both been young and handsome. Something stirred in his heart. Compassion? Remorse? Regret for the days which were gone and would have no tomorrows? He dispatched " Hat " Vaughan, his crony, to offer the friend of his youth two hundred pounds and to promise him three hundred more. But Sheridan, who slept upon a bed with patched sheets and a torn counterpane, who had nothing at all in his pockets save holes, was not to be bought for five hundred pounds. He thanked the Regent for his offer and Mr. Vaughan for his trouble, but he would not accept a farthing. With his hand at his side to still the tearing pain in his chest he politely escorted Mr. Vaughan to the door.

There was no one left in London to whom he could appeal. On May 15, 1816, he scratched a few lines with a hand whose trembling made the characters almost illegible, and sent the note around to Samuel Rogers. Rogers was wealthy; he was generous. He was also, as the author of *The Pleasures of Memory,* a fellow artist.

14, Savile Row.

I find things settled so that one hundred fifty pounds will remove all difficulty. I am absolutely undone and brokenhearted. . . . They are going to put the carpets out of the windows and break into Mrs. Sheridan's room and *take me* — for God's sake let me see you!

A tear dropped upon his hand as he wrote the last words. If he were taken off to prison who would care for Hecca? It was days since she had felt strong enough to leave her bed. Without him she must surely die. And though Richard had learned at last how merciful death can be, he wanted to spare Hecca the terror of facing the end alone.

It was past midnight when his note arrived. But lights still brightened the windows of the banker's house, for Rogers was entertaining Tom Moore, and there was laughter and good talk, and tables gleaming with silver plate. Rogers read the note and the laughter in the room ceased. In that folded piece of paper Death had crossed the threshold. Presently the guests departed. The last carriage clattered away, and one by one the rooms grew dark as the sleepy footmen put up the shutters and snuffed out the candles.

Early next morning Moore hurried around to Savile Row. He brought the money which Rogers had sent and gave it to Sheridan. This morning the sick man was feeling a bit more sanguine. He was always worst at night. During the day his hopes rose, he made plans, he envisioned bright years ahead when he and Hecca should be miraculously restored in health, when an adequate income, derived each day from another impossible source, should sustain them both in luxurious comfort. Then the lengthening twilight shadows fell across the room. Hecca lit their solitary candle and prepared the evening meal. And in the grim and brooding darkness the dreams of the day vanished; each evening he repeated with the poet, "The heart knoweth its own bitterness." He told Moore of a final edition of his dramatic works which was being prepared, and as he spoke his eyes brightened with eagerness. Surely such an edition must have a tremendous sale. The profits resulting would be huge — they *must* be — and the tide of disaster would be turned at last. He could repay Rogers; he could settle with all the world.

Later in the day Smyth, who had been his son Tom's tutor, called to see him. But the high mood with which he had faced Moore had gone. He felt very weak, and he knew that even if the final edition were completed he would never see a penny. So he sent his regrets to Mr. Smyth, waiting in the dismal " parlour " of their apartment, where the dust grimed the furniture and Mrs. Sheridan begged him to partake of some refreshment — lest he go away convinced that their meager establishment contained nothing. " Do let me find you something, Mr. Smyth! " she insisted. He was much too ill, said Sheridan, to receive visitors. Smyth promised that he would return next day; when he did, Sheridan was worse, and Smyth never saw him alive again.

It was June. There were flowers everywhere — even an occasional draggled geranium in Savile Row

[285]

— and the sky remained bright and opalescent until almost nine. Readers of the *Morning Post* were astonished and not a little upset to learn from an article by Mr. Denis O'Brien that Richard Brinsley Sheridan was actually dying in their midst — and in the most dreadful circumstances. Mr. O'Brien was acutely conscious of a fellow Irishman's plight. He urged the generous people of London to assist the poet who was surely one of his country's brightest luminaries. " I say *Life* and *Succour* against Westminster Abbey and a Funeral! " The generous people of London finished O'Brien's article — and disciplined their harrowed sensibilities. A sheriff's officer would actually have seized Sheridan in his bed and blankets had it not been for the intervention of his old friend Dr. Bain.

To his brother Tom at the southernmost tip of Africa Charles Sheridan wrote afterwards that their father had " every attention which could make a death-bed easy." For young Charles possessed his share of the Sheridan family pride, and he could not bring himself to set forth on paper the pity and terror of Richard's last moments. Furthermore he knew how ill Tom himself was, and how few were the days of warm windless sunshine which yet remained to him. And so he penned his tragic and pathetic lie, and the dying man half a world away read it, and was solaced.

Denis O'Brien's appeal bore fruit slowly. Days passed and still no one came publicly to Sheridan's assistance. Not a carriage stopped before the house in Savile Row. The world of fashion pondered the tying of a cravat and exchanged the latest scandal. A few days more dragged by, and then suddenly the swarm descended. Gentlemen and ladies in carriages with armorial bearings upon the doors. Cobwebby muslins and sibilant taffetas; handsome waistcoats and glistening boots; scarves and reticules, scents and snuffboxes. The Duke of York's carriage waited behind His Grace of Argyle's. Lady Bessborough called shortly after the two royal gentlemen had departed. The walls of Sheridan's room dissolved like mist as he listened to her talk, and he smiled happily, imagining himself once more dancing under the great chandeliers at Devonshire House. She was still so beautiful. No matter how tightly they might nail down the lid of his coffin, mused Sheridan, he would still be able to look through it at Lady Bessborough's lovely eyes.

Samuel Rogers came every day. His was the face which Sheridan delighted most to see, and his the only voice save Hecca's which soothed his tortured spirits.

The nation celebrated the first anniversary of the victory at Waterloo, the restoration of sanity and order and the *status quo*. Napoleon was yesterday's nightmare. Impossible to think how once he had terrorized a world which basked now in the sunshine of the Congress of Vienna. Sheridan lay in his bed listening to the commemorative cannon far away, while Hecca sat in the window and described as best she could the people passing in the streets on their way to the parades. She herself was none too well that day. She was very frightened, for Dr. Bain and his colleagues had advised surgery as the only means of restoring Richard's health. Hecca knew that they were simply washing their hands of him, for operations were dreadful things, and only one in every hundred patients recovered. The next day the physicians had changed their minds and Hecca breathed a little easier, since all talk of an operation was forever quieted. But though the doctors expressed themselves satisfied with the patient's condition, to the loving and anguished eyes of his wife he appeared to be growing worse each day.

He continued to talk to her, but she noticed toward the end of the week after the anniversary of Waterloo that his sentences were incoherent, often meaningless. His mind was wandering. He lay staring at the ceiling through long hours, and Hecca's heart froze within her as she listened. He was talking to Elizabeth, to Tom — not a dying man in South Africa, but a tall boy home from school with jests about the masters and complaints about his lessons. Lady Cork, Lady Westmoreland, the Duke of Portland, Pitt, Fox — they were all in that dismal room beside her, crowding her away from the bed. The voice went on — snatches now of the famous speech which he had delivered at the trial of Warren Hastings, when Hecca was a curly-haired child romping in her father's garden. " Richard! " she implored him. " You must rest! " But she could not quiet him; at night when she lay at his side Hecca could hear his voice, even though she could not distinguish his words.

At last his tongue was stilled; he was unconscious. She was now more terrified than ever. When he had raved so endlessly she had known at least that Richard lived. Now as she tiptoed to the bed's side and peered into his still face she realized that so would he lie at last, when the feeble spark which warmed him would have burned itself out. The man on the bed was not Richard, but a simulacrum. With his hands crossed on his breast and his eyes closed he was her husband's statue, that likeness with which they would presently decorate his tomb. She sat beside him, straightening his covers, patiently forcing some thin broth between his pale lips. Sometimes she felt that she too was dead, like Richard; that they both were in their graves together. At such times she prayed that the dream might swiftly become the reality.

The calendar told her that it was July. For days the weather had been sultry, and through their opened windows came the reeking odor of the slums. On July 4th Sheridan regained consciousness long enough to take his last farewells of his wife. Then he closed his eyes once more, and Hecca took up her station beside his quiescent form. The following day the Bishop of London was summoned, and administered the Eucharist. Again the rooms were still. Hester Jane Sheridan sat with her fingers pressed against her husband's feeble pulse. The sun went down outside her window and night fell, and Richard's tired heart still beat. He lived all through that night and the next day and night, but on the 7th of July the thread beneath Hecca's fingers snapped at last. Richard Brinsley Sheridan, aged sixty-five, had died in his sleep.

The news of his passing shocked London into a realization of its loss. One of the few remaining Titans of the grand old century was gone. " There is no one," Creevey declared, " to take the chair he leaves." It was decided at once that he must be buried in Westminster Abbey, and the historic pile where he had touched the pinnacle of his glory threw open its doors to receive him. Sheridan had always hoped to rest in the Abbey beside Charles James Fox, but the Whig leaders could not grant that honor to a man who had been publicly tried for apostasy to his Party. A place was prepared for him near Garrick, at whose obsequies long ago, it was recalled, Sheridan had been chief mourner. The day of his funeral saw the city of London determined to do him honor. People leaned from windows and collected thickly in the streets to watch his coffin pass, and to gape at the princes and prelates who solemnly followed it. Though Grey and Grenville did not attend, the Duke of Bedford — Portland's successor as head of the Party — was one of the pallbearers. Behind him came Lord Spencer and Lord Holland, Lord Lauderdale, the Bishops of London, of York and of Sussex, the Duke of York, Sidmouth and Canning. The trappings of the horses gleamed, the magnificent clothes of all the assembled dignitaries shone blindingly when the sunlight pointed across them. The splendor of the occasion becomes even more remarkable when one remembers the dead man's last lonely hours. Today there was no one in England who failed to do him reverence; a short month ago he could have numbered his friends upon the fingers of one hand — with a finger or two to spare.

The ostentation and display which characterized Sheridan's funeral infuriated Tom Moore, who had been one of the faithful. He published in the *Morning Chronicle* some stanzas whose lilting measure seems a somewhat ill-chosen vehicle for indignation:

> Oh, it sickens the heart to see bosoms so hollow,
>   And friendship so false in the great and high-born;
> To think what a long line of titles may follow
>   The relics of him who died friendless and lorn.
>
> How proud they can press to the funeral array
>   Of him whom they shunned in sickness and sorrow,
> How bailiffs may seize his last blanket today,
>   Whose pall shall be held up by nobles tomorrow.

EPILOGUE

Sighing that Nature form'd but one such man,
And broke the die in moulding Sheridan.

— Byron

RICHARD SHERIDAN was spared the two deaths which followed so swiftly upon his own. On September 12, 1817, his son Tom died in the place of his exile; on October 27th of the same year Tom's forty-one-year-old stepmother closed her weary eyes forever, and was laid to rest in Old Windsor churchyard, not far from a ghost of her husband's youth, the beautiful Mary "Perdita" Robinson.

Sheridan was dead. He had been accorded a funeral such as is seldom given to a private citizen; his bones had been interred within the hallowed precincts of the Abbey. But his reputation was not permitted to remain decently with him in the grave. New detractors arose, and since the dead man could no longer speak, however feebly, in his own defense, they shouted their catalogue of Sheridan's crimes from the housetops. His friends took upon themselves the task of answering the charges and silencing the calumnies, — Tom and Peter Moore; Samuel Rogers; Lord Byron; His Royal Highness, the Prince Regent.

"Prinny" seems at first glance decidedly out of place in that galley of Richard Sheridan's faithful friends and staunch supporters. He had done very little for Sheridan all his life. He had even added to the torment of Richard's last months by sneering at his poverty and his politics, when surely the one was the direct result of the other. Yet it is always possible to assume that the Prince, now that Sheridan was gone, had experienced a change of heart. In spite of all his faults the Regent was a shrewd judge of men. Though he might treat them with unmerited harshness and dispose of them lightly, unfeelingly, he could appraise their characters with clarity and precision.

He said to Peter Moore shortly after Sheridan's funeral: " He was a proud man, sir, a proud man with certain conscientious convictions always operating against his own interests. He was a firm friend and a sound adviser, sir, but he was so systematically jealous of his own honour, that he was always willing to grant what he was never willing to solicit in return — favours which might be interpreted as affecting his own independence." Had the Prince seen fit to make that same statement when Sheridan was defending himself before Parliament in 1812, Richard must surely have died a happier as well as a richer man.

Once more His Royal Highness opened his heart to speak on Sheridan. Of all the eulogies and florid tributes, the miles of verse and prose which his admirers produced, nowhere can there be found a more discerning analysis than the Prince's : " He had an astounding confidence in every man, and although his pen indicated a knowledge of human nature, yet that knowl-

edge was confined to his pen alone, for in all his acts
he rendered himself the dupe of the fool and the de-
signing knave."

Ten days after Sheridan's death Byron, at the Villa
Diodati, composed his *Monody*. It was recited by
Mrs. Davison on the stage at Drury Lane on Sep-
tember 7, 1816.

A mighty Spirit is Eclipsed, a Power
Hath passed from Day to Darkness — to whose hour
Of light no likeness is bequeathed — no Name,
Focus at once of all the rays of Fame,
The flash of Wit, the bright Intelligence,
The beam of Sound, the blaze of Eloquence,
Set with their Sun, but still have left behind
The enduring produce of immortal Mind.

. . .

And here, ah! here, where yet all young and warm
The gay creations of his spirit charm,
The matchless dialogue, the deathless wit,
Which knew not what it was to intermit;
The glowing portraits fresh from life, that bring
Home to our hearts the truth from which they spring;
These wondrous beings of his fancy, wrought
To fulness by the Fiat of his thought;
Here in their first abode you still may meet
Bright with the hues of his Promethean heat
A halo of the light of other days
Which still the splendour of its orb betrays.

. . .

Long shall we seek his likeness — long in vain
And turn to all of him which may remain,
Sighing that Nature formed but one such man,
And broke the die — in moulding Sheridan.

Although he is not often accorded his rightful place among them, Richard Brinsley Sheridan belongs in the company of the great English Liberals. Constantly throughout his long Parliamentary career he opposed the Conservative faction, whose point of view differed from his own merely on the question of time. For neither side is in the least averse to novelty and change *per se*. But the Liberal wants all changes to take place in his own immediate lifetime, while the Conservative admires only those changes which have occurred before his birth. Sheridan championed the cause of the oppressed. He spoke for the victims of persecution and injustice; not only in the case of America, but for Ireland and India as well he advocated the adoption of a more enlightened Colonial policy by England. When " dissenters " of whatever shade of religious thought were denied the privilege of the ballot, Sheridan comprehended the folly of such a course and the danger which might eventuate from the suppression of religious minorities. It is largely due to his effort, though the credit is generally distributed elsewhere, that the Catholic Emancipation was accomplished, and that universal male suffrage was established by the Reform Parliament of 1832.

Many of his speeches take on an added significance today when the rights of the individual are threatened and the horizons are darkened by nations which have invested the abstract conception of the State with powers it never possessed and divinities it never claimed. When we read those speeches carefully in the light of present happenings everywhere we cannot fail to be impressed by the fact that the patterns in the tapestry of history always remain fixed. Succeeding generations merely provide new actors for an old and unchanging drama.

Sheridan lived in an age when dishonesty was rampant and corruption was the norm. He himself remained until the end of his days politically incorruptible. The twenty thousand pounds which the Congress of the United States offered him in recognition of his services during the American Revolution he proudly declined. All around him he saw men who had their "price" and who advertised openly the amount for which they could be bought or sold. But Sheridan valued his honor and integrity so highly that no sum of money could ever tempt him into parting with either.

He was extravagant, supremely careless with money; at one time or another he was in debt to half of London. Yet he never accepted a bribe or sold a "place." As for his debts, they were probably no worse than those of his defamers. Byron summed up the whole question in a letter written to Tom Moore from Venice: "Did Fox pay his debts? Were *his* [Sheridan's] intrigues more notorious than those of his contemporaries? And is his memory to be blasted, and theirs respected?"

Sheridan served his Prince and his Party with devotion, with honesty, and with all the resources of a brilliant and energetic mind. "He made as many

sacrifices," Lord Brougham said of him, " as any pro-
fessional man ever did in the cause of a long and hopeless opposition."

His literary reputation needs no defining. It has
grown, not diminished, in the century which has followed his death. Sheridan placed in the firmament
of the English stage some of its brightest stars. He
enriched the language with phrases which have become
proverbial, with sentences so often quoted — and misquoted — that hardly anyone troubles to acknowledge
their authorship. In an age when conversation was a
career and a reputation for wit was prized above riches,
Sheridan was everywhere regarded as the first among
his peers.

Orator, dramatist, poet, satirist, statesman, wit.
" He ran," wrote Tom Moore, " through each mode of
the Lyre, and was Master of all."

Summary

CHRONOLOGY OF SHERIDAN'S LIFE

1751   Born in Dublin, October 12.
1762   Enters Harrow.
1766   Death of his mother, Frances Anne Sheridan.
1770   Sheridan family moves to Bath.
1772   *Aristænetus* published. Elopement with Elizabeth Linley. Duel with Captain Mathews.
1773   Marriage to Elizabeth Linley.
1774   Settles with wife in London.
1775   Sides with rebellious American Colonies.
       The Rivals (January).
       St. Patrick's Day (May).
       Birth of his son Thomas (November).
       The Duenna (November).
1776   Buys in partnership Garrick's half-interest in Theatre Royal, Drury Lane, and subsequently becomes manager.
1777   *A Trip to Scarborough* (February).
       The School for Scandal (May).
1778   Acquires remaining half-share in Drury Lane.
1779   *The Critic* (October).
1780   Member of Parliament for Stafford.
       Thomas Sheridan's *Dictionary of English Language* published.
1782   Under-Secretary of State in Lord Rockingham's cabinet.
1783   Secretary of Treasury in Coalition Government.
1787   First speech against Warren Hastings (February). Speech at trial of Hastings (June).
1788   First Regency Crisis.

1789	Fall of the Bastille. Fox and Sheridan side with the Revolution.
1790	Split with Edmund Burke.
1791	Temporary estrangement with Elizabeth Sheridan.
1792	Reconciled to Elizabeth. She dies in June.
1793	Beginning of war with France.
1794	End of Hastings' trial. Reopening of Drury Lane.
1795	Marriage to Hester Jane Ogle.
1796	Menace of Napoleon. Sheridan subordinates principles to patriotism. Temporary split with Fox.
1797	Naval mutinies at Spithead and the Nore.
1799	*Pizarro.*
1806	Treasurer of Navy in " All the Talents." Death of Fox. Sheridan succeeds Fox as Member for Westminster.
1807	Defeated at Westminster. Becomes Member for Ilchester.
1809	Drury Lane burned.
1811	Second Regency Crisis. Sheridan becomes Prince's chief adviser.
1812	Loses Prince's favor. Defeated for Parliament.
1813	Arrested and imprisoned for debts (August).
1816	Dies, July 7.

Bibliography

Darlington, W. Aubrey: *Sheridan.* London, 1933.
Drinkwater, John: *Charles James Fox.* New York, Cosmopolitan Book Corporation, 1928.
Fitzgerald, P. H.: *Lives of the Sheridans.* 2 vols. London, 1886.
Hamilton, Clayton, (ed.): *Plays by Richard Brinsley Sheridan.* New York, The Macmillan Co., 1926.
Moore, Thomas: *Memoirs of the Life of Richard Brinsley Sheridan.* 2 vols. New York, 1853.
Oliphant, Mrs. M. O.: *Sheridan.* London, 1902.
Petrie, Sir Charles Alexander: *The Four Georges.* Boston, Houghton, Mifflin & Co., 1936.
Quennell, Peter: *Byron: The Years of Fame.* Toronto, The Macmillan Company, 1935.
Rae, W. Fraser: *Sheridan.* 2 vols. New York, 1896.
Rae, W. Fraser: *Wilkes, Sheridan, Fox, and the Opposition under George III.* New York, 1882.
Sichel, W. S.: *Sheridan.* 2 vols. London, 1909.
Sitwell, Edith: *Bath.* Peter Smith, 1936.

Index

Abington, Frances, Mrs., 132
Absolute, Sir Anthony, in The Rivals, 30, 115, 119
Absolute, Capt. Jack, in The Rivals, 115
Acres, Bob, in The Rivals, 115 f., 118
Adam, William, 218
Addington, Dr., 183
Addington, Lord Sidmouth, 225, 231 f., 290
Admiralty, 209 ff., 232
Alcanor, in Mahomet, 34
Alcock, Mr., 239
" All The Talents," 232, 236 f.
Allen, Ralph, 29
Amelia, Princess, 29, 249
America, 110 ff., 122, 133, 143, 184, 190, 192, 213, 297
André, Maj. John, 75
Andrews, Miles Peter, 72
Angelo, 46 f.
Aristænetus, 59
Armistead, Elizabeth Bridget (Mrs. Charles James Fox), 181, 213, 222
Arne, Dr. Thomas, 121, 154
Art of Speaking, The, 36
Avon, 13 f., 80, 91 f.

Backbite, Sir Benjamin, in The School for Scandal, 200

Bain, Dr., 286 f.
Bastille, 189, 194
Bath, 13 ff., 22–29, 58, 60 f., 63 ff., 72, 75, 80, 82, 84 f., 89, 91, 93 ff., 114, 116, 121, 130, 146, 154, 209
Bath Chronicle, 27, 87, 90 f.
Bath, Maid of, (see Elizabeth Linley)
Battle of Hastings, The, 130
Bear, The, 27
Beaumont, Francis, 66, 132
Beggar's Opera, The, 118
Begums of Oude, 166–170, 172, 175 f.
Belgrave, Lord, 43
Bellamy, George Ann, Miss, 33
Bessborough, Lady (see Lady Harriet Duncannon)
Blackheath, 17
Bladud, King, 14 f.
Bonaparte, Napoleon, 193, 208, 225, 230 f., 234, 250, 255, 271, 277, 280 f., 287
Boswell, James, 219
Bouverie, Mrs. Edward, 195
Bramble, Matthew, in Humphrey Clinker, 28
Bridgport, Lord, 210
Brighton, 173, 235
Brissot, Jacques Pierre, 207
Brooks, 128, 129

[302]

INDEX

Brooks' Club (Almack's), 17, 53, 128, 141, 156, 181, 186, 225, 256
Brougham, Lord, 298
Brummel, George Bryan, 256 f.
Brunswick, Duke of, 204
Buckingham, Duke of, 66, 132
Burgoyne, Gen. John, 135, 166
Burke, Edmund, 20, 52, 97, 120, 122, 133, 136, 143 f., 149, 169 f., 172, 177, 185, 187, 190 ff., 204 f.
Burke, Richard, 135, 144
Burns, Robert, 57
Bute, Lord, 29, 140
Byng, " Poodle," 257
Byron, George Noel Gordon, Lord, 178, 214, 246 f., 257, 259 ff., 261, 263, 266, 268, 270, 275 ff., 279, 293, 295, 297

Callander, Caroline, 226
Camp, The, 108
Canning, Stratford, Mrs., 194 f., 197 f., 200
Careless Husband, The, 3
Carlton House, 154, 158, 160, 181, 243, 252, 254, 266
Carnival of Venice, The, 108
Caroline of Brunswick (wife of H. R. H. Prince Regent), 163, 226, 235, 241 f., 246, 255, 262
Cask Tavern, 91
Catherine II, 204
Catholic Emancipation, The, 123, 139, 227, 236 f., 255, 262, 270, 296
Centlivre, Mrs. Susannah, 24, 125
Chamberlaine, Frances Anne (see Frances Anne Sheridan)
Chamberlaine, Richard, 44, 72
Charlotte, Princess, 242, 246, 261 f.
Charlotte, wife of George III, 179 ff., 184 f., 254, 262

Chatterton, Thomas, 122, 219
Chesterfield, Earl of, 8, 22, 29, 110
Chetwynd, William, 8
Childe Harold's Pilgrimage, 260
Cholmondely, Lord, 213
Cholmondely, Mrs., 38
Cibber, Colley, 3 f., 7
Clandestine Marriage, The, 50
Clare, Viscount, 29, 222
Clarence, Duke of, 241
Clarges, Sir Thomas, 100
Clinch, Laurence, 117 f.
Clio's Protest, 72
Clive, Lord, 3, 147 f.
Coalition Government, 144
Cobbett, William, 238
Cocker, Mr., 274
Colclough, Mr., 239
Colman, George, 50
Commons, House of, 43, 123, 142, 147, 150, 161, 163, 172, 176, 184 ff., 204, 211, 229, 243 f., 250, 268 ff., 274, 280
Congress of Vienna, 250, 260, 287
Congreve, William, 130
Conscious Lovers, The, 24
Constant Couple, The, 24
Coote children, 109
Cora, in Pizarro, 220
Cork, Lady, 136, 275, 288
Cornwallis, Lord, 142
Cosway, Richard, 109
Covent Garden Theater, 3, 8, 33, 36, 113 f., 130, 203, 221, 245
Creevey, Thomas, 235, 290
Crewe, Mrs. (Amoret), 120, 151, 155
Critic, The, 19, 66, 92, 130, 132 f., 220
Cumberland, Duke of, 12, 140, 179, 241, 254
Cumberland, Richard, 130, 133

Dangle, Mr., in *The Critic*, 132
Danton, Georges Jacques, 207
D'Avenant, William, 4
De Camp, Therese (Mrs. Charles
   Kemble), 113
D'Eon, Chevalier, 36
De Genlis, Pamela, 195, 199 f.
De Ligne, Prince, 260
De Staël, Mme., 276 f.
Devonshire, Duchess of, 110, 120,
   136, 150 f., 155, 203, 234
Devonshire, Duke of, 110, 156, 182,
   234
Digges, West, 34 f.
Discovery, The, 40
Doctor and the Apothecary, The,
   189
Dolman, Dr., 85, 88
Don Felix, in *The Wonder*, 125
Dorset, Duke of, 213
Drama of Devils, 113
Drapier Letters, 32
Drury Lane Theater, 3, 5, 7 f.,
   33, 35, 39 f., 52, 84, 119, 122,
   125–129, 136, 153, 189, 217 ff.,
   221 f., 227, 242, 244–247, 264,
   278 ff., 282, 295
Dublin, 33 f., 37, 41, 63, 71, 244,
   280
Duenna, The, 18, 56, 96, 101, 118 f.
Duncannon, Lady Harriet (Bess-
   borough), 151, 155, 216, 243,
   287
Dundas (see Melville)
Dupe, The, 40

East Burnham, 105 f.
East India Company, 148 ff., 152,
   165, 167 f., 170 f., 173, 176
Elizabethans, 6
Ellenborough, Lord, 232
Elliott, Lord, 269

Ellis, George, 157
Elvira, in *Pizarro*, 220
*English Bards and Scotch Review-
   ers*, 260
Englishman, The, 135 f.
Eo, 16
Epsom, 13, 146
Erskine, 232
Essex, Lord, 279
Ewarts, Mr., 83, 91, 103, 105

Fair Penitent, The, 33
Falkland, in *The Rivals*, 115
Fatal Falsehood, The, 128
Ferrers, Lord, 29
Festival of Love, The, 57
Field, Mr., 84
Fielding, Henry, 8, 29
Fitzgerald, Lord Edward, 195
Fitzherbert, Maria Smythe, 113,
   158–164, 181, 227, 235
Fletcher, John, 66, 132
Florizel (see George Frederick,
   Prince of Wales)
Fonblanque, 274
Foote, Samuel, 36, 73, 87
Ford, James, Dr., 125 f.
Foresters, The, 128
Foster, Lady Elisabeth, 110
Fox, Charles James, 17, 20, 42, 52,
   108, 120 ff., 133, 135, 139–142,
   145, 147, 149 ff., 159–163, 165,
   169, 172, 180 ff., 184, 187, 191,
   203, 211, 213, 215, 222, 225,
   227, 231–236, 242, 253 f., 288,
   290, 297
Francis, Philip, 148, 166, 169

Gainsborough, Thomas, 26, 29, 62,
   121, 163, 175, 282
Gamester, The, 24
Gardner, Admiral, 210

INDEX

Garrick, David, 3, 7, 19, 25, 38 ff., 50, 72, 119, 122, 125 f., 136 f., 248, 290
Gay, John, 118
General Dictionary of the English Language, A, 177
George I, 8, 28
George III, 105 f., 109, 111 f., 121, 135, 140 f., 143 ff., 147 f., 150, 163, 179–183, 186, 188 f., 204, 210, 225, 227, 236 f., 241, 249 f., 254, 262
George Frederick, Prince of Wales, 20, 41, 113, 121, 140 f., 144 ff., 158–164, 173 f., 179 f., 184–188, 194, 213, 218, 225–227, 233 f., 236, 241, 243, 250 ff., 255 ff., 261 ff., 265–269, 273 f., 276, 283, 293 f., 297
Germain, Lord George, 135, 213
Gibbon, Edward, 120, 122, 135
Glendalough, Archdeacon of, 34
Golden Rump, The, 8
Goldsmith, Oliver, 7, 16, 29, 50, 114, 122, 136 f., 191
Gordon, George, Lord, 139, 161
Grafton, Duke of, 53
Grenville, William Wyndham, Baron, 225, 232, 236 ff., 242, 248 f., 251–254, 261, 266, 290
Grey, Charles, 172, 191, 215, 217, 232, 236, 242, 251–254, 261, 290
Gulliver's Travels, 32

Halhed, Nathaniel Brassey, 41, 45 f., 55 f., 58–61, 65
Haller, Mrs., in *The Stranger,* 219
Hamilton, John James, 132
Hamlet, 25
Hampstead, 13
Hampstead Heath, 17

Handel, George Frederick, 48, 100, 102, 154, 181, 196
Harrington, Dr., 80, 199
Harris, 114
Harrow, 41 ff., 45 f., 247
Hastings, Warren, 143, 147 f., 152, 165–174, 176, 179, 246, 268, 270, 288
Hatfield, 228
Henderson, John ("Mr. Courtney"), 25
Hernan's Miscellany, 71 f.
Herschel, Willam, 12
Hertford, Lady, 163, 262
Hoche, Lazare, 208
Hogarth, William, 121
Holland, Lady, 275
Holland, Lord, 216, 231, 275, 290
Home, John, 25, 133
Home Rule for Ireland, 143, 237, 280
Hopkins, Miss, 131
Horatio, in *The Fair Penitent,* 33
Howe, Lord, 209
Hoyden, Miss, in *A Trip to Scarborough,* 132
Hudibras, 14
Humphrey Clinker, 28
Huntingdon, Countess of, 29
Hyde Park, 91, 256, 260

Ilchester, 238 f., 242
Ireland, William, 218 f.
Ixion, 65 f.

Jacobins, 192, 208
Johnson, Samuel, Dr., 29, 37 f., 50, 65, 110, 120, 122
Jones, Sir William, 41
Jordan, Dorothea, 219 f.
Julia, in *The Rivals,* 115
Julia und Acres, 116

[305]

INDEX

Junius, Letters of, 53 f.

Jupiter, 65

Kean, Edmund, 279
Kemble, Charles, 113
Kemble, Fanny, 113
Kemble, " Glorious " John, 132, 219 ff.
Kemble, Roger, 26
Ker, Lewis, 46
Kew, 145, 182, 186, 188
Killigrew, Thomas, 4
King Arthur, 113
Kingsdown, 93, 95, 98
Kingston, Duke and Duchess of, 29
Knight of the Burning Pestle, The, 66, 132
Kotzebue, August Friedrich Ferdinand von, 116, 132, 220

Lacy, Willoughby, 125 f.
Lafayette, Marquis de, 192, 207
Lake, Lord, 233, 269
Lamb, Lady Caroline, 261
Lamb, Charles, 84, 131
Languish, Lydia, in *The Rivals,* 27
Lauderdale, Lord, 290
" Laura," 92
Lawrence, Sir Thomas, 29, 62
Lennox, Lady Sarah, 179
Letter to Mr. Pitt, by Sheridan, 187
Lexicographer (see Samuel Johnson)
Licensing Act, 8
Linley, Charlotte, 62, 77
Linley, Elizabeth Anne (Mrs. Richard Brinsley Sheridan) 41, 47, 60 f., 63 f., 66–69, 71–84, 86, 88–91, 95, 99–109, 116, 119, 133, 153–156, 163, 175, 193–200, 214, 245, 249, 263, 288
Linley, Jane, 62, 77, 108, 199

Linley, Maria, 61, 63, 66, 68 f., 73, 78, 82, 198
Linley, Mary (Mrs. Tickell), 47, 62, 64, 82, 100, 106, 108 f., 193, 196–199
Linley, Ozias, 62
Linley, Samuel, 62, 107 f., 142, 198
Linley, Dr. Thomas, 30, 61 f., 64, 68 f., 73, 76 ff., 87–90, 99–103, 106, 118 f., 121, 126, 198
Linley, Thomas (son of Dr. Thomas Linley), 61 f., 81 f., 107, 198
Linley, William, 62, 198
Linnet, Mrs., in *The Maid of Bath,* 73
Literary Club, The, 120
" Little " Theaters — Haymarket, Goodman's Fields, Lincoln's Inn Fields, 7
Liverpool, Lord, 266
Livius, Titus, 55
London, 36, 45, 48 ff., 53, 55, 63, 71, 83 f., 89, 106, 122, 162, 206, 245, 256, 275, 282 f., 288, 290, 297
London, Bishop of, 289 f.
Long, Walter, 66, 68, 71, 73, 76, 104
Lords, House of, 149, 173, 261
Love Epistles of Aristænetus, 58–61, 65
Love's Last Shift, 3, 7
Lunn, Sally, 30
Lyon, Emma (Lady Hamilton), 108

" Macaroni," 17, 19
Macaulay, Mrs. Catherine, 38
Macbeth, 25
Macfadden, Charles, 31
Mackintosh, James, 223
Macpherson, Sir John, 222

[306]

INDEX

Mahomet, 34
Maid of Bath, The, 73
Malaprop, Mrs., in The Rivals, 40,
    115 f., 118
Malone, Edmond, 219
Maria, in The School for Scandal,
    131
Marie Antoinette, 193, 203
Markham, Dr., 121, 144
Marlborough, Duchess of, 12
Marlborough, Duke of, 16
Mathews, Capt. Thomas, 67, 72, 73,
    76 ff., 80, 87–91, 93 ff., 97 f.
Matured Plan of Education for
    Young Nobility and Gentry, A, 45
Melbourne, Lady, 261
Melville, Henry Dundas, Lord, 21,
    212, 246
Mendoza, Isaac, in The Duenna,
    118
Merchant of Venice, The, 24
Middleton, 168
Milbanke, Anne Isabella (Lady By-
    ron), 41
Moira, Lord, 227, 232, 251, 262,
    265 ff., 273
Monckton, Lord, 136
Monody on the Death of David
    Garrick, 136
Monody on the Death of the Rt.
    Hon. Richard Brinsley Sheridan,
    178, 268, 295
Moore, Sir John, 280
Moore, Peter, 293 f.
Moore, Thomas, 38, 43, 54, 107,
    270, 284 f., 291, 293, 297 f.
More, Hannah, 128, 145
Morning Chronicle, The, 18, 248,
    261, 291
Morning Post, The, 105, 286
Mozart, Wolfgang Amadeus, 62,
    107

"Nabobs," 17, 166
Nash, Richard ("Beau"), 16, 22,
    23, 26 f., 82
Navy, 142, 182, 209–212, 232
Nawab of Oude, 167 f., 171
Nelson, Horatio, Viscount, 29, 220,
    242
"New Theater" at Bath, 24
Norfolk, Duke of, 273
North, Lord, 37, 106, 121, 135,
    141, 143 f., 147 f., 250
Northumberland, Duke of, 17
Nourjahad, Tale of, 39, 247, 260

O'Blunder, Captain, 64
O'Brien, Denis, 286
O'Coigley, Father, 223
O'Connor, Arthur, 223
O'Connor, Roger, 223
Ode on the General Fast, 111, 113
Ogle, Hester (see Sheridan, Hester
    Jane)
Old Bachelor, The, 6
Ophelia, 24
Orators, The, 36
Orleans, Duke of, 174
Oronooko, 24
Osborn, Selleck, 22
Ossory, Lady, 114
Othello, 24 f.
O'Trigger, Lucius, in The Rivals,
    115 ff.
Otway, Thomas, 24
Oxford, 38, 56, 58, 60, 65, 95, 106,
    248 f.

Palmer, John, 25, 131 f.
Pamela, 38
Parker, Richard, 212
Parliament, 48, 126, 128, 136, 139,
    156, 169, 185, 204, 216 f., 225,
    230, 238, 250 f., 273 f., 278

INDEX

Parr, Dr., 41, 43, 45, 215, 223
Paull, 238
Paumier, Capt., 93 f., 98
Peake, 282
Peninsular War, 242 f., 262
Pepys, Samuel, 123
Perceval, Spencer, 238 f., 254, 261
Petty, 232
Pierrepont Street, 26, 29 f., 65
Piozzi, Hester Thrale, 29
Pitt the Elder (Lord Chatham), 18, 20, 133
Pitt, William, 20, 121, 139, 142, 149 ff., 156 f., 165, 169, 173, 180, 183–187, 202, 204, 208, 211 f., 222, 225, 228–232, 234 f., 246, 250 f., 288
Pizarro, 132, 220 f., 260
Polesden, 217
Ponsonby, George, 243 f.
Porson, Richard, 219
Portland, Duke of, 154, 182, 225, 238 f., 253, 288, 290
Priestley, Joseph, 29, 121, 203
Proverb Cards, 16
Provok'd Husband, The, 3, 26
Puff, in *The Critic*, 132 f.
Pump Rooms at Bath, 13, 27, 65

Queensberry, Duchess of, 36
Quick, 118
Quilcagh House, 31
Quin, James, 26, 50

Rabelais, François, 55
Rajah Cheyt Singh, 167 f.
Ranelagh, 48
Regency, 141, 147, 181 f., 185, 187 f., 204, 225, 250 f.
Rehearsal, The, 66, 132
Relapse, The, 67, 127
Requiem, 235

Restoration, 6, 54, 57, 127
Retaliation, 136, 191
Reynolds, 129
Reynolds, Sir Joshua, 20, 109, 122, 137, 198, 245
Rich, John, 36
Richardson, Joseph, 215 f.
Richardson, Samuel, 37, 50
Richmond, 43
Richmond, Duke of, 206
Rights of Man, 190 f., 193, 208
Rivals, The, 4, 40, 113–118, 128, 131, 133
Robespierre, Maximilien François, 207
Robinson, Mary (" Perdita "), 20, 42, 127, 145, 293
Rochefoucault, 207
Rockingham, Marquess of, 20, 143
Rogers, Samuel, 122, 276 f., 283 ff., 287, 293
Rolle, Squire, 161
Rolliad, The, 108, 150, 157, 215
Rosy, Dr., in *St. Patrick's Day*, 15, 118
Rowe, Nicholas, 5, 33
Rowlandson, Thomas, 121
Royal Marriages Act, 159
Royal Theater, 33
Rudliche, in *Hernan's Miscellany*, 72

St. Anne's Hill, 213, 234
" St. Cecilia," by Reynolds, 109, 198, 245, 282
St. John, 169
St. Patrick's Day, 15, 118
Salisbury, Lady, 151
Salisbury, Lord, 180
Savile Row, 283–286
School for Scandal, The, 120, 129, 131, 174, 200, 270

INDEX

Scott, Sir Walter, 217, 235
Scrace, 27, 75
Sefton, Lord, 257
Selden, John, 240
Shall I, Wasting in Despair, 57
She Stoops to Conquer, 114
Shelburne, Lord, 143
Sheridan, Alicia (Mrs. Le Fanu),
    30, 34, 37, 46, 64, 71, 214
Sheridan, Charles Brinsley, 215,
    217, 267, 277, 286
Sheridan, Charles Francis, 30, 34,
    46 f., 71, 74 f., 93, 97
Sheridan, Elizabeth, 30, 34, 46, 64,
    71, 74
Sheridan, Elizabeth Anne (see
    Elizabeth Linley)
Sheridan, Frances Anne (Chamber-
    laine), 33, 37–40, 44, 47, 115,
    120, 247
Sheridan, Hester Jane, 200, 213–
    217, 229, 233, 248, 263, 275–
    278, 281 f., 284 f., 287–290,
    293
Sheridan, Mary, 196, 198, 200
Sheridan, Richard Brinsley, 4, 6, 10,
    15, 18–21, 30 ff., 34 f., 37–61,
    65 f., 71 f., 74 f., 79–101, 103–
    108, 110 f., 113–120, 125–136,
    139, 141–145, 147, 149 f., 153–
    158, 161 ff., 165, 169–178,
    181 f., 186–189, 191–197,
    199 ff., 204–208, 211–223, 225–
    233, 236–239, 242–248, 250–
    254, 260–265, 267–271, 273–
    279, 281–291, 293–298
Sheridan, Thomas (son of Richard
    Brinsley and Elizabeth Linley),
    119, 153, 156, 196, 198, 200,
    213, 215, 217, 226 f., 233, 248,
    253, 263–267, 278, 285 f., 288,
    293

Sheridan, Thomas, 29 f., 32–40, 42,
    44–49, 54, 58, 64, 95, 105, 119,
    153, 177
Sheridan, Dr. Thomas, 31 f.
Siddons, Mrs. Sarah, 52, 175, 219 f.
Siddons, William, 26, 52
Smith, 131
Smock Alley Theater, 32, 34
Smollett, Dr. Tobias, 28
Smyth, 285
Sophocles, 55
Soubise, 36
Spencer, Lord Robert, 41, 209–212,
    232, 290
Stafford, 136, 139, 141, 236, 239,
    282
Stanhope, Lady Hester, 36
Statesman, The, 128
Steele, Richard, 24, 71
" Stella," 32
Sterne, Laurence, 72
Stewkley, Lord, in *A Journey to
    Bath*, 115 f.
Storace, Stephen, 189
Stranger, The, 219
Sumner, Dr., 44 f.
Surface, Charles, in *The School for
    Scandal*, 131, 200, 216
Surface, Joseph, in *The School for
    Scandal*, 131
Swift, Dean, 31 f., 36, 54, 177
Sydney Biddulph, 37 ff.
" Sylvio," 92

Tancred, 33
Taxation No Tyranny, 110
Taylor, Michael Angelo, 173
Teazle, Lady, in *The School for
    Scandal*, 132, 214
Theocritus, 55 f.
Three Tuns, The, 27
Tickell, 108, 135

Tilburina, in *The Critic,* 92
Times, 11
Tone, Wolfe, 208
Tooke, Horne, 238
Tories, 141, 161, 183, 185, 188 f.,
    192, 234, 266
Townshend, Sir John, 135, 182
Tragedy of Douglas, The, 25, 133
Trip to Calais, A, 87
Trip to Scarborough, A, 6, 127 f.
Tryfort, Lady, in *A Journey to*
    Bath, 40, 115
Tunbridge Wells, 13, 146

Vanbrugh, Sir John, 3, 6, 8, 26, 127
Vaughan, " Hat," 283
Vauxhall Gardens, 48
Vergil, 55
Vortigern and Rowena, 219

Wade, Captain, 82
Walpole, Sir Horace, 8, 17, 29, 114,
    121, 139
Waltham Abbey, 96 f.
Waltz, The, 259
Wanstead, 213
Ward, Sarah, 26
Warren, Dr., 183
Waterloo, Battle of, 281, 287 f.
Watier's Club, 256
Wedgwood, Josiah, 29, 122, 156
Wellesley, Hon. Arthur (Duke of
    Wellington), 121, 242
Wells, The, 109, 196 f., 199
Wesley, John, 29

West, Benjamin, 109, 180
Westminster, 151, 236, 238
Westminster Abbey, 174 f., 286, 290
Westmoreland, Lady, 275, 288
Wexford, 239
Whigs, 139, 141, 147, 150 f., 157,
    159, 161, 181, 183, 185–188,
    190, 234, 242, 246, 250, 264 ff.,
    269 f., 290, 297
Whiskerandos, Don Ferolo, in *The*
    Critic, 132
Whitbread, Samuel, 217, 246 f.,
    264 f., 273–276, 278 f.
White's Club, 53, 256
White Hart, The, 27, 93
Whyte, Samuel, 37, 41
Wilberforce, William, 139
Wilkes, John, 135
Wilkie, 61, 65
Willis, Dr., 183, 186
Willoughby, Miss, 20
Windham, William, 172, 232
Windsor, 141, 180, 182, 185, 241,
    250, 281
Wither, George, 56
Woffington, Peg, 7, 33 f.
Wood, Brothers, 27
Woodfall, William, 141
Wooton Bassett, 273 f.
Wordsworth, William, 57, 122, 190
Wycherly, William, 6

Yarmouth, Lord, 262 f.
York, Duke of, 121, 185, 241, 257,
    287

Publish'd Dec.r 15.th 1784 by T. Malton No.6 Conduit Street.